Finding the Trapdoor

Finding the Trapdoor

ESSAYS, PORTRAITS, TRAVELS

Adam Hochschild

Syracuse University Press

Copyright © 1997 Adam Hochschild
All Rights Reserved

First Edition 1997
97 98 99 00 01 02   6 5 4 3 2 1

The pieces in this collection first appeared, sometimes in slightly different form, in the following publications: "Paragon of Porkers: Freddy the Pig" in the *New York Times Book Review;* "Magic Journalism" in the *New York Review of Books;* "The Grand Bargain in South Africa" in the *Village Voice;* "The Private Volcano of Malcolm Lowry" in *Ramparts;* "Empire's End: A Moscow Journal" in *West* magazine, with portions also in *Newsday* and the *San Francisco Chronicle;* "Summer of Violence" and "Isle of Flowers, House of Slaves" in the *San Francisco Chronicle;* "Fishhooks and Chickens" in the *San Francisco Examiner Magazine;* and "Finding the Trapdoor" in *Zyzzyva.* All the others were first published in *Mother Jones.* Permission to reprint these pieces from the listed sources is gratefully acknowledged.

The paper used in this publication meets the minimum requirements of American National Standard for Information Sciences—Permanence of Paper for Printed Library Materials, ANSI Z39.48-1984. ∞

Library of Congress Cataloging-in-Publication Data
Hochschild, Adam.
    Finding the trapdoor : essays, portraits, travels / Adam Hochschild. — 1st ed.
      p. cm.
    ISBN 0-8156-0447-5 (cloth : alk. paper)
    1. World politics—20th century—Moral and ethical aspects.
    2. Politics, Practical—Moral and ethical aspects.   I. Title.
    D445.H58   1997
    909.82'8—dc21   96-52066

Manufactured in the United States of America

For Judith W. Klein
(1947–1996)

Adam Hochschild was born in New York City in 1942. After graduating from college, he worked as a newspaper reporter in San Francisco, and as an editor and writer at *Ramparts* magazine. In the mid-1970s, he was a cofounder of *Mother Jones* magazine and was an editor there until 1981. Since then, Hochschild has mainly devoted his time to writing books. They include *The Unquiet Ghost: Russians Remember Stalin, The Mirror at Midnight: A South African Journey,* and *Half the Way Home: A Memoir of Father and Son* (reprinted by Syracuse University Press). His articles and reviews have appeared in many publications, including *Mother Jones, Harper's, The New York Times Magazine, The New York Times Book Review, The Village Voice, The New Republic, The New York Review of Books, The Washington Monthly, The Nation, The Los Angeles Times,* and *The Washington Post.* He has also been a commentator on the National Public Radio program *All Things Considered.*

Hochschild's books and articles have won prizes from the Eugene V. Debs Foundation, the World Affairs Council, the Society of American Travel Writers, and the Overseas Press Club of America. He and his wife, Arlie, a sociologist, live in San Francisco. They have two sons.

Contents

PART THREE   *War and Other Literary Pleasures*

Acknowledgments

My thanks go first of all to my wife, Arlie. Always, gently, my best critic, she read all of these pieces in manuscript, usually several times. By example, she has taught me so much about perception that sometimes I think I see the world through her eyes. She was with me on several of the trips described here, and was in my heart on all of them. Hermann Hatzfeldt was also a traveling companion, both on a few of the trips in these pages and on others there wasn't room for. Without him, I never would have gotten to spend a remarkable week in a dugout canoe on the Mirití River.

I'm also grateful to the many friends who read early drafts of these pieces, especially to my former colleagues at *Mother Jones* magazine, where many of the articles had their first home in print. Only a writer who has worked with a demanding, sensitive, perfectionist group of coworkers knows what a huge help it can be, and how often a skilled editor can draw out of you something you otherwise didn't think you had to say. I owe much to all of them, particularly to Jeffrey Klein, Deirdre English, and Doug Foster.

Editors at more than half a dozen other publications also published articles in this volume in their first incarnations; without the invitation and encouragement of one of them, Howard Junker of *Zyzzyva,* I never would have written "Finding the Trapdoor." My gratitude also goes to the friends who were willing to do a critical reading of the final collection, to help me make the parts add up to a whole: Janusz Bardach, Harriet Barlow, Patricia Labalme, Elinor Langer, Paul Solman, Lawrence Weschler, and the late Ruth Russell. And finally my thanks to Cynthia Maude-Gembler and her colleagues at Syracuse University Press, for giving these pieces a second lease on life.

Adam Hochschild

San Francisco, Calif.
January 1997

ix

Introduction

Once during the 1980s I was in South Africa to write about the country's long and bitter conflict. In a desolate rural town, government-supported vigilantes had thrown a grenade through the window of a black activist's home. Miraculously, no one was killed, although a sleeping child was injured. The next day, several of us drove out to look at the scene and to interview witnesses, an odd little convoy consisting of myself, a French diplomat, a *New York Times* reporter, a human-rights worker who knew the area, and a news photographer. When we reached the cinder block house, the photographer got out of his car, took a look at the window, and exclaimed: "Damn! They patched it up." No picture.

At the time I felt appalled by the photographer's crassness. But as I recently sifted through several decades' worth of articles and essays to choose the ones for this book, I was struck with how often, like him, I have been more attracted to places where the windows are broken than to those where they are patched up. And so you will find many more pieces here about countries like El Salvador and the former Soviet Union than about ones like Holland or Denmark. (Although my favorite spot of all, least in need of any patching up, I unexpectedly came upon in benighted, violent Colombia.)

Why are writers more attracted to describing evil, like the throwing of that grenade, rather than good? People have surely asked that question ever since Sophocles and Aeschylus. In recent years I think I've come to understand the answers better. I remember when I first tried to plow through the *Oresteia* trilogy of Aeschylus as a college student. I could not even keep the names straight in this bewildering saga of revenge and betrayal ignited by Agamemnon's sacrifice of his daughter to the gods. It all felt beyond comprehension: too bizarre, too foreign, too remote from modern experience and certainly from my own.

But I reread the *Oresteia* recently, shortly after spending six months in Russia interviewing people about their memories of the Stalin years. With a cold shiver of recognition, I suddenly felt the plays all too close to what I had just been listening to for months. How different is Agamemnon's appalling sacrifice of his daughter from someone denouncing—as millions of Soviets did—a neighbor, a coworker, or a relative to the secret police? Is that not also a human sacrifice, also done to propitiate the all-powerful gods, who might otherwise condemn you to death? And what about Agamemnon's father, who tricked Thyestes into eating the flesh of his children, disguised as the food of a feast? Reading about that today, I find it hauntingly like the end of Nikita Mikhalkov's fine 1994 film about Stalin's purges, *Burnt by the Sun,* where secret policemen allow a happy little girl to steer the car that, unknown to her, is taking her father to his death. Is she, also, not being tricked into feasting on the flesh of a loved one? We live in a century that has seen too many such feasts.

Few other places open so wide a window onto human darkness as did Stalin's Russia, but some of the ones in the following pages offer a glimpse: a slave traders' fortress in Senegal, Mississippi before the civil rights laws, El Salvador, apartheid-era South Africa. And ultimately such places interest us, writers and readers alike, because evil raises so many more questions than good. Where does it come from? Why does it persist? And how we would behave if brought face to face with it? Would we do battle bravely? Give in? Run away? Sacrifice someone else to save ourselves?

Some of the people in this volume, like Patrick Duncan in South Africa, Victor Serge in Russia, or Jan Yoors in Nazi-occupied France, faced such moral choices in their lives, and that is certainly part of what drew me to their stories. Others here faced moral dilemmas of a different sort. How does a torture victim behave when he has to sit down in the same room with his former torturers today, as part of the same government? How does a group of Amazon Indians, or of French mountain villagers, maintain its traditional culture amid the temptations of modern consumerism? Can a former white racist leader find redemption? One of the great rewards of writing is that you get to travel not only to distant countries but also into the lives of people wrestling with such dilemmas. And the journey usually changes the writer as well, although in ways at first not always easy for him or her to see.

What follows in this book, then, are some of the unpatched windows I've been lucky enough to look through. The pieces in the first two sections involve personal encounters with people and with places, some of them experiences central to my life. The glances through windows in the third section are mainly vicarious—encounters with books, although some of these, too, are meetings whose effects have long stayed with me.

These pieces, incidentally, need not be read only in a proper sequence. Think of them instead as pictures in a gallery, which you can skip or linger over, looking at them in whatever order that fancy takes you.

Readers of my book *Half the Way Home: A Memoir of Father and Son* may recognize passages from it in two or three of these pieces. But I hope they will forgive me this bit of self-plagarism, for these words are put to quite different work here, in the articles where they first appeared.

For this collection, I have made minor revisions in almost all the pieces. However, because occasionally the point of a story is to give the feel of something like the end of the old era in the Soviet Union or the start of the new one in South Africa, I have not tried to bring any political reportage up to date, except to name a few people who for their own safety could not be identified when an article was first published. Otherwise I felt it was best to leave the pieces stand as a series of snapshots from particular moments in time; hence at the end of each article is the date it first appeared.

Prologue

Preceding page: Boris Sergievsky (1888–1971).
Courtesy of National Air and Space Museum.

Finding the Trapdoor

Unlike other mammals, writers are not born into the world knowing how to make their own particular noise. Almost from the beginning, wolves howl, hogs grunt, bears growl. They need no M.F.A. programs in growling, or summer workshops in discovering the grunt within. Even if separated from their families at birth and raised by some other species, they still know the right sound. But writers are different: all too easily they mistake someone else's sound for their own. For many years, that's what happened with me.

Ever since I could remember, I had wanted to write novels. As a child I loved reading them; in high school a kindly, encouraging freshman English teacher helped me hear the chords and echoes that could lie below the surface of a piece of fiction. One day he gave me an extra-credit assignment to read and write about a couple of short stories. One was John Galsworthy's "The Apple Tree." It is the tale of an upper-class Englishman, out hiking in the country, who falls in love with a beautiful Welsh farm girl. He swears eternal devotion and promises to come back to the farm so they can elope. But then he lapses into his usual social world, fails to return to the farm, and soon marries a conventional woman of his own class. Years later, he learns that the farm girl has killed herself in grief, and sees that his life has been wasted.

I was at an age when I wanted every story to have a message, and the moral of this one, to me, was unmistakable. The conventional wife in the story was the existence of a lawyer or businessman that parents, teachers, and family friends seemed to expect of me. The radiantly beautiful farm girl was the alluring alternative: my life as a writer of fiction. Unlike that of the hero of the story, I

3

vowed, my life would *not* be wasted. I would make the right choice.

The English courses I took when I went on to college only strengthened my assumption that the greatest of all human achievements was to write novels. But I was eager to be finished with formal education and to enter the real world beyond. Soon after I graduated, I moved to California in 1964 and began working as a newspaper reporter. Hadn't journalism been the route toward literature for Stephen Crane, for Mark Twain? I hoped it would be the same for me, providing some "material" for my *real* writing, my novels yet to come. The newspaper articles I wrote, I was sure, were not yet the real me. One thing about being twenty-one or twenty-two is that constant sense that the real you is yet to come. At one level this is frustrating, but at another it's a deep comfort, for it lets you off the hook when anything you do falls short of full, glorious, fame-producing self-expression.

I soon began to write short stories, most of them set in the various down-and-out milieux I was seeing as a reporter in San Francisco. I was constantly racing to the scene of fires, robberies, murders, and suicides. Working in a newspaper city room in those preelectronic days was noisy and exciting. You banged away on a manual typewriter, and, near deadline, a copy boy stood by to run each page of your story to the city desk the moment you finished it. Overhead, pneumatic tubes whooshed and thumped as they carried copy and proofs to and from the typesetters. On the wall, a bell connected to the San Francisco Fire Department's alarm system clanged away, and the moment it gave the *ding-ding, ding-ding* signal for a second alarm, a reporter and photographer began running for a car. On the city desk, a police radio poured forth an unending static-laden litany of woe and disaster. One afternoon, listening to it, the city editor, a small man with a big voice and suspenders, suddenly rose in his seat, pointed at me, and bellowed: "Hochschild! There's a woman having a baby in a taxi! Go!" I was so rattled when I got to the scene that I didn't even notice whether the baby was a boy or girl. I was happy: this was my material, the real world in all its gritty glory, soon to be immortalized in my fiction.

Besides experience in journalism, there were other classic ingredients to being a successful young novelist, I knew from my reading and my college courses. It was best if you lived in a pivotal, glamorous time and place, like Paris in the 1920s. And ideally you should be, like Hemingway and Fitzgerald, the voice of your generation. All that seemed easy: I was living in the San Francisco Bay Area; it was the mid-1960s; and, with the Vietnam War, the country was in the midst of the greatest generational conflict it had ever seen.

Another classic criterion for being noticed as a young writer I could not meet. For, if possible, you should be from a poor background, like Chekhov or Dreiser. Alas, my family was distressingly well-off. My father, with whom I had a tense and difficult relationship, was a big businessman. More frustrating yet, in my rebellion against him I couldn't feel I was the voice of my generation, of sons against fathers during this tumultuous decade. He was remarkably liberal, as opposed to the Vietnam War as I.

However, my parents were out of sight, on the other side of the country. I seldom talked about them with my friends, and would not have dreamed, in what I wrote, of revealing much about the world I had come from. One of the few people who knew was my wife, Arlie, then a graduate student, later to become a professor at Berkeley and a superb writer of social science with an artist's eye. She and I lived, if not in Chekhovian poverty, at least in conspicuous simplicity. We drove a VW Beetle, and our threadbare furniture came from a Salvation Army store.

At home, I was not doing my fiction writing in a proper Paris garret, above a brothel or sawmill (like Hemingway's apartment), but I had almost the equivalent. Our two-room apartment was in a pleasant, slightly dilapidated brown-shingle building in Berkeley, and underneath the glassed-in sun porch in back, where I wrote, the ground had subsided. The floor slanted, and pencils rolled away from me on the top of my Salvation Army desk. I had to saw an inch and a half off the two near legs to make the desktop level.

After some two years of newspaper work, I moved on to a job writing for *Ramparts* magazine. But my articles there, like my unpublished short stories, were in my mind only small steps toward the big breakthrough, my first novel. I planned one out, and wrote several chapters and an outline of what was to come. Miraculously, in 1969, a New York publisher gave me a contract and a $5,000 advance (more than $20,000 in today's money). I was deliriously happy. Still in my mid-twenties, I was on my way. My career—my real career—was launched.

By now I was no longer working at *Ramparts.* When people asked me what I did, I loved saying that I was writing a novel. This gave me an identity, and in a strange way I think I cared about that most of all. The actual novel felt important, of course, but as I look back at it now, I think it mattered so much to me mainly because it let me think of myself as *being* a writer. I got occasional offers of free-lance magazine assignments, but I turned most down: I was doing my novel, and almost anything else, I felt, would be something lesser. Would Proust or Tolstoy have paused to write a profile or a book review?

When anyone asked what my novel was about, I said, enigmatically, that I preferred not to talk about it. I knew, from reading *Paris Review* interviews, that we real writers seldom described works-in-progress. The creative process was complex and delicate, and could easily be disturbed by insensitive questions from ordinary mortals. For the same reason, as I worked, I showed my manuscript to almost no one.

I imagined my own *Paris Review* interview to come. I would talk about the major literary influences on me, about my adventurous newspaper days, and about the breakthrough with my first novel, after which it was all smooth sailing. I would talk—but only when pressed—about what episodes in my life had inspired those in my fiction, as I turned the dross of everyday reality into the gold of art. I would have some wise words of advice for younger writers. And then I would wait for the interviewer to notice the slanting floor and the sawed-off desk legs.

.   .   .

I worked on the novel steadily. One of the few times I wrote something else was to spend a couple of days jotting down some childhood memories that bubbled up with uncommon insistence when an uncle of mine died. A swashbuckling Russian who had been a fighter pilot in the First World War, he had worked his way through Europe as a cabaret singer, flown explorers around Africa, and then shocked everyone in the family by marrying my father's shy, staid sister. But however vibrant a presence he had been to me as a boy, he was a figure from another era, who seemed to have nothing to do with the American rebels of the sixties whose literary voice I hoped to be. I filed those pages away at the back of a drawer and forgot about them.

After several years, I finished the novel and mailed it off. I waited expectantly for the great praise I was sure my manuscript would get. Then came a terrible blow. My editor told me he had decided not to publish it. It had never occurred to me that this might happen. Didn't I have a contract, an advance already paid? More important still, hadn't I been telling people for several years now that I was a novelist? I felt like a groom abandoned at the altar when the wedding guests are already seated, the organist is already playing. I was crushed. My editor, I was sure, had committed a major felony against American literature.

I showed the manuscript to many other publishers. No luck. I tried sending it around in England—hadn't Joyce also been spurned by narrow-minded publishers in his own country? No luck there, either. There was a recession in the publishing industry, I told friends; there were mergers, acquisitions, dark forces at work; it's harder than ever to get a decent book published these days . . .

Worst of all, after a gap of many despairing months, I reread my manuscript once again and began to see why no one wanted to print it. I had followed all the rules—the prose sparkled, the generations clashed, the stream-of-consciousness passages were all in lowercase italics, the symbols coyly awaited discovery by alert critics—but the characters were stiff and one-dimensional. The novel lacked the sound of a human voice.

．　　．　　．

Chastened, with a sense of having wasted several years, I went back to what I then thought of as my lower-ranking trade, journalism. In the mid-1970s, some friends and I started *Mother Jones* magazine. We were lucky in our timing, for it was in the wake of the Watergate scandal, where two journalists had forced a president to resign, and the country was ready for a new magazine with an antiestablishment, investigative edge. And I was lucky personally: I had talented colleagues, meaningful work, and the excitement of being part of a magazine that caught on.

Unexpectedly, I found myself learning something enormously useful from being one of the magazine's editors. When editing, what you have to do all day long is what writers find hardest: cutting. You cut passages out of stories to make them fit on the available pages; you reject other pieces because they are not good enough; you say no to an unending stream of queries. The job demystifies words. It reminds you, as you look at letters to the editor and reader surveys and listen to what subscribers tell you, that readers are impatient and busy. You have to compete for their attention. Is this article going to keep someone reading for six thousand words? Or is it only worth two thousand? Or should we drop it entirely—even if it was written by an old friend, by a famous writer, or by one of us? You learn that no piece of writing is sacred. The reader, not the writer, comes first. And you learn that nothing has value just because *you* wrote it.

During those years as an editor I wrote very little, still nagged by a lingering sense of my earlier failure. Every once in a while, I would skim through the manuscript of my old novel, and a feeling of humiliation would wash over me once more. Eventually I began writing occasional pieces again. At first these were, like most of what we ran in *Mother Jones,* political commentary or investigative reporting. I was dimly aware, though, that others could do this better than me. Then one day quite a different sort of idea came to me.

For several years I had been admiring the books of Victor Serge, an anarchist who fought with the Bolsheviks in the Russian Civil War. A fine writer and a man of luminous moral intelligence, he spoke out for free speech and democracy, and was harassed, jailed, and exiled by Stalin. Suddenly, reading Serge's memoirs, I realized that on one day in October 1919, at the site of an old observatory just outside Petrograd, Victor Serge and my beloved Russian uncle, Boris Sergievsky, had fought on opposite sides of the very same battle. In 1978 I decided to go to Russia, find the battlefield, and write about these two men I admired, who each stood for something so different. I did so; it's the piece that begins on page 65 of this book.

Once I had written the article, I found myself feeling something I had not experienced before. It was not a sense that I had written anything great or lasting. I merely felt that for the first time in my life, I had written something fully in my own voice. Almost everything else—the other magazine and newspaper articles, the unpublished novel and short stories—were, I now saw, in one way or another in someone else's voice.

My voice, curiously, was not what I had expected. It seemed like a long-lost identical twin, who turned out not to look like what I thought *I* looked like. For one thing, it had none of the rhetorical flourishes or instantly recognizable style of some of my favorite novelists. For another, this voice of mine was not writing novels at all, but nonfiction. Furthermore, my voice was still in part that of a reporter: traveling about, interviewing people, describing people and places I had seen. What I'd learned in my first trade still had some use after all. Perhaps the distinction I had always made between writing and mere journalism was an illusory one.

.   .   .

Not long after this, as I was nearing my fortieth birthday, my father died. Much of my life, and my very becoming a writer, which had at first upset him greatly, had been a quiet rebellion against his hopes and plans for me. And now he was no longer there. It's as if you spend all your life with one hand braced against a wall that threatens to topple over on you. Then suddenly one day the wall vanishes. It is hard to find your balance.

I still had that persistent dream that my real work was as a novelist. And so in 1981 I left my job as an editor and spent some months working on a new novel. But like the first, it felt wooden and lifeless. At least I was now self-aware enough to see this. I felt all roads blocked. As a last resort, I decided to work on a memoir. Writing one was something I had long thought about but had been sure I wouldn't do for years. The memoir I had sometimes imagined, finally revealing some information about my private life to a surprised world, was supposed to be a late, minor appendage to my career as a novelist, as Conrad's memoirs are to his. It felt all wrong to be doing it first. I figured I would write the book, then put the manuscript away for some years. I would try to publish it only after I had produced the novels that, I hoped, were still somewhere inside me.

Most unexpectly, the memoir came tumbling out quickly. Telling myself that I wouldn't try to publish it right away had mysteriously opened a lock, a lock I hadn't even realized was fastened. Writing the book barely felt like work, more like writing a letter to a friend. To my further surprise, I realized that I had long ago written the opening pages: those childhood memories of my uncle Boris, quickly jotted down and filed away a decade earlier, then used more recently in that article from Russia. I finished a rough draft of the book in two and a half months.

I revised the manuscript and showed it to friends. They generously gave me much useful criticism for which I will be forever grateful. In the preceding fifteen years I had learned this: forget all that coy concealment about work-in-progress in those *Paris Review* interviews. Talking about your writing, trying it out on people, watching closely to see where they get interested and where they get bored is the most precious tool a writer has. If a piece of work doesn't accomplish the job you want it to, you can go back and try again. That's a luxury that an aircraft designer or a bridge engineer doesn't have.

One day I realized I had abandoned another earlier belief: that a writer must toil ceaselessly on the Great Book and not waste any time on lesser work. While working on my memoir I was, I noticed with some surprise, doing more other kinds of writing than ever: op-ed pieces, a book review column for *Mother Jones,* a regular commentary for National Public Radio, and more magazine articles that felt to me to be in that new voice I had found. At bedtime, I found I was telling stories to my five-year-old younger son, with a regular stable of oddball characters. Sometimes we would take turns, each carrying the story a lap farther.

Instead of distracting me from work on the memoir, all these things seemed to help, as if limbering up some additional literary muscles I hadn't known about before. By accident, I had learned another important secret: that each of us does not have just one voice, but many, and that speaking in one of them can help bring the others to life. "Any proper writer ought to be able to write anything," Kingsley Amis once said, "from an Easter Day sermon to a sheep-dip handout."

My feeling of not wanting to publish the memoir for a long time evaporated, replaced by the simple vanity of wanting people to read it now. It would not, after all, be the life story of a famous novelist, only of a human being. *Half the Way Home: A Memoir of Father and Son* was published in 1986. I've written several more books since then, but this first one was a turning point that made it possible for me to go forward.

Two unexpected things happened after the book appeared. The first occurred a year or so later. One day I pulled out the manuscript of that early unpublished novel, expecting to feel a failure once again for having wasted several years on it. But as I read through it this time, something struck me like a thunderclap. The manuscript was, I saw, a first version of *Half the Way Home.* True, it was a novel, not a memoir. The main character was a young woman, not me. Her parents were largely not my parents. She grew up in a different part of the country. But the underlying feelings I was trying to evoke—clumsily and unsuccessfully this first time around—were the same. Like some biographer poking through his subject's attic, I had discovered my own first draft. So: all that time and effort had not been wasted after all. I felt as if an enormous burden had been lifted from me.

The other thing that has happened since *Half the Way Home* came out is this: When I run into people who have read the book, or get letters from them, sometimes they begin by saying, "I read your novel . . ." At first, my impulse was always to correct people, to say that the book is clearly labeled a memoir, that I didn't make anything up, that it's all true. Today I am more bemused. Slips of the memory reveal something, like slips of the tongue. What I think the "I read your novel" shows is that we are accustomed to turning to nonfiction for information, and to novels for character and emotion. After all, isn't this exactly what I, too, had believed for years—thinking that if I wanted to portray a character, to make a reader feel, I could only do so by writing novels?

Now I feel much more relaxed about all this. The important thing is to convey what you care about, to evoke those feelings in others, and to make your characters live and breathe and walk off the page, whether you're writing fiction, nonfiction, or something in between. Often the right form turns out to be something entirely different from what you had once imagined. My own, it appears, often seems to be some mixture of history and first-person reportage, and the more leaps between them the better. After all, is there anything more exhilarating than time traveling? And characters are everything. Searching for good ones and for the meanings embodied in their lives has taken me, physically or intellectually, to some times and places I wouldn't have missed for anything: to remote corners of Siberia in the Stalin years and today; to the Congo in the time of Joseph Conrad and King Leopold II; to Andrei Sakharov's apartment in Moscow; to coal miners' shacks in Appalachia; to a day on the campaign trail with Nelson Mandela. Amazingly, I even get paid for doing this.

The people I have encountered, both in person and in the revealing paper trails left behind in history, are far more interesting than any it would be in my power to make up. Novelists write, in part, by imagining alternative selves, living in different places and circumstances. We nonfiction writers get to go out and find those selves and talk to them. I think we have more fun.

.   .   .

A writer's search for a voice goes on for a lifetime. Sometimes I think of that searcher as being like a would-be singer, ready to give a concert, who is trapped in a pitch-black house. This may sound like a bizarre image, but it is always the one in my mind. The lights in the house are off; the doors are closed; mysterious screens and barriers stand everywhere; floor-length blackout curtains cover all the windows. You stumble around in the dark, banging into things, shouting but not heard. You have only a limited amount of time—that's what life is, after all—to find the magical opening, the window or door through which you can stick out your head and sing, so that those outside can hear you at last.

Bumping about in the darkness, most of us tend to grope toward the traditional grand aperture: those French windows of the novel. Find them, fling them open, and there you are on the balcony, ready to sing your song. There are other traditional openings, too: the smaller window of the short story, the doorway of the poem.

But now, I am beginning to see, there are all sorts of other ways out of the darkened house, and each of them lets your voice out: dormer windows, a little wicket for the meter reader, skylights that swing open, chimneys you can poke your head up, the secret trapdoor hidden under the rug. Someday, perhaps, I'll stumble upon those French windows and write a novel. But if not, I won't be disappointed. Recently, and certainly unimagined in my *Paris Review*–reading days, I have found myself writing very short stories for very small children. My kids have now grown up, and those stories simply need somewhere to go. What passage out of the house is this analogous to? Maybe to that little flap the cat pushes through to get in and out of the backyard. In any case, it's something that won't be found by someone looking only for the French windows. But to me it feels like a real opening out of the house nonetheless. I plan to keep looking for more.

1996

PART ONE

Gypsies, Russians, and Other Heroes

Preceding page: Jan Yoors and his Gypsy *kumpania,* Yugoslavia, 1936. *Courtesy of Marianne Yoors.*

A Gypsy for Our Time

Most epic voyages of discovery begin with an ocean crossing or a trek through unexplored wilderness or a passage across trackless desert. But one of this century's more unusual odysseys—a journey between cultures, across several continents and through war and prison—began by accident in a Belgian village on a warm spring afternoon in 1934. And the voyager was then a child.

Twelve-year-old Jan Yoors was playing in a field near his home when he noticed smoke from a campfire. Going closer, he found a semicircle of fifteen covered wooden Gypsy wagons. Several Gypsy boys ran out to meet him. They played in the grass together; then the boys taught Yoors a few words of their language and invited him to share their dinner. "It was then," Yoors writes, "that I committed my one great semi-conscious error: I stayed five more minutes."

That night he shared the Gypsies' sleeping place—feather quilts spread on the ground. "We lay on our backs and looked up into the starry sky. . . . I noticed a shooting star and, eager to share this with Nanosh, pointed out to him where it had passed, far away. In a hushed, husky voice he told me never to do this again: for each star in the sky is a man on earth. When a star runs away it means that a thief takes flight, and if you point a finger at a shooting star the man it represents is likely to be captured."

When the Gypsies moved camp the next morning, Yoors went with them. His five minutes stretched into some eight years. During that time his *kumpania,* or extended family, roamed from Spain to Poland, Czechoslovakia to Turkey. The men traded horses; the women told fortunes. Pulika, the wise and resourceful *kumpania* leader, allowed Jan Yoors to come and go at will. And so, some winters, he returned to his amazingly tolerant parents for several

15

months, and then headed off across Europe in the spring to find Pulika's *kumpania* once again.

Unlike many others who have tried, Yoors was accepted by the Gypsies from the start. This was because when he first came he was a child. A few years later, and he could not have slipped through the door into this magical world. Looking back on the day of his first meeting with the boys from the caravan, Yoors writes in *The Gypsies,* the book in which he describes these travels: "As sometimes happens between very young human beings, there was from the beginning a feeling of great ease, almost one of having met before."

A feeling of having met before. When I first came across Jan Yoors's books and began insistently pressing them on others, I found that they were usually as deeply affected as I. One friend described how, for several days after finishing the last page of *The Gypsies,* he had a feeling of overwhelming sadness, almost of bereavement. We returned to the subject in conversation for months afterward. I began to discover something of a network of Yoors's admirers; it was not a cult, however, for there was no cult figure: we readers had no idea where Yoors was now.

The source of his books' peculiar appeal is, I think, this: Jan Yoors is one those rare people who have lived out a myth. At its deepest layer that myth is a secret wish we all share: to be born again in a different place and a different time—a time and place more intense, more heroic and closer to the core of life than our everyday existence. Yoors was reborn like this, shedding his old life for a new one. And he found the life of this splendid, earthy, free-wandering race of Gypsies to be even richer than he had imagined. The boldness of Yoors's running away to join them—and this is the source of my friend's sadness—feels almost like a reproach to those of us who stayed behind.

As the young Jan Yoors was drawn more deeply into Gypsy culture, what appealed to him most was the Gypsies' love for the "heroic, perpetual present." They are not trapped by attachment to possessions, time, or place. When he so movingly describes episodes from his life with his adoptive family in *The Gypsies,* Yoors virtually never mentions what countries these took place in. For the important thing is not the destination but the journey. Gypsies, he says—the true Gypsies, or *Rom*—are always on the move and never settle in one place. In their language there are no words for the names of days, months, and years. It matters only if it is winter, a season they dread because they have to camp several months in one spot, or spring and summer, when they can roam free once again.

Caught by the strange appeal of his writing, I began to wonder what had become of Yoors himself. If he were alive he would be in his fifties. Was he still among the Gypsies? And could their culture survive in an age of jets and television? I imagined Yoors robust and vigorous and of course out of doors, by a Gypsy campfire in a forest or meadow, in a caravan rolling down a European country road. Yet he must have lived in Britain or the United States for a long time, for his books are written in an English of great beauty. One of them carries a puzzling note of acknowledgment "to all those who share my roof." As it turned out, I did not have to look far to find him. I began in the handiest place to start searching for someone in the English-speaking world, the Manhattan telephone book. And there he was.

.   .   .

A block away, New York University students with books under their arms line up at the Xerox machine in the Copyquick shop. Then there is the shaded expanse of Washington Square, filled, this hot summer day, with hundreds of people in shirtsleeves and with policemen patrolling in pairs. A few houses past the square, a door is opened by a handsome woman with an intelligent face and a light accent. "Do come in."

I momentarily have the impression of having stepped into a museum. The large, sparsely furnished central room of this house has a high ceiling, and on its walls hang several vast tapestries, ten to fifteen feet long, bold and abstract. Strong brown and black splashes cover light backgrounds with shapes vaguely resembling huge waves or flames. Entering the room, I see that the entire length of one wall is covered with a high wooden loom, with rollers as thick as telephone poles. On it, a new tapestry is half woven.

Across the room, a man raises his head and smiles. He is in a wheelchair, which he rolls across the floor. Jan Yoors looks utterly different from the person I expected. His hair is gray and long, falling an inch or two below his ears. His face is pale, not tanned, and the hair and his tortoiseshell glasses make him look not like a

Gypsy but a scholar, perhaps, who has just emerged from the library stacks.

I ask Yoors about the wheelchair and he explains: he has no legs. They were both amputated when a circulatory ailment came on very suddenly about three years ago. It is hard to take this in. But he does not return to the subject except when I bring it up; in five minutes I've completely forgotten that I'm talking to someone in a wheelchair. His bearing asks for no pity. It is not that he defies pity, like someone who seems to be bravely overcoming a handicap. To his own injury Yoors simply pays no attention.

However, my asking him about his operation has reminded him of a Gypsy story, and he is already in the middle of it, gesturing extravagantly. "When I was in the hospital, we told no one. Absolutely nobody. We didn't want people coming all day with their sympathy; we just wanted to resume our normal lives. I wanted to get back to my work at the loom here. But the very night I get home from the hospital, the phone rings at three o'clock in the morning. Someone is speaking Romany [the Gypsy language, a descendant of Sanskrit], so my wife gives me the phone. It is a Gypsy, whose voice I don't know, calling from Copenhagen, which is now a sort of world meeting place for Gypsies. He calls me by my Gypsy name. 'Vanya,' he says, 'We've heard the news. We are coming.'

"Three weeks later, another phone call. Also at three o'clock in the morning. This time from Barcelona. 'Don't worry,' he says. 'We are on the way. This is Nene. We have been traveling many years in South Africa. Rafi and his *kumpania* are coming from Australia. They will meet us in Montreal and then we will all come to you.' Nene? Rafi? And then he explains in his Gypsy way: 'We are the sons of Ruva. When we last saw you, you were shaving; we were not.' Ruva I remembered—a Gypsy I knew in Spain, about thirty years ago. I only dimly remembered that he had had small children.

"Three weeks later, they call again. 'Vanya, we're here.' There were thirty of them—eleven adults and nineteen children. They stayed at a hotel at Coney Island. They turned the place upside down; the children had races with the elevators. They came to see me every day. We roasted whole pigs in the fireplace for them. When we went out—they liked Chinese restaurants—the procession would stretch over a whole block. People would stop their

cars and stare at us. They were all following me in my wheelchair.
I must have looked like a Mafia don with his entourage. They
stayed three months, coming every day. And then, suddenly, they
left. I don't know where they are now. But . . ." Yoors smiles,
spreading his hands, palms up, ". . . someday they'll come back."

The large room we are talking in is not only the workroom
and living room of this house but also something of a traffic circle;
people pass in and out carrying weaving materials and big wooden
boxes of vegetables. Three of them are children, aged nine to thirteen, and, as Yoors calls to them, I realize they are named after
members of his old Gypsy family. Yoors's wife, Marianne, who had
met me at the door, is from Holland; her sister Annebert, also a
gentle-featured woman in her fifties, is working at the loom as we
talk. She pushes a wooden shuttle back and forth, then packs the
horizontal threads of wool yarn tightly into place by flicking a
screwdriver rapidly down between the vertical threads with a constant, gentle thud, thud, thud. From time to time she is joined in
her work by two dark-haired Japanese women—Motoe and Masumi. Everyone goes by first names only. But, when required by
the outside world, they all use the last name of Yoors. Here, in the
middle of Greenwich Village, is a miniature, patriarchal Gypsy
kumpania.

"It is better this way," Jan Yoors says. "I don't get into those
stand-off battles with my children the way most American parents
do. We may get into a fight, but the showdown never comes,
because the child then gets involved with one of the other adults.
. . . No, I don't think of it as a commune. A commune is a would-
be thing you put together because for some idealistic reason you
want to live communally. Here we share a common work, and so
sharing the household is a natural outgrowth of that. On a normal
commercial loom, each worker works his own square meter; here
we all work together."

However, the tapestries are signed with Jan Yoors's name. He
does the original design—full-scale, on a huge sheet of paper,
called by artists the "cartoon" and pasted up behind the loom as a
sort of road map for the weavers; then he and the four women all
pitch in to do the actual weaving. The finished tapestries hang in
museums, offices, and public buildings throughout the United
States and Europe.

The household revolves around Yoors. When he needs to at-

tract the attention of someone in another room, he make a quick
clap-clap with his hands, and one of the women comes instantly to
his wheelchair. There is something disturbing about all this patri-
archy. Finally I realize that what I am feeling is not so much anger
as disappointment. One wants heroes whole. But they seldom
come that way. Yoors senses my disapproval; he mentions that his
daughter does not like it when, during visits by Gypsies, the men
and the women go to separate rooms. Yoors says this about his
daughter's feelings with a distinct note of pride: he plainly values
her Gypsy-like independence of mind, despite its clash with the
culture he loves. One also wants cultures without such contradictions, but perhaps they also don't come that way.

.   .   .

We go back to the tapestries. "The Gypsies love them," Yoors says,
"but they are always a bit puzzled. They ask: 'But what do you
need them for?' For them, attachment to an artifact is something
neurotic. They don't like photographs or monuments. You should
not have to *make* something to be happy. Happiness is people—
family, other Gypsies, having feasts. There is no pride in career."

Are Gypsies still traveling the world today, as they did when
he started living with them in the 1930s?

"Of course. In western Europe now the camper truck has replaced the wooden wagon, but they still call it by the same
name—*vurdon.* And they still park them in a circle at night. Here
in America the *vurdon* is usually a Lincoln Continental. In some
parts of the world, nothing has changed at all. In 1967 I was in
Uzbekistan, in Soviet Central Asia. We were driving along a road.
A Russian guide was showing me local art objects. And all of a
sudden I saw a train of fifty wooden wagons. *Fifty* of them! 'Ahhh
. . .' I said, 'I'm getting out here.' I traveled with them for a whole
week. It was wonderful. You might think they would have difficulty getting around in the USSR, which has internal passports,
laws against nomads, and so on. But they managed. Whenever we
came to a village, the police would come out. The Gypsies would
apologize for having no permits and then say, 'But we are only
going to our cousin's wedding. It's not in this village, but the
next.' 'Oh, you mean over in Otokino' (or wherever), the police
would say, figuring they'd let the authorities there deal with the
problem of all these unauthorized people. 'Yes! Otokino! That's it,'

the Gypsies would say, and would make a big show of asking directions. And the police would say, 'O.K., move along, then.' They had been traveling for *months* this way, all across the Soviet Union. The Russians have something of a soft spot in their hearts for Gypsies, after the third vodka, anyway."

Gypsies, Yoors says, adapt their work easily to fit the needs of whatever country they are in. In South America, they are often tinsmiths. In Mexico, they travel in trucks with battery-powered film projectors, showing movies in small villages without electricity. In the United States, they knock on people's doors and offer to fix dented fenders. Everywhere the women tell fortunes.

Gypsies are divided into four principal tribes and many more subtribes. Very tribal in his own feelings, Yoors has no use for some Gypsies—particularly those who have abandoned the wandering of the true *Rom* and settled down for good in one country, sometimes becoming heavily involved in violent crime. Others, like his adoptive Lowara tribe, he claims, have an extremely strict code of honor, although he admits this applies to their dealings with each other rather than to those with the *Gaje* (non-Gypsies). One American Gypsy Yoors knew, for instance, found himself without his tools on a fender-mending expedition. It was a Sunday and hardware stores were closed, but grocery stores were open. So he filled in fender dents with liverwurst, then painted them over.

I ask him what the survivors of the Gypsies he once traveled with do now.

"Oh, they tell fortunes, and they sell rugs, for cover."

Cover for what?

"Please!" Yoors holds up his hands in protest. "They are my kin."

. . .

Yoors was eighteen years old and in France with his Gypsy band when the Germans invaded. He felt torn between two worlds. Gypsies have never, as a group, taken part in warfare. The decision Yoors faced was doubly difficult, for Pulika wanted him to marry Djijo, a young woman of the *kumpania* to whom he was deeply attracted. "Having seen the luminous shore," Yoors writes, "I decided not to cross over to it." Regretfully, he left the Gypsies and furtively made his way to German-occupied Paris, planning to slip from there to England and join the British army. Waiting for his underground passage out of the country, he took refuge in a nunnery.

One day a man knocked on the door of Yoors's room. He was an agent of British Intelligence. He had come to tell Yoors: We want you to go back—and to organize the Gypsies for us.

In his second book, *Crossing,* Yoors describes the events that followed. After many weeks on the road, he found his *kumpania* again and was greeted with great rejoicing. After the welcoming feast, he and Pulika talked of the war now enveloping them. Standing in a meadow at night, the fiery young idealist argued with the skeptical sage. This time, this war, Yoors told Pulika, the Gypsies would have to break with their ancient tradition: Nazism was too terrible; in Germany itself Gypsies were already being sent to concentration camps. Pulika then spoke eloquently about how the purpose of life is love; history is a record of lost illusions. "Do not accept their ideological passions," he told Yoors. "They are lies . . . more easily believed than truth, and courage about death often disguises cowardice about life. Leave to others the quest for eternal certainties . . . one day you will learn again to open the closed fist."

Then, abruptly, Pulika told Yoors he would establish liaison with the Resistance.

Pulika hastily arranged a meeting of the *kris,* an assembly of the leaders of all the major *kumpanias.* It is the Gypsies' supreme court and decision-making body. The traditional coming together of hundreds of wagons was out of the question because of German troops patrolling everywhere, and so the *kris* took place at a provincial French tavern. To authorities who were suspicious of so many people gathering, Gypsy leaders explained they were assembling for the funeral of a venerable old Gypsy named Bengesico Niamso—Romany for "cursed German."

Instead of being in the customary forest clearing, the Gypsies sat uncomfortably in tubular chrome chairs; when an elder poured out the ritual libation to buried ancestors, the brandy ran along the linoleum floor. The *kris* made the decision to join the battle against the Nazis, and in the months ahead Yoors worked with a growing network of Gypsies throughout France, who used their wagons to carry arms to the Resistance. Often, hidden in metal storage bins under the wagons, were British pilots who had been shot down. Here the Gypsies' unaccustomed participation in a *Gajo* war felt natural to them, for they were carrying out a long tradition of helping men on the run from the police.

.   .   .

Gypsy beliefs endured through the war's worst hardships. Once Yoors and Pulika were hiding out in a forest, cold and hungry. They made contact with a French Resistance group that offered them a meal of freshly cooked pheasant. Pulika refused it. Despite their love of feasting, true *Rom* will never eat wild game, "because it is wild and free like ourselves."

After some months, Yoors and many of his Gypsy comrades were captured by the Germans. He was thrown into solitary confinement in La Santé prison in Paris. One night he heard a distant voice echoing out from another cell in the labyrinth, calling in Romany: "*Romale tai Shavale, Tshurara tai wi Lowara, ame Rom sam.*" (Gypsy men and youths, Tshurara and Lowara [members of two feuding tribes] alike, we are all *Rom*.) "The cry in the night was never identified, but it did not matter," Yoors writes. "It brought back to me a clear and strong vision of a long single line of Gypsy wagons and horses, moving relentlessly toward the horizon."

Somehow that vision kept him alive, through six months of intermittent torture, more than a year of imprisonment and the knowledge that the Germans were trying to wipe the Gypsies off the face of Europe. After the war, he learned that half a million Gypsies, including Pulika and virtually all his family, had died in Nazi death camps.

Yoors himself was saved by accident, a curiously appropriate one for a man who has lived a double life. A clerk mistakenly switched his file with that of another prisoner, and he was unexpectedly released. The Germans then realized their error, and twenty-four hours later they had posters with his picture all over Paris. But he managed to rejoin the Resistance and finally escaped across the Pyrenees to Spain. There he regained his health while staying with Gypsies. It was two of them who were to visit him in New York some thirty years later.

It is eerie to think that this man sitting in front of me, in a Greenwich Village town house, cultured, cosmopolitan, discussing what was in this morning's *New York Times,* was once under Nazi torture. He avoids the details in his book, so I ask him about it only hesitantly.

"You should understand that I was really crazy for a while afterwards. For years after the war I had nightmares. When I went to a restaurant—I had been arrested in a Paris café, you see—I always had to be facing the door and be near an exit. That was really why I came to America in 1950; I wanted to get as far away from the Germans as possible. I have only been able to even write about the experience recently; something about having the operation on my legs, experiencing pain again, although this time there were doctors and nurses there trying to make it better, not people trying to make it worse.

"What did they do to me? I was held under water for a minute, two minutes at a time. In a way it was experiencing death, the first sensations of drowning. But it showed me that above all I wanted to live. When I first went into the war I did not know that; that had been what Pulika wanted to tell me, that I foolishly wanted to die in the fight against Hitler. But the drowning—each time it showed me I wanted to live.

"Then came the electrodes. It is not pain, exactly, but an intensity of sensation, so intense you can't stand it. But it made me realize that all our other sensations were mild. I wanted to experience a positive intensity equal to that negative intensity. I experienced despair, total despair. But if it goes that deep, it must go that high. If we never experience much despair we can never achieve ecstasy."

.   .   .

Jan Yoors is rolling along the crowded Bleecker Street sidewalk as the Japanese weaver Motoe pushes him in his wheelchair, zigzagging in and out among hawkers, dog droppings, and scraps of windblown garbage.

"You want to find Gypsies? It won't be difficult here," he says. "They are everywhere. They've done well here. The U.S. has the largest percentage of college-educated people in the world; that prepares them for psychoanalysis—and for fortune-telling. And then lately the Gypsies have been cashing in on being an ethnic minority, getting foundation grants and money from the churches and Small Business Administration loans. To them this ethnic minority business is just one more strange custom of the *Gaje* to take advantage of, like wanting to have your fortune told."

We turn a corner, and Yoors and Motoe scan the next block. "By the way," he says, "don't believe any of this stuff you read about Gypsy kings. There is no such thing. It's another thing to fool a *Gajo.* Any Gypsy who enters a hospital, for instance, is automatically a king. He gets better treatment."

In his books, Yoors talks about other misconceptions *Gaje* have about Gypsies. For example, novelists who've created Gypsy characters, like D. H. Lawrence in *The Virgin and the Gypsy,* or Prosper Mérimée in *Carmen,* often imagine that Gypsy freedom includes sexual freedom as well. But in real life, says Yoors, Gypsy women, at least, are highly puritanical and monogamous. Even writers who have visited Gypsies firsthand usually come back with the image Gypsies want to give them: of a sinister and mysterious tribe, with exotic rituals and preternatural intuition. It is an image Gypsies have been cultivating for centuries, because it helps scare off the police and is good for the fortune-telling business. Among themselves, Gypsies tell no fortunes.

"Stop," Yoors says suddenly. "Here's one." We are in front of a storefront with a sign: READER/ADVISOR. PALM READINGS. TAROT. COFFEE GROUNDS READ. Motoe steps inside and talks to a young, dark-haired, unsmiling woman who puts her head through a bead curtain. Then Motoe comes out to the sidewalk: "She says it's closed now. Nobody is here. We must come back later."

But Yoors calls in Romany through the open door, and the woman comes outside immediately. She is perhaps twenty-two or twenty-three, with olive skin, jet-black hair and eyes, and high cheekbones. As she and Yoors talk, she quickly relaxes, crosses her arms, and leans smiling against the door frame. Their talk is formal-sounding; no interruptions, no short yes or no answers. Part of it, by each of them, involves reeling off a list of names.

The sound of spoken Romany is full and sensual. It is not precise, like French, or businesslike, like German, but full of deeper, rich tones, like a mixture of Italian and Russian. Every once in a while the woman uses an English phrase, but only in relation to time: "six months ago," "three, four months ago." Suddenly I realize that the list of names she is giving is of Gypsies who have died.

(Yoors confirms this later. "When a Gypsy man and woman

talk, if they are not husband and wife, the talk is tribal talk, not personal talk. She is a Rusuri. They are a tribe that left Russia right after the Revolution and came to New York via France in the thirties. They 'own' New York now, and they're having a feud with the Bimburas, who came here via South America and Chicago.")

At one point the woman nods her head at Motoe, and Yoors says something in which I recognize, from his books, the word *bori,* Romany for daughter-in-law. ("That made it all right for her to be with me," he explains afterward. "She is obviously not my daughter, and she is too young to be my wife. If she was not a relative of some kind, it would not be proper for us to be on the street together.")

While they are speaking, a very small boy, perhaps two years old, looking almost too young to talk, emerges from the shop. The boy has the same dark hair and olive skin as his mother. He seems very sturdy and healthy. He looks us over carefully, then begins riding a bright red, blue, and yellow tricycle in circles. Unexpectedly, it seems sad: how will this child riding his plastic fluorescent toy on New York sidewalks ever feel any sense of Gypsy identity?

Suddenly he rides right up to where I'm standing, next to Yoors's wheelchair, and whacks me boldly on the calf with the back of his hand.

"*Rom sin?*" (Are you a Rom?) His saucer eyes look straight up at me.

I shake my head.

He thumps his fist proudly on his chest. "*Rom sam!*" (I am a Rom.)

·   ·   ·

At the heart of Gypsy freedom is the ability, when trouble looms in one country or opportunity beckons in another, to slip across national borders. Yoors describes one such crossing in *The Gypsies:*

> I clearly remember stealthy long marches into unknown countries, by night. On one such march the horses' hoofs were padded with straw and bound with strips of colored dress material. Rain fell steadily. For days Gypsy wagons had been massing near the border. One night they all converged and fell in with the long line of other moving wagons, to punch through the border en masse. Leaving the roads, we traveled cross-country

through rugged terrain. The caravan plodded through the flailing rain. At times it slowed down to a crawl and we waded ankle-deep in the slippery mud, pushing, shoving, urging the horses on with low clicking sounds. At other times the wagons would suddenly hurtle forward, pitching and swaying. Unrelentingly, the *Rom* pushed onward, leaving behind a trail of deep mud mashed by numerous horses, wagon wheels and people on foot. A low, repeated whistle came from the direction of the lead wagon and slowly passed down the staggered line of wagons. The sound was deep and low and strangely reassuring, in contrast to the unrelenting howling of the wind, the splash and suck of horses and men wading through the mud and the occasional wail of an infant quickly hushed. Suddenly the startling sound of loudly pounding hoofs told that we had reached a paved road. The oncoming wind smelled of smoke from wood fires. We had finally caught up with other Gypsies camping nearby, probably waiting for us at this spot. We were met with subdued joyous greetings. We tethered the horses at the backs of the vans, rubbed them briskly and covered them with blankets, tarpaulins or pieces of carpet. The wind whipped the many-layered skirts of the women.

Back in Yoors's house, I ask him about the border he crossed in his own life. Does he have any regrets about crossing back, into the world of the *Gaje?*

"No." He shakes his head emphatically. He is holding a bobbin of red wool weaving yarn for Masumi, which she winds deftly into a ball. "The Gypsies have a saying—*yekka buliasa nashti beshes pe done grastende*—with one behind you cannot sit on two horses. I had to choose. I could not see making my life with them. For all its beauty, it was a limited world. After all, if I had stayed I would now be an itinerant horse dealer." He stops and smiles. "But you know, if my parents had ever tried to stop me, I would still be a Gypsy today."

In the room where we are talking, his tapestries surround us. I am struck again by their size and by the large, bold shapes on them: visual pulses of color two and three feet high. In most tapestries you see a pattern; here you see vigorous, active motion.

"In some ways I am more of a Gypsy than ever," he goes on. "If I cannot work on a grand scale, I do not work. I like to think of that as an equivalent of the splendor of Gypsy life." As he nods at them, I realize for the first time that he is also the maker of three or four large bronze sculptures that sit on wooden pedestals in various corners. He points also to a striking charcoal drawing of a headless nude, black on a brown background, that almost fills an entire section of wall, her legs and shoulders butting against the frame, as if trying to break free. "People ask me: 'Why not make a bigger drawing? Then you could fit the head in.' But if I made a bigger drawing, I'd make the body bigger too. It is what is unseen in a person, or a drawing, that makes them interesting."

How does Yoors feel about young Americans of recent years—hippies, runaways, people who have figuratively considered themselves Gypsies?

He tips his head and frowns slightly, as if I have not asked quite the right question. And I can see what he means: he has thought of his own life in terms not of defiance but of affirmation. His story is not of running away but of finding a new home, first with the Gypsies, then with his art.

Finally his face relaxes. "I answer you . . ." (his hands, palms together, make a swerving motion) ". . . Gypsy fashion. Once in Elat on the Red Sea I met an American hippie, as far away from anything familiar as he could get. He lived on a mountain cliff—an open cliff with only the stars overhead. He had the shortest shorts and the longest hair I have ever seen. I stayed for supper. He was fussing around, opening cans; 'I'm putting my kitchen in order,' he said. Then he took me to his 'library,' a single board with a row of books on it, and took out to show me an issue of *Esquire,* which had an article that mentioned *him.* And then, worst of all, he began talking about *his* mountain." Yoors leans back in the wheelchair and smiles. "So. You see?"

. . .

The central ritual of Gypsy life is the *patshiv,* the great feast. It can celebrate a birth or marriage, but most often is unplanned, given to mark the chance meeting with a caravan of friends, relatives, or fellow tribes people that luck has brought to the same crossroads. Great *patshiva* become a part of Gypsy legend. Pigs and chickens are "borrowed" from local peasants, and hedgehogs are caught in the fields; all are cooked over an open fire, highly seasoned with black pepper and wild garlic, and served with fried onions, tomatoes, and red peppers. The guests pick out choice morsels to feed each other, and sing songs to each other. Even the dead are included; the living speak and sing to them.

At the end of *The Gypsies,* Yoors tells how Pulika's caravan was crossing Europe in 1940 when one day a French horse dealer casually remarked that he had bought a horse from another Gypsy a few days before. Without appearing curious, Pulika asked a few questions. Early the next morning, all the young men of the camp were sent out in *taligas*—open carts—fanning out across the countryside in the direction the other Gypsies were said to have gone. Yoors and a companion drove their cart farther and faster than the others, slept in a farmer's field that night, then cut through a pine forest and finally came out onto an open plain. "Suddenly we became aware of a long line of Gypsy wagons a great distance ahead of us, slowly moving in wide lazy curves like a languorous and fat summer snake." At last, when night had fallen and the campfires were lit, they caught up. The wagons were the *kumpania* of Milosh, Pulika's younger brother, who had, with incredible difficulty, made his way from German-occupied Eastern Europe to France in search of Pulika. The brothers had not seen each other for seventeen years. The *patshiv* lasted for days.

It is not a *patshiv,* but there seems something celebratory when I sit down to dinner with Jan Yoors and the four women of his unusual household before leaving. It is a hot summer evening, and we eat outdoors on a tiny patio. There are high walls on each side, but I am more aware of the island of night sky above. In this little well beneath the rooftops of the city, we are cut off from most noise. It is very peaceful. Motoe and Masumi speak softly to each other in Japanese, Marianne and her sister Annebert in Dutch; Yoors, I, and the three children talk in English about their day at school. At the end of the meal is Gypsy-style coffee: Turkish coffee thick with fine grounds, poured from a copper pot into brown ceramic bowls that look like miniature flowerpots.

Yoors is talking once again about the Gypsies' capacity for enjoying the present. He tells of meeting one Gypsy, who was known as "the Millionaire"—not because he had a million francs or zlotys or whatever, but because he had *spent* a million. To the Gypsies, he says, all wealth is for celebrating, not hoarding: when Gypsies die, all their possessions are burned.

Looking around, I notice one thing that has given this cramped space we are in its spaciousness: a giant design, ten feet or so high, in black paint on the whitewashed wall opposite me. "It's the Japanese character for fire," Yoors explains. "Fire is a very Gypsy thing. The process is the actuality. It does not construct something for the future. Its present is everything. And when it is dead . . ." (he smiles and spreads his palms wide) ". . . it is gone."

.   .   .

For Jan Yoors, the fire did not burn long. Though he did not talk about it during my visit with him, his heart condition was steadily worsening; the loss of his legs was only the first sign. A few months after I saw him, he suffered a massive heart attack. Three days later, still unconscious, he died. He is buried in Long Island's Green River Cemetery, in a special plot where the bodies of Jackson Pollock and other artists also lie.

Yoors designed tapestries at a pace that far outstripped the rate at which he and the four women could weave them. He left behind many designs at his death, and his household plans to continue weaving from them for years. This bit of artist's immortality might please his Gypsy friends, for it contains an echo of their own culture. The Gypsies believe, Yoors wrote, that the soul of a dead man lives on as long as do people who knew him and remember him. Only when the last of them are gone does the soul finally die.

1978

Aristocratic Revolutionary

The first real talk I had with Patrick Duncan was on his lawn. In his country, apartheid-era South Africa, as in so many nations, important political talk took place on lawns, streets, park benches—places hoped to be out of range of the hidden police microphones everyone assumed were present indoors. I noted this down as the first of many lessons from the time my life intersected his. For this story, although mainly the tale of a remarkable man who managed to be both aristocrat and revolutionary, is also the story of a nineteen-year-old boy beginning his political education.

The conversation I speak of took place in 1961. As a college student on summer vacation, I was traveling through Africa; finally I reached the continent's end, Cape Town. I had heard a good deal about Patrick Duncan and was eager to meet him. Although a white man, he was in the forefront of the battle against South Africa's apartheid system, which then denied more than 80 percent of the country's population the right to vote because they had black or brown skin. The long, brave struggle for justice and equal rights in South Africa had captured my imagination, as it had that of so many people elsewhere in the world. Duncan was the editor of an antiapartheid newspaper and was angrily denounced in the progovernment press. In the 1950s, when South Africa's police state had not grown quite as severe as it became later and mass protest meetings were still allowed, Duncan was one of the handful of white people ever invited to speak to these black crowds. He had been jailed three times for his beliefs.

Paradoxically, Duncan had come to all this from the top of his country's elite. His father, Sir Patrick Duncan, had been a cabinet minister and then governor general of South Africa in the 1930s. As a teenager, Pat traveled the country with his father in the governor general's official train, called, with apparently unintended irony, the White Train. Years later, one of the times he was imprisoned for his antiapartheid work, the police colonel who arrested him turned out to have been in the honor guard at his father's state funeral.

A mutual friend had told me about Duncan and had given me his phone number. When I called him up on arriving in Cape Town, he invited me to his house for dinner. The man who met me at the door wore a suit and tie and had piercing blue eyes. The ruddy skin of his face stretched tightly over the bones. He spoke with an impeccable Oxford accent quite different from the broad, slangy singsong of other white South Africans, and he spoke emphatically, precisely, always in complete sentences. At first I was puzzled and disappointed. For Pat and his gracious, British-born wife, Cynthia, lived in an elegant house in one of Cape Town's wealthiest white suburbs—a house with stables, a large garden, and, in the British fashion, a name: Keyser House. There were dark-skinned servants, a British nanny for their four children, and even a swimming pool in the shape of Africa. All this seemed terribly wrong to me, not at all my idea of how a revolutionary should live.

At the end of the evening, however, Duncan asked me to come out on the lawn with him. He paced up and down with an energetic, restless limp, the result of a childhood bone disease that had required many operations and left one leg unable to bend at the knee. (A famous picture showed him under arrest after leading a demonstration, on crutches.) His way of speaking was breathless and passionate, as if he were always thinking: there is little time, little time, we must get right to the point. Once, later, as if it fitted into the same category, he told me simply that as a matter of principle "I never read fiction."

"*Your country*," he said, as he limped back and forth on his lawn under the night sky, "holds *this* country in the palm of its hand." President Kennedy had been elected less than a year before. Pat Duncan was convinced that here at last was an American president who—if only someone could explain things to him properly—would force South Africa to change its ways. Although the South African government had taken away Duncan's passport, he told me that twice during the past year he had journeyed secretly to Washington in unsuccessful attempts, through various family connections, to talk to the president. He said that as an American who had been to South Africa and seen the injustice of apartheid first-hand, I had an important message to tell people when I went home.

This was heady stuff for a young student who, in his own way, was also under the spell of the Kennedy mystique. That night I sat for a long time on a seawall near where I was staying in Cape Town, watching the ocean waves pound, unable to sleep.

.　　.　　.

The next day I went to the office of the newspaper Duncan edited, a biweekly called *Contact*. It had bold black and red headlines about security police raids, labor organizing, and student resistance to apartheid. South Africa's blacks were hungry for such news, and there were few other places they could get it. This was a period of vast optimism in Africa: elsewhere on the continent a score of territories were winning independence from British and French colonial rule; the problems that would follow had not yet appeared; surely South Africa's liberation, everyone felt, must also be near.

Contact was loosely aligned with the Liberal Party of South Africa, a small opposition group, multiracial but mainly white, that favored Western-style democracy. But the paper also reflected Duncan's own quirks. One of these was a belief that United States intervention was the best hope for South Africa. This conviction was coupled with an extraordinarily vigorous anticommunism. Second only to apartheid as a subject of *Contact*'s attacks were the Russians. South Africa's tiny community of antiapartheid whites was sharply divided: Liberals and Communist sympathizers (the party itself was outlawed), often spent as much time attacking each other as they did the government. Years later I heard reports that *Contact* had some CIA funding. Duncan was no one's puppet, but he was so enthusiastically pro-American that if Washington had offered money, I'm sure he would have accepted.

The *Contact* office was right across the street from the South African parliament. "That's the room they watch us from: the one over there with the curtains drawn," an editor told me. Soon after I arrived, a staff meeting began. Over sandwiches, pickles, and beer, Pat and the other editors and writers talked about the stories they were planning with a group of the paper's Coloured, or mixed-race, sales agents, who picked up bundles of *Contact* every two weeks and sold them on the streets of Coloured districts around Cape

Town. The group also discussed an American naval flotilla then making a "goodwill visit" to the city. To everyone's dismay, the U.S. Navy was putting its sailors ashore in racially segregated groups, so as not to offend their white South African hosts. "If only," Duncan said in that earnest way of his, "if only I could get out there and *talk* to the admiral. I'm sure I could make him understand."

Later that afternoon, Duncan asked me to come home with him. On the way out the office door, he said impulsively, "But you're leaving in two days and you haven't seen the Cape! I *must* show it to you." Three of the *Contact* Coloured sales agents were standing on the sidewalk outside the building waiting for a bus, and, on a second impulse, he invited them to join us. (Pat always did things on sudden impulses. Before one of his secret trips to the United States that year, another antiapartheid activist told me, Duncan had unexpectedly shown up at the man's house at 7:00 one morning to say: "I'm leaving for America today. Do you want to come?")

The area around Cape Town is heartbreakingly beautiful; I felt at the time it was lovely beyond anything that so unjust a country deserved. The city itself climbs a slope that steepens to a sheer cliff: the striking, flat-topped Table Mountain, often with a thin white "tablecloth" of fog rolling off the top. To the south stretches the rocky Cape Peninsula, which points downward like a finger near where the Atlantic and Indian oceans meet. It was along this peninsula that we drove in Pat's Volkswagen van for several hours, along the tops of cliffs, past beaches and coves. Pat knew an amazing amount of natural history, and kept up a nonstop commentary on the rocks, the flowers, the tide pools. The three Coloured newspaper salesmen listened in polite awe. They had never seen any of this territory, although they had lived nearby all their lives: they had no cars, and the beaches were almost all for whites only.

That evening at his house, out on the lawn in the dark again, I asked Pat if on my next summer vacation from college I could come back to South Africa and work for his paper. He said yes.

·   ·   ·

The following spring, just before I was to leave for South Africa, my plans were almost upset. A new government edict confined Pat Duncan to Cape Town. This came on top of an existing ban on his attending political meetings. The next step, everyone thought, would be house arrest. Pat had no illusions about the nobility of martyrdom; he wanted to continue the fight against apartheid. And so one night in May 1962 he defied his confinement order, left his house after dark, switched cars with some friends on a country road, drove 750 miles through the night, and slipped across the border into neighboring British territory.

The tiny, impoverished kingdom that was then the British colony of Basutoland is today the independent country of Lesotho. It lies amid southern Africa's highest mountains. Map lovers know it as one of the few nations surrounded on all sides by a single other country—South Africa. As an island of British territory, Basutoland was at the time considered safe from the South African police, and so it served as a refuge to many South African political exiles. For Pat Duncan it was a logical base: as a young man, he had spent a decade as a civil servant in Basutoland, much of the time as a traveling magistrate. He had thrown himself into the job with typical enthusiasm, writing a book on the territory's tribal law and customs, and becoming fluent in its language, Sesotho. Before I left the United States, he sent me a message that I should come to Basutoland and meet him there.

And so, several weeks later, on the last leg of a long journey, I found myself on the once-a-day steam-powered train that crawled slowly across the South African veldt and up into the hills to Maseru, Basutoland's capital. One of the people sharing my compartment was another American: portly, breezy, recently retired. I asked if he was staying long in Maseru. No, he said, only an hour or so—which I knew to be the time the train waited before it made the return journey back downhill to South Africa. What was he going to do there? "Oh, nothing. Get out and walk around a bit." When I pressed further, he proudly pulled a worn pamphlet out of his pocket. It was the chart of international mailing rates published by the U.S. Post Office, which listed all nations, colonies, and territories in alphabetical order. Beside the names of most of them were red check marks. This man was, methodically, visiting every country in the world. As our train pulled into Maseru, I felt I had truly arrived at the ends of the earth.

·   ·   ·

In Basutoland, I spent several days with Pat Duncan. He was full of energy and plans. He was sending a steady stream of columns and editorials to his paper in Cape Town. And he had just made a major political decision, which was to join the Pan Africanist Congress, one of South Africa's two major black organizations. The PAC had recently split off from the much older African National Congress, charging, among other things, that the ANC was too much under the influence of white communists. Both groups had been banned and had gone underground in South Africa itself. The PAC's militant opposition to both apartheid and communism made it the political home Pat was looking for, despite the group's black nationalism. Black PAC exiles in Basutoland seemed to trust Pat but to be baffled by him. He was the organization's only white member.

Pat said I should travel on to Cape Town and work with the staff now putting out *Contact* in his absence. And this I did, filled with dreams of being a crusading reporter in a country that had scandalous injustice waiting to be exposed on all sides. But things turned out otherwise. The political situation was very tense: the African National Congress and other underground groups had begun staging attacks on power stations and government buildings, and the government had rushed through draconian new laws in response. *Contact* and the tiny handful of similar publications feared being shut down; their staffs went to work each day half expecting to be arrested by nightfall. One day the police raided the office of another antiapartheid publication in Cape Town. The *Contact* people thought I would be deported immediately if I was seen at the paper, and so I never went to the office or out on assignment, and worked only in my tiny rented room. What little work I did consisted mainly of copyediting articles and of correcting the English of Africans who wrote letters to the editor. The letters made up in feeling what they lacked in grammar, and I tried to leave the basic wording pretty much alone.

> Sir: Although I am small, I am pulling a heavy wagon. Whenever we give for freedom we must forget our differences. . . . If we are too critical amongst ourselves it gives the enemy a chance to be strong. . . . Anyone who breaks through the iron chains of oppression must be heartily welcomed by all Parties, as long as his manifesto is, "Africa must be free!"

Or:

> Sir: Although our being tongue-tied by our oppressors and colonial powers hinders our progress towards freedom . . . I feel that justice will eat up injustice until one day injustice falls dramatically dead.

Meanwhile, certain that *Contact* would soon be banned, Pat was preparing to publish it from his place of exile, Basutoland. He had decided to build up a cadre of people prepared to clandestinely take the newspaper from there into South Africa once this became necessary. He figured the task would be easy: more than a hundred thousand Basutoland Africans worked as migrant laborers in South Africa, mostly in the mines. A steady flow of them crossed the border at all times, wearing their traditional dress, a blanket fastened around the neck. "We'll just get some of these chaps," Pat said, "to carry bundles of papers under their blankets."

.   .   .

Images from the summer:

A headline in a white paper: 400,000 WHITES FLEE ALGERIA. The Johannesburg railroad station—a vast, modernistic structure with a graceful vaulting roof, all built, at great expense, so that white and black passengers never meet. The slogans on walls everywhere: AVENGE SHARPEVILLE! Six months in jail if you're caught slogan-writing. A morning scene in Johannesburg: a garden wall with graffiti from the night before; a white matron in a white dress, hands on hips, supervising a black servant whitewashing over the offending words.

In the *Cape Times,* a story on the "banning" of 102 people under new legislation running side by side with a story on Yves St. Laurent's new collection. A parade through the streets of Johannesburg of white mercenary "freedom fighters," who had helped topple the leftist government of the Congo. Little everyday things one would take for granted elsewhere that here, on the verge of civil war, seem suddenly absurd: the white orchestra conductor's formal black tailcoat at a concert, a bookstore displaying the *Journal of the South African Racing Pigeon Society,* a newspaper story: CHAIRMAN OF RUGBY BOARD LODGES COMPLAINT ON QUALITY OF SPORTS COMMENTATORS.

A party: a group of young black men are dancing, bobbing up and down with the music; a young white woman is dancing enthusiastically in their midst, but can't get the rhythm right—her head goes up when theirs bob down, down when theirs bob up.

.   .   .

I traveled around South Africa a good deal that summer, by train, bus, hitchhiking. Once I got a ride atop a truckload of wonderfully aromatic onions, another time with a trader who bought diamonds from wildcat miners and sold them in Europe. But I did not fully absorb everything until long afterward. Looking over a predictably indignant newspaper article I wrote soon after I returned home, I see that I left out every experience that raised too many uncomfortable questions. Here is one:

I am crossing South Africa from west to east. I have reached a town in one of the remote, desparately poor and overcrowded rural areas set aside for blacks. The following day I must be in the city of Durban. I have a twenty-four-hour journey ahead of me: all day on a bus, which connects to an overnight train to Durban. I show up at the bus depot early in the morning. But as the bus rolls in, I realize I must have missed something in the timetable. For on the side of the bus is a sign: SLEGS VIR NEI-BLANKES/NON-EUROPEANS ONLY. Almost all South African transport is segregated, and in this part of the country there are many more black buses than white. The only white bus of the day on this route, it turns out, comes too late to connect with my train.

I explain my predicament to a dour Afrikaner official at the bus depot. He shakes his head. The law is the law. "*Ach,* man, you just must wait."

Meanwhile the white driver of the blacks-only bus I had hoped to take overhears my pleading. He confers with his ticket-taker, also white. He turns to me and says, "All right, mate. Come along with us. We're breaking the rules by taking you. We could get in trouble. So don't tell anyone."

The two of them sit in a little compartment at the front of the bus, walled off like an airliner's cockpit. The ticket collector insists on giving up his seat for me, and sits on an upturned crate. At stops, he opens the door into the rest of the bus, collects ticket money, then shuts the door and sits down again. Both men are Afrikaners. They insist on giving me food and cigarettes. They ask my impressions of South Africa. I try to stay off politics, and say instead how spectacular is the scenery. And it is: through the large front window of the bus I get a magnificent view of brown hills, the black paths of grass fires, eroded scars of red earth, and the vast open spaces rolling out to a horizon that in Africa always seems wider and more distant than any other horizon in the world.

Suddenly, in midafternoon, some sort of scuffle breaks out among the African passengers. An argument, shouting. The ticket collector, a strong, husky man, lets out an oath in Afrikaans, gets up, and goes through the door into the passenger compartment. He picks up one of the two arguing black passengers by the back of his shirt collar, spins him around, and gives him a brutally hard kick in the buttocks that sends the man sprawling to the far end of the aisle. Then he turns around, comes back to our little cabin in front, and shuts the door.

The bus doesn't stop. The ticket collector and driver resume talking with me: rugby, weather, movie actresses. I feel horrified. I feel I should do something, say something, speak up, get off the bus. But I say nothing and feel guilty. Our conversation continues, awkwardly, until they leave me off at the railroad station, in time to catch my train. I thank them profusely, remembering once again that they had risked getting into trouble for my sake, because I was a fellow white man.

.   .   .

Looking through a dusty suitcase recently, I found the breathless diary I kept that summer of 1962, more than half my life ago. Why is it always so embarrassing to read your juvenilia? One reason, I think, is that it is usually written in someone else's voice. A voice deliberately echoing other voices, wanting that imagined reader-over-your-shoulder to exclaim, By God, this is as good as Conrad! The voice in my diary, however, is not literary, but political. It is a State Department voice. I wrote about how eloquently Patrick Duncan summed up South Africa's injustices, and then added, "And he has a keen appreciation of the part the U.S. can play."

Although I fancied myself to be a leftist, enough so to have had many long arguments with Pat, I still secretly had the illusion that he and many of my South African friends—white and black—had then: that the United States would wake up, and would at last live up to its heritage and support the movement against apartheid. It was an attractive fantasy, above all because it offered me a role. I prepared lists of people to talk to when I got home: influential journalists, people my family knew in the government, foundation executives.

But gradually the hopelessness of this project became clear to me, and my resolve fell away. Why expect the United States to square off against a country in which it has millions in investments? And which is so staunchly anticommunist?

It is hard to fix a moment when my understanding of all this began—which meant understanding that international politics works in economic and not moral terms. But I remember staring at the directory board in the lobby of the U.S. embassy in Pretoria, and being astonished by the long list of military attachés we had there. One result of that summer was that I do not think in terms of "we" anymore. As in "Why are we in Vietnam?" When *that* question came up a few years later, it was no sudden shock. South Africa helped me lose my political virginity.

.   .   .

Around me, South Africa's long-simmering conflict edged ever closer to civil war. You could see it on people's faces. And then one day in August newsboys on the streets of Cape Town waved papers with banner headlines proclaiming the arrest of the country's most wanted man, who had eluded capture until now, Nelson Mandela. Overnight more slogans appeared on the city's walls and buildings: FREE MANDELA! (And who had tipped off the police about Mandela's whereabouts so that they could put their roadblock in the right place? Only many years later would it be revealed: an American diplomat.)

The time I spent in South Africa then was a watershed in my life. It was my first experience with people engaged in serious politics, whose beliefs were not merely opinions voiced in the classroom or across a dinner table but commitments that could affect someone's comfort, freedom, even life. One man I knew fairly well was later hanged. Another, a burly, vibrant black activist with a humorous glint in his eyes and a fine singing voice, was eventually driven out of his mind by police torture. Two others later spent years in jail. Another, not much older than me, saved himself from prison by turning state's evidence on his friends, and lives under that cloud still. Dimly, unable to assimilate it all at the time, I had the sense that summer that I was traveling back and forth across a battlefield.

Twice in the months after I had first seen him, I traveled back into Basutoland from South Africa, to visit Pat Duncan and to report on some tasks he had asked me to do. One of these was to quietly talk with people in Johannesburg and Cape Town, to find out which of *Contact*'s current street vendors, and who else, would agree to keep on distributing the paper covertly, for Pat was still planning to publish it in exile after it was banned in South Africa. People knew they could be putting themselves at risk of long jail terms by agreeing to do this, but nonetheless, many volunteered. I took their names to Pat, suitably encoded, in case I was searched crossing the border.

Meanwhile, Pat had jumped enthusiastically into another project. Although a classic liberal to the core and once an ardent Gandhian, there was one hope he had now abandoned: that change in South Africa would come nonviolently. He felt, as did many others, that the time had come for symbolic acts of sabotage. Basutoland, he thought, would be the perfect base: a rural, mountainous country with a long border with South Africa. It was still a British colony, but in several years was scheduled to become independent.

Most of Basutoland consisted of roadless, dry mountainsides dotted with small, extremely poor villages of round mud huts. Scattered through these mountains every ten or twenty miles were trading posts, owned and run by Englishmen or white South Africans.

Pat purchased two trading posts that had gone out of business. He planned to reopen them, operate them as a cover, and then gradually start to use them as bases from which to mount guerrilla raids against electric power lines and other such targets across the border, in South Africa itself. I was in Basutoland when he closed the deal purchasing these trading posts, and he invited me along when he went for the first time to inspect them.

It was an extraordinary journey. Pat and I and Joe Molefi, a big, quiet man who was an official of the Pan Africanist Congress, drove until the road ended, rented small, rugged horses from some missionaries, packed saddlebags with food, and set off on a dirt path across the mountains.

Pat was in his element. Whenever we met people walking the other direction, they hailed us with a long, melodic, trailing-off greeting that sounded like a dying shout, and translated as: "Where . . . are . . . you . . . coming . . . from?" Pat carried on animated conversations with them in the Sesotho language. The men wore blankets and conical straw hats; many were carrying their belongings as they made the first stage of the long journey to the gold mines near Johannesburg. There was little work in the villages here; to support their families, these young men had to go off to the South African mines for nine months at a time. Ahead of them lay an examination by company doctors: is this piece of human machinery fit enough for backbreaking work? Then a bunk in a cinder block barracks; work shifts in a cacophony of drills and conveyor belts a mile under the earth; meager savings sent home.

We spent the night at one of the trading posts Pat had bought, whose previous owners had closed it down some months before. The local chief came to greet us; later we went to sleep on the floor. My summer was of course winter below the equator, and we were some five thousand feet above sea level. To protect ourselves against the bitter cold we shared a single blanket and much South African brandy. I remember arguing about capitalism and socialism with Pat far into the night.

The next day, we rode twenty-five miles. I have often thought that if I could relive one day of my life, this would be it. We would gallop to the top of a rise and then suddenly, exhilaratingly, see dozens of miles ahead through the clear, cold mountain air, knowing that no car, no road, no telephone was within two days' ride of us. The horizon was rimmed with sharp, jagged snow-topped peaks.

Pat was in the lead; even here, he wore a tweed jacket and tie. At one point, as we were crossing an open plain, he exuberantly decided to give his horse a rest: he got off and ran, tweed jacket, necktie, and all, limping on his bad leg and leading the surprised horse for a mile or two. When we arrived that night at the second trading post, he fell asleep exhausted.

A month later, I visited him there again to report on the work I had been doing in South Africa, just before I was to go home. Pat was by now busily stocking the store with supplies and preparing to open it soon. The guerrilla warfare plans were temporarily on hold until the business was going.

I stayed two days. Each morning Pat got up at 7:00 and donned his coat and tie. He rang a gong at 7:15, and from 8:00 on was at work, leading local villagers in rebuilding partitions, shelves, and counters. In the evening we read and talked by the light of a fire and kerosene lanterns.

When I left, Pat came out of the mountains with me as far as the colony's capital of Maseru, to see his allies in the Pan African-ist Congress office there. This time we traveled a different route, riding some miles across the rocky mountains to another trading post, owned by someone else, which had a short grass airstrip. We arrived there, unannounced, in the late afternoon. As was the cus-tom here, the white owner and his wife put us up for the night, so that we could get a ride back to Maseru with the small plane that would be bringing the trading post its twice-weekly load of sup-plies the next morning.

The trading post operator was a white South African named Eric Rust. His instinctive hospitality toward fellow white men in the mountains was in conflict with an obvious suspicion that Patrick Duncan, the famous antiapartheid activist, was up to no good here. Nonetheless, skin color momentarily outweighed politics, and the Rusts gave us dinner. We ate off a white tablecloth, sherry before the meal, brandy after, like people in one of those old *New Yorker* cartoons of black-tie dinners in the jungle. The conversation was strained. Rust kept getting up from the table and going over to the store next door to check on things, as if he thought his African clerks would cheat him if he left them unsupervised for long.

After dinner Rust showed me around his trading post. It was a place where Africans brought their corn to have it milled into flour, and where they could buy canned goods, soap, trinkets, cloth. Rust also showed me his elaborate shortwave radio. He ex-plained that he and the other white traders scattered around the mountains, most of them many miles from a telephone, got on the radio at fixed times three times a day to check in with each other. "That way, if we don't hear from a chap, we can head over right away, to make sure he's not in any kind of trouble."

Surrounded by hundreds of thousands of black people in a ter-ritory that was scheduled soon, to his dismay, to become theirs,

Rust did not specify what he thought the "trouble" might be. As I went to sleep that night, I noticed, propped against the wall in the corner of the guest bedroom, a rifle.

. . .

After several months in South Africa, I returned to the United States for my last year at college. I stopped on the way in England, with all sorts of messages Pat wanted me to deliver, for mail to there from Basutoland had to pass through South Africa and might be opened. There were London newspaper editors to be asked to keep up the pressure on South Africa, and friendly M.P.s to be urged to ask certain questions in Parliament. Finally, still pursuing his scheme to begin cross-border raids into South Africa, Pat asked me to go and see a British friend of his who had done behind-the-lines work during World War II. I was to ask him if he could send Pat, in Basutoland, someone who knew something about explosives.

I found this man, now an Englishman of some eminence with his cloak-and-dagger days well behind him, at his elegant country house. He was obviously fond of Pat, but when I relayed Pat's unexpected request, he looked as if he had swallowed a centipede. He said politely that he would think about the matter, and changed the subject.

The following year, I saw Pat when he came to New York to testify at the United Nations against apartheid. He still cherished the idea that if you could only *talk to the right people,* the U.S. government would turn sharply against South Africa. He managed to meet Robert Kennedy and Adlai Stevenson, and was elated at their friendly, albeit noncommittal, response.

America thrilled him: the size, the friendliness, the vitality of New York, the way Chicago, "this tre*men*dous city, a *thou*sand miles away from the sea, is a *port!*" One afternoon, to try to prove to him that he had too many illusions about the United States, I took him on the subway to Puerto Rican Harlem. He limped on his bad leg up narrow stairways and through hallways as we knocked on doors in tenement buildings with paint scaling from the walls and uncollected garbage piled high by the stoops. He was shocked and depressed, but his faith in the United States was unshaken.

That year—1963—was the last time he came to the United

States and the last year I saw him, although we continued to correspond regularly. His health was never strong, and although we did not know it then, he had only a few years left to live. I felt warmly toward Pat as a person, but soon I reached a point in my political life where I felt I had nothing more to learn from someone like him. I had decided, with the somewhat hazy definition my generation had of the term, that I was a radical; he was a mere liberal. I became active in the movement against the Vietnam War; he saw America as the hope of the world. And he was, moreover, a *white liberal,* a category of people all too frequently made into heroes by the American press, a category that any hardheaded realist (like me) knew was insignificant in South Africa's future struggle. For a decade or so after the last time I saw him, I seldom thought of him, except as someone with whom I had spent a youthful, adventurous summer.

Then one day in the late 1970s, some work took me to Chicago. While there I met the author Studs Terkel at the radio station where he records his syndicated interview show. South Africa came up in our conversation, and I mentioned the summer I had spent working there. When he heard Pat Duncan's name, Terkel said that he had interviewed Pat many years ago, on one of Pat's visits to the United States. I asked if he still had the tape.

It was late afternoon. Terkel kindly found a vacant studio, put the tape in a machine for me, turned it on, and left for home. It was a strange scene: the studio where I sat had several soundproof glass windows that faced other recording studios or control rooms, all empty of people now, at the day's end. It was as if the array of meters and knobs and switches before me were redoubling itself in mirrors, an electronic catacomb. Then suddenly, its cadences registering in flickering needles on dials, out of the speakers came the voice I had not heard in fifteen years—clipped, breathless, intense, in those Oxford-English complete sentences, urging listeners that as Americans they must *act* in South Africa, come in on the side of justice before it was too late. I felt profoundly moved, as if some part of me were recaptured, some circle completed.

In the following weeks and months I often thought back over my time in South Africa. It had been a watershed in my life; that much I had always dimly known. But why was Pat Duncan's image half-censored from my memory? That had to do, I saw now, with my life before I even met him.

In each of those long horseback rides over the Basutoland mountains that summer, we had always been stopped by Africans we met on the trail. Sometimes they spoke some English, learned in a village school or in the South African mines. I remember one man: an intent, frowning, somewhat suspicious face, a blanket pulled tight around his shoulders. He seemed to pull it tighter and to look me over carefully for a moment before repeating the ritual greeting: "Where . . . are . . . you . . . coming . . . from?"

I answered with the name of the trading post we had left a few hours before. But of course that was not the real answer. Where are you coming from? The most important place I was coming from, and one that I had tried to forget during the summer and had mentioned to nobody, was from a family where my father had been the chief executive of a mining company that made most of its money by investing in southern Africa. One of those mines was even in South Africa itself, and it was not impossible that this man who questioned me on that mountain path might be returning to work in it, where the profits from his hot, dangerous, ill-paid labor thousands of feet below ground, flowing across oceans, dividing among holding companies and joint ventures, and subdividing among shareholder dividends and executive salaries, had helped pay for my education, for my being able to see enough of the world to grasp how economic imperialism works, for the very luxury of being able to fly all the way to South Africa and take part in the antiapartheid movement.

Where are you coming from? There was a further layer of answers. I think now that I had come both to South Africa and to radical politics generally out of guilt. I felt implicated in an injustice by having benefited so much from the profits of multinational capitalism. I therefore had to prove my innocence, to prove that I was *not* of the ruling class or of its outlook. It was this that unconsciously first drew me to Pat Duncan. Was he not also someone born on the wrong side? But this same feeling led me to a puritanical disapproval of the aristocratic side of his life: his formal dress, his big house with the servants and swimming pool in Cape Town. It seemed wrong to enjoy any material comfort when people were suffering. Part of my unconscious definition of political commitment then was that you had, in some way, to suffer with them.

There is a character type that the South African writer Nadine Gordimer captures brilliantly in her short story "Which New Era

Would That Be?" The story is told through the eyes of a black man: "These were the white women who, Jake knew, persisted in regarding themselves as your equal. . . . These women—oh, Christ!—these women felt as *you* did. They were sure of it. They thought they understood the humiliation of the black man walking the streets only by the permission of a pass written out by a white person. . . . There was no escaping their understanding." Later in the story a white woman refers nervously to her sense of guilt, and an African character shrugs "as if at the mention of some expensive illness he had never been able to afford and whose symptoms he could not imagine."

The guilt-stricken white liberal, familiar both in this country and in South Africa, is exactly what Pat Duncan was *not*. I now think that one reason I felt so ambivalent toward him was that, unlike me, he felt no guilt. He never tried to vicariously partake of anyone else's suffering. And, furthermore, he never pretended to be anyone other than himself—and that self happened to be one that enjoyed the life-style of the upper class. He never denied that he was a governor general's son. He came to political action not out of a sense of guilt, but out of a burning passion for justice. It has taken me several decades to see how important a distinction that is.

. . .

Pat never did turn his trading posts into bases for sabotage raids. In 1963, while he was on a trip to Europe to drum up opposition to apartheid, the British government banned him from returning to Basutoland. It was just as well, for his guerrilla warfare plans were wildly impractical. He would have been immediately traced as the source of any sabotage on the South African side of the border. Successful guerrillas evade capture by blending invisibly into the jungle or into the local population—difficult things to do if you are the only white man for miles in all directions, in a countryside with no trees.

His other project also came to naught. He never did publish a banned *Contact* from Basutoland and smuggle it into South Africa under the blankets of mine workers, for, ironically, the South African authorities never banned it. They thus avoided protests from Pat's influential friends overseas. Sapped by police harassment and increasing debts, the paper died a year or two after Pat had left Cape Town.

Unable to reenter either South Africa or Basutoland, Pat went on speaking tours in England and Scandinavia. He wrote a book about South Africa and articles for magazines and newspapers around the world. Because he spoke French, the Pan Africanist Congress sent him as their representative to Algeria—an important post, for the PAC was beginning its own attempt at guerrilla warfare, and many members were going to Algeria for military training. Although it was then the most militantly socialist of the African countries, Pat liked Algeria more than he expected, and was interested in its experiments with worker self-management.

The final chapter of his life was more difficult. The South African government stripped him of citizenship. The PAC was riven by factional struggles; after one of them Pat lost his job, although he remained as the organization's only white member. He turned to an early concern, which I had seen signs of that day after I first met him, when he had driven me past the cliffs and tide pools of the Cape Peninsula—the earth. As far back as 1943, distressed at the farming methods Europeans had brought to southern Africa, he had written a pamphlet urging "a form of agriculture that will not destroy the soil. And this must be the first [aim of postwar peace]. If it is not, there may be no others." Even now, in the mid-1960s, while continuing to speak and write on South Africa, he wrote a book called *Man and the Earth,* a prescient statement of the basic beliefs of what, some five years later, emerged around the world as the environmental movement.

Pat wanted to stay in Algeria: he liked the country, he felt it to harbor no racism, and it was Africa. He found a job with a hunger relief organization. But after a few months he had to go to England for medical treatment, for what was diagnosed as aplastic anemia. Only by doing some research in medical books did he discover what the doctors initially hadn't told him: that the disease was fatal. He was forty-eight years old. He went to Oxford, and said to the warden of his son's college, "Take care of my boy, because I'll be dead in six weeks." He was right. The end came in 1967 in a London hospital; he did not have time, as he had hoped, to return to the continent he knew was his home.

.   .   .

During one of his spells in South African jails, Pat wrote: "For ten years now I have been living a directed life; with few exceptions, every book I read, every person I meet, my very holidays, all I try to do, has been done with a purpose: to do what I can to put an end to the colour bar and to bring political equality to South Africa."

Pat had one sterling quality that stood out above everything else: he was deeply angered by human suffering. When confronted with it, he always tried to do something. In this way, his personal feelings and his political life were one.

A friend told me a story about Pat. Once a Japanese sailor was taken off a ship after an accident at sea, and was brought ashore at Cape Town. He had been badly injured and was dying. At the time there were no diplomatic relations between South Africa and Japan, and no one could be found in the city who spoke Japanese. Pat read about this in the newspaper, and thought it outrageous that a man should die alone, in a strange country. For two days, until the sailor died, he visited him at Groote Schuur Hospital, bringing him fruit and flowers, trying to talk to him in sign language. In miniature, this was what Pat Duncan did in his political life. He was not dismayed by the impossible. He hated to see anyone suffer. He followed his passion. And he was himself. Wherever his spirit is now, I know it is still wearing a coat and tie.

1985

Broad Jumper in the Alps

If you were playing some open-air parlor game in which you had to deduce the nationality and occupation of strangers, you might guess that John Berger was an Italian orchestra conductor. Italian because of the great warmth of his large face and expressive, dark-browed eyes; a conductor because he talks so much with his hands, face, and body—shrugging, gesturing, outlining ideas in the air, as if constantly trying to break through a barrier surrounding what can be conveyed in mere words.

Berger is, at this moment, standing outside the house he lives in, wreathed in the dense, steamy smoke of engine exhaust in freezing air. His constantly moving hands and torso are signaling a visitor at exactly what speed and around obstacles of exactly what shape to back a car out of a narrow, winding, snow-clogged drive-way. John Berger is not an Italian conductor but anyone who guessed the right label in that parlor game would not have the complete answer. Berger is British, but has lived outside of Britain much of his life. He is a Marxist of sorts, but writes about things other Marxists tend to ignore, like the nature of love. He is a novelist and screenwriter, but one who for some years painted pro-fessionally and whose books still frequently erupt into drawings and diagrams. He first became known as an art critic, but his work also includes—often all in the same book—fiction, poetry, report-age, and the utterly unclassifiable, such as a piece comparing, among other things, how Homer and Walt Disney look at animals.

Most paradoxical of all, the house with the snowbound drive-way is in the village where Berger has lived for some years—an isolated hamlet of several dozen old wooden houses, far up a rugged valley in the French Alps. Nearly everyone else in the val-

ley earns a living with their hands. Berger says he intends to spend
the rest of his life here.

.   .   .

Although friends had long urged John Berger's books on me, for
some years I never picked them up because I know so little about
art; why read an art critic? But when I began reading him several
years ago, I grew intrigued, although not, as perhaps one should
be, because of Berger's controversial analysis of Cubism or his
much-praised book on Picasso. Rather, I liked Berger because he
was the first writer I've run across who could explain why so much
fine art is boring.

You know what this feels like. Perhaps it is a Renaissance
painting of winged cherubs ascending to heaven, perhaps an eighteenth-century landscape, perhaps a crucifixion or a haloed saint.
You hear or read an expert explain why the damned thing is a
great work of art. You look at it, remain totally unmoved, and
begin to feel intimidated because you cannot "appreciate" this
piece of high culture in the proper way.

What Berger does is to set aside the mystique surrounding art,
a mystique that mainly considers matters of technique and style,
and which classifies artists into schools and ranks them on a scale
of greatness. In addition, he looks at why pictures were painted in
the first place. For example, in his book *Ways of Seeing* (also a BBC
television series), Berger talks about a Gainsborough portrait
called "Mr. and Mrs. Andrews." He quotes a few conventional art
critics, who mention the picture's "sensitively observed" cornfield
and the couple's enjoyment of nature. But then Berger asks: "Why
did Mr. and Mrs. Andrews commission a portrait of themselves
with a recognizable landscape of their own land as background?
. . . They are not," he answers, "a couple in nature as Rousseau
imagined nature. They are landowners." He goes on to talk about
how only those who owned land could afford the "enjoyment of
. . . nature." The sentence for poaching in the Andrews's day was
deportation to Australia; for stealing a potato, a public whipping.
"The function of portrait painting," Berger says elsewhere, "was to
underwrite and idealize a chosen social role of the sitter. It was not
to present him as 'an individual,' but, rather, as an individual
monarch, bishop, landowner, merchant and so on."

Clearly this is not Art Appreciation 101. By talking about

painting as a reinforcer of class divisions, Berger turns conventional art criticism on its head. "It has been said that European painting is like a window open onto the world. Purely optically this may be the case. But is it not as much like a safe, let into the wall, in which the visible has been deposited?" In *Ways of Seeing,* Berger shows you still lifes, landscapes, portraits of merchants with their hands resting on globes, and summarizes: "Oil painting, before it was anything else, was a celebration of private property. As an art-form it derived from the principle that *you are what you have.*" Then he makes one final, dazzling leap. Our pervasive, much-deplored, modern advertising, he says, is not a tawdry comedown from the great aesthetic tradition of Western painting. It is its *continuation,* in only slightly different form. The main difference is that advertising celebrates the hope of possession of property, not its actual possession.

I oversimplify greatly. For Berger's writing is not that of someone trying to debunk art, but of someone who loves it greatly. He is sensitive to the subtleties of an extraordinarily wide range of painting: he writes about medieval frescoes and Jackson Pollock with equal gusto. Yet what makes him so interesting to read is the way he combines this very sensitivity with a thoroughly unromantic analysis of why the art got painted. From that very combination new questions arise. What, he asks, are the tensions you can see in the work of Rembrandt between his unparalleled perception of human nature and the role of his portraits as status enhancers for those who paid to sit for them?

Berger asks other provocative questions which, in my limited reading, few critics address: why do European artists depict passive female nudes and not—as in other cultures—active sexual love? Why does a Turkish artist see landscape differently from Corot? Read Berger closely and a visit to an art museum becomes a different experience. But these days he is not to be found in museums.

.   .   .

A light snow is falling as we head along a narrow, climbing, mountain road. John Berger is driving, but talking intently. He is oblivious to the car and has forgotten to shift gears. "He goes through a car about every five years," Beverly Bancroft, the American woman with whom he lives, tells me later. As we now roar along in low gear, Berger speaks over the noise of the motor. "It's an extraordinary thing, this area. You drive fifty miles from Geneva, and in some ways you've driven a couple of centuries."

It becomes clear as we head farther up the valley that these are not the Alps of tourists, but a different set of mountains, whose sides are too rocky and steep for skiers. At one point we pass a small factory belching clouds of dense black smoke. "Yes, of course that's highly polluting," says Berger. "But the company threatened to close down and move away if the local authorities made them fix it. So they've left it alone. Unemployment here is so severe they cannot afford to lose still more jobs."

The family we are going to pay a call on, Berger says, has fifteen cows and eight children. There is another mission for this visit as well: one of the children, a plumber, has just fixed some of Berger's pipes, and Berger wants to take him a bottle of Scotch. I ask if this is the usual rate of exchange.

"No, it's much more complicated. There is very little exchange of money in this community. But there is always a price for everything. It's usually not an immediate price, however; the payment may be over a period of months or even years. But it's seldom money. And the payment may also not just be between one individual and another, but between families. Gérard spent several days fixing my plumbing, for instance, so obviously the whiskey is not enough. But for the last several summers we lived near his family in the *alpage* [the high-altitude pastures] and helped them there with the haying, with getting animals into the barn in the evenings and so on."

The peasant family's house is stone and square. They all welcome Berger, whom they call *Djon,* and glasses of white wine instantly appear. Three grown sons are there. They and their parents and Berger trade local news, about snow levels and the weather, about so-and-so's car, which slipped off the road and had to be towed, and, a good deal, about death: another family who had a cow die, a young boy who was killed in another mountain road accident, someone's mother who just died. When he talks, Berger rides right over the division of language: his French with this family is sprinkled with "I mean"; his English, with me, with *"bon."*

It is hard to judge whether this is the same kind of talk these people would have among themselves if Berger were not there. They seem relaxed and at ease with him, but I wonder what they really think of this strange Englishman who has come to live among them and write about them. There is no way to ask directly now. At one point the father of the family asks me what I do and I say I'm a journalist. *"Ah,"* he says, placing me. *"Vous êtes de la même parti que Djon."* The same political party? The same type? The same profession? From his tone of voice perhaps he means: you have the same forgivable eccentricity as he.

.   .   .

Later that evening we are back at Berger's house. It is a farmhouse, probably built in the eighteenth century, he says. It has cold running water only; across the driveway is a two-hole outhouse with snow drifting through cracks in the walls. From the outside, like most houses in the village, Berger's home seems quite large. Once inside, you realize the reason: most of the downstairs is a barn. "This architecture is really quite energy efficient," Berger explains. "The walls are extremely thick; the hayloft provides additional insulation on top; a dozen cows generate quite a lot of body heat. It's almost the equivalent of having a small furnace going down below."

That would be splendid if John and Beverly kept cows. But unfortunately they don't, and the house is near freezing temperature. I borrow several sweaters and sit close to the old iron stove in the kitchen. All the houses we have visited have such a stove; it does multiple jobs: cooking, keeping a kettle of hot water simmering, drying dish towels that are hung above it, keeping an iron warm and—of most interest to me now—heating the room. Berger constantly feeds the stove with big chunks of coal or with wood, which, like other townspeople, he has gathered in the communal forest.

He is almost always in motion: chopping wood, dashing off to get something, rearranging the smoked hams that hang from a rafter in the empty cow barn. Although he shows me his ice-cold study with desk and typewriter, it is hard to imagine him using it: I can better picture him writing by dictating, on the run, to someone trotting along behind. This constant physical activity is a form of communication between him and his farmer neighbors. He tells me, for instance, about a team of Italian mountain woodcutters who come here from across the nearby border; Berger learned about their lives not with notebook or tape recorder, but by going out and cutting trees with them.

We return to the question of what has drawn him to this village. Even Berger's admirers on the Left often ask, "But why is he so interested in *peasants?*" Unspoken is the feeling that there is something dead-end about the subject. Which is strange, for peasants of one sort or another do, after all, comprise more than half the people on earth. In one article, Berger writes about the questions the existence of peasants poses to what we think of as development, or modernization. They represent, he says, people "who have scarcely lived the division of labor." They are a preconsumer society. Finally, their closeness to the earth makes them identify its well-being with their own. Berger adds ironically: "This is what is labeled—especially by urban revolutionaries—their love of property.

"When I wrote my book about migrant workers, *A Seventh Man,*" Berger says across his kitchen table, "I realized that I really knew rather little about village life, that is to say peasant life. The things written about peasants seemed to me to be so much viewed from the outside that they were inadequate, really urban views of the village. This is true of modern sociology; this is true of Marxism—where it had disastrous consequences in the Soviet Union. Although I had no illusions that I ever would be completely a part of peasant life, I wanted to participate in their experience."

Along with this wish, Berger also came to feel that time was short. "In twenty-five years, if the Common Market economic planners have their way, there will be no more peasants here. In Europe, as in America, corporate agribusiness is replacing family farmers. Already in various parts of France there are deserted villages, where everyone has left because they can't make a living anymore. But the difference between here and the U.S. is the thousand years of tradition bound up with that farm culture."

As Berger talks, his face wrinkles, squints, frowns, constantly changes shape. It is far more than intellectual interest, he says, that keeps him here.

"I feel at home here in a way I have felt nowhere else, certainly not in England. From the age of three or four I have always had the sense of being not quite at home. In some ways this is very curious, because my parents were very good to me. From the age of twenty onward I knew I wanted to leave Britain as soon as possible. I don't feel French particularly, but I do feel at home in this village, accepted for who I am. I only recently recognized, looking back over my work to date, that all my writing, really, is about emigration of one kind or another. And in some ways I think you can say emigration is the quintessential twentieth-century experience."

What has he found in the culture he has immigrated to? Berger talks about one quality he likes very much: the Alpine peasants' disdain for money. "You see this everywhere, almost a *shame* people feel about having to deal with money. When you owe somebody money, it's extremely difficult to persuade them to accept it. Even in the cattle market, where they are dealing with strangers, watch the peasants when they hand over money: you can see they don't like it. If it's anything more than a few francs, the deal is always hidden, as it were, by the fact that they drink together when the money is exchanged. There is a complicated and subtle thing here: I do not mean that peasants don't love money, openly or secretly; they do. They want it; they know money offers them a little protection. But for them money is a necessary evil, not, as in bourgeois culture, an automatic good.

"I also find that peasants are extremely observant. They notice infinitely more than other people. It's not a virtue: it's *necessary* for them to see at the first possible sign when an animal is sick, or what the likely change in the weather will be a day or two later. I find that if I'm worried or sad about something, even if I say nothing, people here will notice immediately, whereas friends in the city might not."

Berger's isolation from those friends is less than might appear: there are summer visitors; he travels to England once a year and to Paris and Geneva more often. He has no telephone, however. Now he takes a break from talking to make salad, and soon I eat dinner with him, Beverly, and their four-year-old son, Yves. One of the questions I plan to ask him later is: What limitations does he feel in what he can talk about with people here—is all conversation about snowfall and sick cattle? I get a partial answer, unexpectedly, just as we are having dessert.

An excited pounding suddenly comes from the wooden front door. Then it bursts open—there are no locks in this village. A young man with a broad, open face rushes into the kitchen and embraces John and Beverly. "*Je suis sauvé! Je suis sauvé!*"

It turns out that Armand, thirty-three years old, has just come back from the doctor's. The doctor has told him that a growth on his throat was not the cancer he had feared. He is saved.

Berger produces a bottle of *gnôle,* the clear, homemade apple brandy that is the staple drink in these parts, and quickly explains to me that the previous week, when Armand thought he was fatally ill, he had held a farewell party for all his friends. Now, in Berger's home, after the initial toasts, kidding, and rejoicing, the talk takes a philosophical turn.

Armand: People who ask too many questions can never be happy.

John: But is happiness as a constant state ever possible? Aren't there just moments of happiness occurring along a continuum?

Armand: You can only be happy if you express all that is in you. Why are some people so reserved that they never speak their minds, express themselves, say what they truly think?

John: I believe that you can only do that when you feel a dream of power, of possibility, of the ability to change your life. Today, *you* can, because you were saved.

We raise our glasses once more to Armand's salvation, and the talk goes on.

. . .

When we talk about someone's mind, we usually do so with analogies to the vertical. X is a towering figure among historians. Y has written the most profound book on this or that. It is as if each field of thought has heights to be scaled or depths to be plumbed, but is still a *field,* with borders. But I think of John Berger's mind as being horizontal. He is a broad jumper of the intellect.

He is always making links where no one else has. Between the famous photograph of a Bolivian colonel pointing to Che Guevara's dead body and the Rembrandt painting of a doctor in an identical pose pointing to a cadaver before a group of medical students. Between the struggle of Third against First World today and the tensions of city dweller against peasant as painted by Millet.

One reason Berger can so easily leap the fences between traditional fields is that he never got any formal training in what they were. He left school at sixteen and served in the British army at the end of World War II. After that came art school and some years as an artist. Early in his career he also worked in television, both as a producer and an on-camera performer. "The first series of programs I did were for schoolchildren, about animals. Each time I had an animal in the studio: an iguana, a donkey, a mongoose, or whatever. The idea was to show the animal, talk about it, and so on. This was live, and all kinds of things happened: the iguana jumped to the ceiling, hiding behind the lights, and there were still fifteen minutes of airtime to fill. The chimpanzee became hysterical when the lights went on and leapt into my arms, sobbing like a child. I had to pacify her while talking and still end the program exactly on the dot, no overrunning, no falling short; you had to end within five seconds of a given time. It was good discipline."

In an age of specialists, Berger roams free. In conversation, too, he is immensely, graciously curious about everything that comes his way: a farmer's troubles, the latest twist in French politics, the way sunlight streams through a snow-laden tree branch, news from abroad. I continually have to remind myself that I am interviewing him, not the other way around.

Ever the emigrant, Berger experiences his curiosity as a kind of intellectual traveling: "Every time I'm attracted toward doing a book on a new subject, it's like landing in a new country. But once I've learned to live there, I'm still impelled to go elsewhere, to not settle there."

When you look at Berger's work carefully, the links between his book-countries become clearer. One concern is that of community. Works as disparate as *A Fortunate Man,* his loving portrait of the life of a rural British doctor, and his screenplay for *Jonah Who Will Be 25 in the Year 2000,* about a group of people in Geneva in the aftermath of the failed student rebellions of 1968, both ask: what are the possibilities for true human community in an age full of pressures against it? It is the same concern that has drawn Berger to write of the peasantry here in the French Alps, a community that may not last.

Another Berger theme is the worldwide tension between urban rich and rural poor. This is visible most clearly in my own favorites among his books, *A Seventh Man,* and his films, *The Middle of the World.* Both are about migrant workers. In some parts of Europe, migrant laborers live nine to a three-bed room—three men sharing a bed in shifts. They come from Turkey to Germany, from

Greece to Sweden, from Africa to France. (And, for that matter, from Mexico to the United States.)

In *A Seventh Man,* which, like many of his books, is profusely illustrated by his longtime collaborator, the Swiss photographer Jean Mohr, Berger and Mohr move through workers' barracks, factories, and the back alleys of Europe's cities. Beneath Geneva, a city whose major industry is international conferences, they find a huge sewer line under construction, the hazardous underground working conditions made worse by the fact that the hundreds of migrant laborers on the project have no language in common. Berger combines various migrants' experiences into one epic journey from distant, poverty-stricken village to city factory job in an unfamiliar land. He tells the story almost in a sort of blank verse, and all from the rural newcomer's point of view: why are there no animals in the streets of Düsseldorf, Lille, or Stockholm? Are they hidden?

Berger coauthored three screenplays in French with Alain Tanner, which Tanner, a Swiss, then directed. The heroine of *The Middle of the World* is a migrant, a woman from southern Italy working as a waitress near Geneva. The film is the story of her three-month love affair with a married Swiss engineer. Across the subtly etched barriers of class and traditional sex roles, their love does not last. Although totally devoid of rhetoric, this is one of the most profoundly feminist films ever made.

The same consciousness of the difference between the rural and the urban underlies much of Berger's art criticism. For example, Berger says, the shape Picasso's genius took was largely determined by the fact that he was an "invader" of industrial Europe from feudal Spain. At the end of that study, Berger makes one of those marvelous mental broad jumps. One reason, he says, that Picasso became restless and repetitious in his later work is that he ran out of subject matter. The tragedy is that the greatest visual genius of our time did not seek to portray the whole world: Picasso should have gone to India, Berger says, to Africa, to anywhere he wanted in the Third World to see and to paint.

Finally, closely linked to the other themes, is Berger's constant eye on the corrupting power of money and the marketplace. In the gentle, wry *Jonah Who Will Be 25 in the Year 2000,* which has something of a cult following, a supermarket cashier undercharges people she likes or old folks who are hard up. In his concern about the commodification of everything, Berger is influenced by the early Karl Marx. But where Marx saw liberation from this pressure in a communist future, Berger finds it more in the past, among that vanishing class that Marx and his followers scorned, the peasantry.

Like all innovators, Berger sometimes cuts his original path with too broad a stroke. There are rough edges; he sometimes overstates his case; and it is possible to pull out passages from his thirty-odd years of work that make him sound far less subtle than he is. Another flaw is his occasional stretches of obscurity. For example, there are some foggy patches in his lyrical, brilliant but difficult novel *G,* a strange tale that involves British country houses, the first airplane flight across the Alps, South Africa during the Boer War, civil war between Slavs and Italians in Trieste, and a mysterious Don Juan character who shows up in most, though not all, of these places. (Berger won Britain's Booker Prize for the novel, then promptly gave half the money to labor organizers working with cane cutters on Caribbean sugar plantations owned by Booker McConnell, Ltd., the prize's donor.) One incident, in which the hero of *G* comes across two dead horses in the forest, left me totally baffled. I asked Berger what it meant. "Several people have asked me," he says, "and the answer is, I don't know. It was a dream I had and I was impelled to put it in the novel."

Whatever his flaws, Berger is a writer who gives you new eyes. Reading him makes you look at things differently: the power relations visible in a portrait, an advertisement, a photograph, all the world's taken-for-granted surfaces. One day, for example, after I had immersed myself in Berger's writing for several weeks, I was visiting somebody in a hotel where the elevator operators wore uniforms with epaulettes, gold buttons and braid. Why, I suddenly wondered, the military overtones?—and military in a symbolically old-fashioned way. Surely it is cheaper to build automatic elevators, or at least to let elevator operators wear their own clothes, like bank tellers or store clerks. Then it occurred to me that the uniforms hark back to an earlier, more pronounced form of the master-servant relationship, when the line between household servant and soldier, both in service to a medieval master, was not so distinct. For a fleeting moment then, the visitor to the Sheraton or the Hyatt Regency partakes of some temporary echo of the role of the castle lord. A trivial thought, and no doubt somebody has had it before. But it never would have crossed my mind if I hadn't been reading John Berger.

.   .   .

My last day with Berger is spent driving up and down snowy valleys on various errands. He picks up several bags of coal for his stove from the local coal merchant, who has a shed full of huge bins with almost as many varieties of this essential item as a supermarket would have cereal brands back home: hard coal, soft coal, Russian coal, coal dust compressed into pellets, and more. We stop and visit a pottery shop, which has been operated by the same family in the same building for two hundred years. We deliver another bottle of whiskey in return for some favor given. Berger shows me the house of the local madwomen: "They are three sisters, and they're all a little mad. They don't talk to anybody; they threaten to burn down buildings, but they're not in fact dangerous. Everybody knows their story: one Sunday when they were teenagers they all went to mass, and when they came home they found that their father had cut his wife's throat in a fit of jealousy and then hanged himself. So everyone knows why the sisters are the way they are. If they lived in a town, of course, they'd be locked up in an institution."

Finally, driving up a road cut into a cliff and peppered with warning signs about avalanches and tire chains, we cross a high bridge over a gorge, and Berger shows me the now-deserted house of the woman who was the model for the chief character of the haunting novella, "The Three Lives of Lucie Cabrol," in his book *Pig Earth.* The house is perched on the outside of the cliff-hugging road, some two hundred yards directly above a rushing stream. The woman who lived here was murdered, a long time ago; "everyone knows by whom, but they don't want to deal with the police." Snow begins to fall, and we climb back into the car and head back down the bleak valley.

What is one to make of Berger's choice to live in this spot? For an American equivalent you must imagine Susan Sontag, say, settling in a mining town in Appalachia. Permanently. In the United States the whole notion of going to live in the country became for many people, in the late sixties and early seventies, an escape from the politics of the time. Yet Berger's journey is just the opposite: a deeply political man, he has become an advocate and recorder of a whole culture in danger of being destroyed. How effective at that can he be when he is not a peasant himself? Just as Berger says that peasants pose a question to industrial society, so his decision to live here raises the question: how successfully can one emigrate?

In his work, Berger has not got this question entirely in focus yet. You can see this in *Pig Earth,* his first book about this region. Berger's introduction and conclusion talk about the differences between himself and the villagers, between peasants and city dwellers; in between are poems and short stories of varying length. Although one can learn about village life from these stories, for me they do not fully work as fiction. In realist fiction we have come to expect a certain emotional closeness of writer to story: either the story happened to the writer, or something like it did, or the writer was somehow an intimate part of the world in which the story took place. But Berger has just told the reader he was not a part of the world of *Pig Earth* until recently. So the "I" of several of the stories seems too discordant with the newcomer's "I" of the introduction. There are psychological limits to emigration, and, in this book at least, Berger has bumped up against them.

·   ·   ·

Since I have had dinner at John and Beverly's house for several days, I invite them out to eat the final night of my stay. It turns out there is only one place to eat out in this village—the Café La Doxie. And, as I discover when I stop by during the day to reserve a table for the evening, they serve only one dish: cheese fondue. I ask Madame La Doxie if we can reserve a table for three at 8:00 P.M. "Fine," she says. "I have the wine. You bring the cheese."

During the day I buy some Gruyère cheese at the nearest grocery, which is several miles down the road. At 8:00 P.M. John, Beverly, and I take it to the café. Except for the fact that there are several small tables instead of one large one, this kitchen and dining room could be part of someone's house instead of a café. Evidently the building is both. A yellow-white mound of raw lamb's wool, waiting to be spun, sits in a corner.

Mme. La Doxie already has the wine simmering on the omnipresent wood stove. "Quick," she says, "we must cut up the cheese." All four of us go to work, with fingers, a kitchen cleaver,

Berger's penknife. The fondue begins to bubble; we are apparently the only customers here. But are we even customers? Berger insists that Mme. La Doxie join us at the table. She is a small, ancient woman in a black dress, with sparkling eyes and cheeks like shrunken pomegranates. She is eighty-seven. She is the only person in the village, I notice, whom John does not call by the familiar form, *tu.* Soon, in comes her forty-two-year-old son and his nine-year-old daughter, and they join us too.

After the meal, I ask for the check. However, it appears there is no such thing at this café. Pressed repeatedly, Mme. La Doxie says at last, "You can pay me twenty francs for the wine." Berger, directly behind her where she cannot see him, shakes his head at me and points a finger upward: I should offer more. "Forty francs," I insist, in a sort of upside-down bargaining. She makes a big show of refusing the money; finally I stuff it into her cash drawer.

Following this, as if to deny that any sort of business transaction has taken place and to put our whole encounter on a non-monetary basis, she produces a bottle of *gnôle,* and her son reaches into a cupboard for some homemade sausage—deeply smoky, with the meat and fat in gravel-sized chunks. It bears the same relation to vacuum-packed-in-plastic salami as fresh salmon does to a frozen fish stick.

"Pour her some more *gnôle* and she'll sing," Berger says to me in English. Mme. La Doxie does sing, in a surprisingly sturdy voice: a sweet, melodic song about a handsome young chimney sweep and a young woman who says, yes, you can come and sweep my chimney again. The double entendre is gentle, not bawdy, and the song is a touch sad.

They explain to me that chimney sweeping is what young men from this area traditionally did when they migrated to Paris to work—spending ten or twenty years there, accumulating enough money to come home and buy a flock of sheep. They swept chimneys then with a weighted small pine tree at the end of a rope; now the job is done with chemicals and brushes. It was mainly men from the Alps who were sweeps: having been mountain shepherds as boys, they had no fear of steep roofs. While on them they sang, partly to advertise their presence to the next house.

"Oh!" Beverly says. "Remember the chimney sweep who was here a few years ago and swept our chimney? And he sang so beautifully."

"Yes!" says Mme. La Doxie. "And he came here to the café and sang for his dinner. Later he sent me a postcard."

She rummages in a drawer and finds it. It is unsigned, in florid handwriting, with some lines from the chimney sweep's song.

> *Souvenir d'un petit rammonage*
> *D'un petit rammoneur*
> *Qui rammone de tout son coeur*
> *De ville en village*

> In memory of a little chimney sweeping
> By a little sweep
> Who sweeps with all his heart
> From one town to the next

That was three years ago, she says; the man has never come back. There are few chimneys left to sweep. Here in the café, as elsewhere in the village, rising fuel prices have meant that the old brick chimneys are boarded up, except for an outlet for a galvanized iron pipe from the stove. And that cannot be swept; you just take it apart by hand once a month and shake out the soot.

We say our good-byes. As we file out of the café, the snow crunches under our boots, and the chimney sweep's song echoes in my ears like an elegy . . . and, as Berger says about the peasantry itself, like a question. Granted, chimney sweeping was dirty, dangerous work and should not be romanticized. But there are almost no trades left today where people sing on the job. And what does it say about our world that this is so?

1981

Two Russians

The most vivid memories I have of my childhood are of the summer evenings when Boris's plane took off.

Boris Vasilievich Sergievsky, captain in the Imperial Russian Air Force, World War I fighter pilot, winner of the Order of St. George (which entitles the bearer to a personal audience with the tsar, any time of day or night), test pilot for the Pan American Clippers of the 1930s, tenor, gourmet, lover, horseman, and adventurer, was, miraculously, my uncle. One day he had flown his plane down from the sky and, to the complete shock of all her relatives, had married my father's sister. From that point on, life in our family was never the same.

When I was a boy, my parents and I shared a summer home with Boris and his family, in upstate New York. Boris had long retired from aerial combat and test piloting, and now operated an air charter business in New York City, flying people anywhere they wanted to go in a ten-passenger Grumman Mallard that could put down on land or water. On summer weekends, he flew north to join his family, landing on a lake near our house. Then, on Sunday evenings, he would take off to return to work in New York.

Each time, Boris warmed up the plane's engines on shore, watched by a cluster of admiring children. I knelt with my fingers in my ears, a few feet from the right wing tip. Through the cockpit window I could see the intent faces of Boris and his copilot. Their eyes checked instruments on the panel; their lips moved in a mysterious technical jargon I could not hear; their hands reached up to adjust a wondrous galaxy of knobs and switches and levers. First one motor, then the other, gave out a long, shattering roar so loud you felt as if you were standing *inside* the noise. The aircraft rocked and strained at its wheels; the saplings at the edge of the

forest behind it bent toward the ground. Finally the engines qui-
eted to a powerful whoosh, Boris released the brakes, and the plane
rolled down a ramp into the water.

Boris taxied out to the middle of the lake, the propellers blow-
ing a wet wind back over us on shore. Suddenly a great white tail
of spray spread out behind the plane. Its wheels now folded into
its belly, the Mallard lifted higher and higher in the water, transformed into a shape of sleek grace. A motorboat or two raced
alongside, then were quickly left behind. At last, triumphantly,
the plane broke free of the water and rose into the dusk. The
engines' roar echoed off the lake; the very mountains vibrated. A
plume of water drops trailed from the fuselage, then faded to a fine
mist, then to nothing. Rising into the sky, Boris dipped a wing
and turned toward New York.

.   .   .

This is the story of two men, two lives, two approaches to life—
totally different, yet brought together for one brief moment by
history. Whether the best of what each represented can be recon-
ciled with the other, I leave to you to judge.

My uncle Boris is the first of these two heroes, and certainly
the one with the more commanding physical presence. He loomed
above my childhood landscape, an elemental life force. Looking at
pictures of him today, I am startled to find him quite ordinary in
size.

Boris had a square, Russian face, a sturdy tree-trunk body, and
a laugh like the Mallard's motors warming up. He loved people
and knew everyone from airline presidents to the man who ran the
restaurant in the Eiffel Tower. But his closest friends were all Russians; when they came to visit on summer weekends, the language
threaded through my days like music that summoned up a time
and place far away.

Nearly half a century after the Russian Revolution, Boris's
friends still talked of estates and sleigh rides and the beauties of
old St. Petersburg. Here, among their fellow princes, counts, and
generals, it was their rank in that vanished world that counted, no
matter how they had fared in the new. One of Boris's friends
played the accordion in a Russian restaurant; another, who, I was
told, had been the equivalent of attorney general under Tsar
Nicholas II, drove a New York taxi. One princess, a cousin of the

Imperial Family, signed our bilingual guest book simply as "Vera of Russia."

The party never ended. Russians celebrate everything twice, it seemed: Christmas on Christmas Day and on Christmas Eve, birthdays on your birthday and on the birthday of the saint you're named after. We feasted on *shashlik, piroshki,* and, best of all, Siberian *pelmeni*—delicious little meat-filled dumplings in broth. According to Boris, who cheerfully claimed that nearly everything important had been first invented by Russians, *pelmeni* was the ancestor of wonton, ravioli, and other inferior imitations. At meals there was much toasting, to chants of *"Pey-do-dna!* (drink to the bottom) *Pey-do-dna!"* When the mood was right, after dinner Boris stood by the piano and, fixing his eyes first on one and then another young woman among the guests, sang arias from *La Belle Helène, La Traviata,* and other operas and operettas. During one interlude of his amazingly varied life, when he had been stranded in Europe for a few months without wars or airplanes, he had sung professionally.

If you had asked me about Boris ten years ago, I would have described him as a *Reader's Digest* Unforgettable Character. And, indeed, his biography is remarkable. He spent two years as an infantry officer in the Russian army in World War I, then later he served as a fighter pilot, developing a new method of attack (approach the German plane head-on from a slightly higher altitude, wing-over quickly, and attack from the rear before the back-seat machine gunner can swivel around). Afterward he fought in the Russian Civil War, escaped from a Bolshevik prison, arrived penniless in the United States in 1923, and then spent fourteen years as chief test pilot for his old schoolmate Igor Sikorsky. Along the way, he had his taxiing seaplane sunk by a tidal wave off the coast of Chile, flew oil prospectors up Colombia's alligator-infested Magdalena River into the Andes, and flew live boa constrictors downstream, to be made into snakeskin shoes and handbags. He set more than a dozen different world aviation records for speed and distance. Some of them—since they are for types of aircraft no longer made, like four-engined seaplanes—still stand.

Although it has taken me a long time to see just why, Boris meant a great deal more to me than the sum of his feats. And that feeling stems partly from the contrast between his life and my own. I was the only child of elderly parents. As a boy, I was frequently sick, painfully shy, always overprotected. A succession of governesses hovered nearby, their job (performed with too much success) to make sure that nothing unseemly ever happened to me. I went to an Anglophile, all-male elementary school where the desks were bolted to the floor, the boys called the teachers "sir," and even the nine-year-olds had to wear coats and ties. I was irredeemably well behaved.

Across that gray and decorous sky, my uncle Boris flamed like a shooting star. He was Tom Jones parachuted by accident into a Henry James novel. For him, life was celebration, lust, adventure. Unlike anyone else I knew, he reveled in earthiness. Once I remember him telling me about some battle he had fought in, during which a bullet had hit a fellow officer standing next to him, not seriously wounding the man, but nicking an artery. "And Ahhhdahhhhm, his *blawwwd* vas awwwwl awwwver me!" Boris slapped his knee and roared with laughter, "I vas *rrrret* from het to foooooot!"

Boris loved friends, airplanes, champagne, steak tartare, horses, and, above all, beautiful women, whom he always managed to find wherever his airplane set down around the world. Once at an elegant New York dinner party, the hostess asked each guest at the table to answer the question: what was the most memorable experience in your life? When Boris's turn came, he said only a few words: "Bathing a princess—in champagne."

I suppressed much of my feeling for Boris for a long time. It was more comfortable to think of him merely as an exotic character, a figure from an old home movie, colorful but no longer relevant. There seemed no other way I could reconcile the affection I felt for him with what became important to me as I grew up: civil rights, radical journalism, the antiwar movement of the 1960s. How could I, with Cuban posters on my wall, admit that someone who meant so much to me still had two pictures of Tsar Nicholas II on his?

It wasn't until I was almost thirty that I came to feel differently. I found myself thinking about Boris more and more. He lived robustly in the present; he enjoyed life to the full; he repressed nothing. Of how many people could I say that? Certainly not of myself. In my own struggle to put the constrained and emotionally frozen little boy of my childhood behind me, I had to admit that this monarchist lover of Holy Russia was, ironically, one of the best models I had.

As an act of homage to Boris, or to that part of him I wanted in myself, I learned to fly a glider. I wrote to him about the experience, the first letter I'd ever sent him. He wrote back a beautiful note in the handwriting of Russian émigrés—many curls on the letters and a few false starts where Cyrillic characters had been in midstroke reluctantly converted to Roman ones. He said that he, too, had flown gliders, and appreciated the beauty and the silence, although perhaps someday I would learn to fly power planes also; then I would no longer be limited by air currents, and the whole world would be mine.

On a visit home a few months later, I went to see him and my aunt. We had just had our first child, and Boris grunted with satisfaction when he saw my wife breast-feeding the baby, "just like we used to do in Russia." As with the *pelmeni,* he seemed about to claim that Russians had invented breast-feeding. We talked warmly for some time, but he was old and ill; we knew it was probably the last time we would see each other.

I remember waking one morning a few weeks later and realizing that I would never again stand on the lakeshore, feel the spray on my face, and watch the Mallard thunder across the water and into the sky. I think it was at that moment that I first felt what age is, what death is.

. . .

During that last visit I was struck by one thing Boris said. I had asked him about his early days in Russia and where he had lived and fought; I had begun to think that someday I would visit those places myself. He told me with particular feeling about his time in the White forces during the Russian Civil War. The army he was with battled eastward into Russia, pushing back the Bolsheviks. In the fall of 1919, the Whites reached the outskirts of Petrograd (as St. Petersburg had been renamed in 1914; it was to become Leningrad in 1924). The capital of the old Russia was within reach, the tide of the war might be turned. "But there were only fifteen thousand of us," said Boris. "Lice everywhere, carrying typhus. There was much dying. And then, outside Petrograd, we were met by a much larger army under the command of Trotsky himself. We could do nothing . . ."

Like most of my friends in the New Left, I did not know much about those times. Arguing over the Soviet Union had been a matter for the previous generation of American radicals, not my own. I knew more about the Cuban Revolution than the Russian. Soviet history seemed distant and . . . somehow embarrassing: it had produced so much blood and suffering and, finally, a country of stultifying grayness. I think we didn't want to acknowledge that its makers had anything whatever in common with our own politics. But Boris's description of this lost battle triggered something. I began to do some reading.

Perhaps there are true scholars, but most of us read history selfishly. We are drawn to a period because we would like to have lived then. We are drawn to a historical figure because we would like to have lived that person's life. Such heroes are hard to come by in the Russian Revolution. Despite all the harrowing tragedy of his later life, in which he and several of his children were murdered by Soviet agents, Trotsky remains aloof, a brilliant intellectual and self-taught military genius, but with much blood on his hands. Lenin is even less appealing, a harsh, rigid man who took visible pleasure in sending his enemies to the firing squad. And the paranoid Stalin took mass killing to a scale seldom matched in history.

It was only after some months that I came across the writings of another and quite different person of that period, the first whom I wholeheartedly *liked,* both as a political activist and as a human being. He and Boris are the chief characters of this story. And at one time, I was to discover, their paths crossed.

Victor Serge was also Russian. But while Boris was born near a palace (his mother had a minor post at the tsar's court), Serge was born in exile, in a slum. As a child he often had only bread soaked in coffee to eat. His parents were Russian revolutionaries, who had fled to Belgium at the time of Serge's birth in 1890. On the walls of the Brussels apartment where Serge grew up, he recalled, "There were always portraits of men who had been hanged."

Serge never finished school. He left home when he was in his teens, lived in a mining village, worked as a printer, and finally made his way to Paris. There he lived with beggars, read Balzac, and grew fascinated by the underworld. But soon the revolutionary in him overcame the wanderer. He became the editor of an anarchist newspaper. For refusing to testify against some comrades, he was sentenced, at age twenty-two, to five years in a French maximum security prison. Released in 1917, he went to Spain to join a short-lived anarchist revolt. Finally, Serge managed to make his way to revolutionary Russia—the homeland he had never seen.

He arrived there in early 1919. The country was now swept by the Russian Civil War. This brutal conflict, which took several million lives, was between the Bolsheviks and the counterrevolutionary White forces—mostly led by former tsarist generals, and supplied by England, France, and the United States. Serge had no doubt the Whites had to be defeated, and he fought in the Red Army. But he was agonized by the other battle the Bolsheviks were fighting, against virtually all the other parties of the Left. The Bolsheviks had dissolved Russia's first democratically elected legislature, and were now busy executing many of their political opponents.

Victor Serge spent most of the next seventeen years in Russia. Almost alone among the shrill and angry voices of that time, his is one that today rings clear and true and admirable. Serge threw himself totally into the Russian Revolution, but he never abandoned his passion for civil liberties, and his sympathy for the free spirits who didn't toe the Bolshevik line. "The telephone became my personal enemy," he writes. "At every hour it brought me voices of panic-stricken women who spoke of arrest, imminent executions and injustice, and begged me to intervene at once, for the love of God!"

Yet the White armies were attacking from all directions; Serge felt it was no time for intellectuals, however accurate their criticisms, to be on the sidelines. He worked as an official of the Comintern and as a militia officer. At one point he was in charge of examining the captured archives of the Okhrana, the tsarist secret police. At the same time he argued ceaselessly against the arrests, the closed trials, the death penalty for political prisoners.

As he watched the ever more oppressive Soviet bureaucracy, Serge was more convinced than ever that political power should be decentralized—to the small community and the workplace. With such ideas, he quickly got into trouble. In 1928, he was expelled from the Communist Party. Stalin blocked him from further government jobs and clapped him in jail. A few days after his release from prison, Serge wrote, "I was laid out by an unendurable abdominal pain; for 24 hours I was face to face with death. . . . And I reflected that I had labored, striven and schooled myself titanically, without producing anything valuable or lasting. I told myself, 'If I chance to survive, I must be quick and finish the books I have begun: I must write, write. . . .' I thought of what I would write, and mentally sketched the plan of a series of documentary novels about these unforgettable times."

Over the next two decades, during which he was imprisoned again, sent into internal exile, and finally allowed to leave Russia, Serge wrote those books. His opposition to Soviet tyranny meant that his books would never be published in the USSR, but his radicalism kept them out of print in America for most of the cold war as well. His work constitutes one of the great political testaments of our time, above all his *Memoirs of a Revolutionary 1901– 1941,* which is as fine and as lasting as anything by Orwell.

Serge was part of that generation that at first saw the Russian Revolution as an epochal step forward from the system that had just given Europe more than 12 million dead in World War I. Serge's great hopes make all the more poignant his clear-eyed picture of the gathering darkness as the Revolution turned slowly into a vast self-inflicted genocide, the time when, as a character in one of his novels says, "we have conquered everything, and everything has slipped out of our grasp."

Above all, there is something deeply human in Serge's voice. You can see it in photographs of him as well: kindly, ironic eyes that seem to be both sad and amused by something, set in a modest, bearded face. In one novel three members of the Trotskyist opposition meet on skis in the woods outside Moscow. They talk of the injustices around them, agree that things are hopeless and that probably prison and death await them; then they have a snowball fight. In his *Memoirs,* Serge describes fighting White saboteurs on the rooftops of Petrograd in the summer of 1919, "overlooking a sky-blue canal. Men fled before us, firing their revolvers at us from behind the chimney-pots. . . . The men we were after escaped, but I treasured an unforgettable vision of the city, seen at 3 A.M. in all its magical paleness."

I admired Serge's writing, and for other reasons too, which I did not yet fully understand, I felt drawn to this man. As I read his books and learned more about his life, he became almost as immediate a presence for me as my uncle Boris. Finally, tracing their lives, I suddenly realized something. On an autumn day in 1919 on a hillside near the old imperial capital, at one of the turning points of twentieth-century history, these two heroes of mine had fought on opposite sides of the very same battle.

What could be seen at that battlefield today? Were there any remnants left in Russia of Boris Sergievsky's dashing, aristocratic world or of Victor Serge's revolutionary one? I decided to follow these two adoptive roots, so to speak, back to their origins.

.   .   .

In the great plaza before the Winter Palace, squarish tour buses stand packed together like rows of shoeboxes. Even though the cold war is as frigid as ever and the Soviet Union firmly in the grip of a sclerotic Communist Party bureaucracy, Leningrad still welcomes the Western tourist dollar. But we are not here to see the usual tourist sights. We turn instead down a side street lined with weathered stone buildings whose half-open doors lead to enclosed courtyards that speak of mystery, seclusion, and time past. We enter one. My wife, Arlie, and I mount the worn marble steps, and on each of the four floors we knock on doors and ask. No one remembers. Finally, on the top floor, a tenant says, "Wait. I'll get someone. She has lived here many years."

We remain on the landing, in front of the communal apartment's huge wooden door, which has beside it seven doorbells for the seven families who live inside. A woman comes out: stocky, broad-faced, with gold teeth and slightly suspicious eyes. She says she is sixty years old; she has lived in this apartment since she was seven. No, she says, defying my arithmetic, she does not remember this man Serge. She shakes her head firmly, arms crossed on her chest. Another *nyet* when I ask if we can come in. Evidently she fears getting into trouble if she allows a foreigner into the apartment. Anyway, she adds, the whole place has been remodeled, so it is not the same as when this man—is he a relative of yours?— lived here.

Curiously, despite the "no"s, she is happy to talk, and we stand on the landing for more than half an hour. I peer past her, trying to glimpse inside. The apartment had been hastily abandoned by a high tsarist official, according to Serge's description, and still had a grand piano. In the bookcase had been the collected *Laws of the Empire,* which Serge burned one by one in early 1919 for heat.

I bring up Serge's name again, and suddenly her eyes narrow. "This man—was he an anarchist?"

"Aha, so you *do* remember him!"

"No," her arms cross again firmly; she shakes her head. "Absolutely not."

That evening we walk to another part of Leningrad, to the Smolny Institute, a spot with ties to both Serge and Boris. Before the Revolution, the Smolny was Russia's most exclusive girls' finishing school, under the personal patronage of the tsarina. Boris's mother studied here. In 1917 the Bolsheviks took the school over as their headquarters and planned their coup d'état from its classrooms. Victor Serge had his office here. From here he heard the guns of the White armies attacking the city. Now the building is closed to the public; the grounds are a park. Fountains play; a warm breeze rustles the trees. Two old men talk on a bench. There is no suggestion of the history that took place at this spot; it is ghostly by its absence.

By 10:00 P.M. the sun has set, but the sky still glows with the luminous "white night" of the far northern summer. Back at our hotel, I am still thinking about the woman at Serge's apartment. I check some dates in his *Memoirs*. If she told me her age correctly, she was ten when the police knocked on that same door at midnight and arrested Serge the first time. And she was fifteen when, in front of a pharmacy that still stands on a nearby corner, he was arrested again and sent into exile in the Urals. Fifteen years old. A family she shared a kitchen with. Can she really have forgotten? Does she only remember the "anarchist" from some later denunciation? Now I notice another passage in the *Memoirs*. Serge says that in the mid-1920s, the Soviet authorities moved a young secret police officer "plus his wife, child and grandmother" into the communal apartment to keep an eye on him. The dates fit. Was this woman the child?

.   .   .

When people ask what Arlie and I are doing in Russia, I tell them about the search I am on. In Leningrad the question once comes from a woman who speaks good English, Natasha Ivanova. She is strikingly beautiful, in her early twenties, but with something about her eyes that makes her look older than would an American of the same age. When I mention that we had tried to visit the Smolny Institute, where Boris's mother went to school, she extends her hand, palm down: "Do you see that ring?"

It is a large, elaborate silver ring, with some kind of crest on it.

She looks me straight in the eye. "It's my grandmother's graduation ring—from the Smolny Institute."

I peer more closely. Worked into the ring's coat of arms is a date. 1917. *The last class.*

We have only one more day left in the city, and we spend it with Natasha, from breakfast until she puts us on a train after dinner. Her grandmother, born into the nobility, still lives. She is seventy-nine. At one point, during a taxi ride, we ask Natasha about other members of her family. Of her father, she says only, with peculiar firmness, "He lived for many years in the Far East." When we get out of the cab and are beyond earshot of the driver, she explains: suspect because of his aristocratic parentage and a job that put him in contact with foreigners, her father spent eighteen years in Stalin's prison camps. He escaped and was re-captured, trying to swim across the Amur River to China. At one point he was held—and tortured—in the same Leningrad prison where Victor Serge had been jailed a few years before. She is weeping. It is, she says, only the second time she has told her full story to anyone. The first was to a schoolmate, who scorned her for being the daughter of a prisoner; she resolved never to tell anyone again.

Natasha is studying English literature at the university here, but has a summer job as a guide with Intourist, the state tourism agency. There is a secret police office in every major hotel, she says; she was summoned to one recently and grilled for information about an American she had been guiding, a China expert. Natasha tells us about the many months of training she took to become a guide, an hour each day after work. They taught her the proper commentary for the city's monuments and cathedrals, and taught her how to answer embarrassing questions.

"Tell us about the embarrassing questions."

She smiles with malicious pleasure and takes out a worn pocket notebook in which she has taken class notes in microscopic handwriting. "So," she says, "You are interested in Russian history. Ask me something."

"What about Stalin?"

"Ah, Stalin!" Natasha finds the right page. "When Stalin was on the throne"—she winks—"oh, excuse me, when Stalin was first secretary, it is true he made certain mistakes. But he was a great military leader. And many of the bad things done in his name he did not know about. They were done by Beria. Now *he* was a very bad man."

She asks, "What particularly would you like to know about Stalin?"

"Well, what about the prison camps? The purges? How many people were killed?"

"Please!" She raises a finger and declaims dramatically from the notebook as if it were the script of a play. "Don't rub salt in the wounds."

Natasha is far less interested in Victor Serge's story than in Boris's. Born nearly forty years after the Revolution, she still considers herself a princess. "We would like to think," she says, "that there is something honorable in that." She is immensely proud that her grandmother, like only a few other aristocrats of the day, was a republican, who believed Russia needed democratic elections.

And does her grandmother, the survivor of Boris's world, remember her days at the Smolny Institute? Yes, yes, Natasha says. "She remembers the parties. When it was a girl's birthday, they served a duck with a silver chain around its neck and a cake with a gold coin baked inside—the birthday girl got it in her slice. And once when the tsarina visited Smolny, she dropped her handkerchief. The girls found it, and tore it into tiny strips so they could each have a piece." So far as Natasha knows, her grandmother is the last living graduate of the Smolny Institute in Russia; the others are in exile or dead. "Sometimes I feel as if I am . . ." Natasha says, "what is your word for those large animals that died a long time ago? I am . . . a dinosaur."

.   .   .

From Leningrad we travel south, sharing a second-class railway compartment for twenty-four hours with two Ukrainian peasants who are heading home. We are like people from Mars to them. They have never before in their lives spoken to a foreigner.

Victor and Eva are chunky, open, very gentle with each other and full of questions about the United States. Do people live in houses or apartments? How many hectares has Arlie's parents' farm? They have never talked with someone like me who speaks Russian, but badly. When I indicate I haven't understood something, Victor repeats the same mysterious idiom with more enthusiasm; Eva repeats it more loudly. With great fascination Victor looks for long minutes at my pocket Russian-English dictionary; he has not seen anything like it before. Life on their state farm near Kiev has been good to them; they have their own home, their private vegetable garden. I ask them what they think about the Russian Revolution, but draw a blank. Their parents were illiterate; their sense of history beyond that generation is hazy.

In their warmth and generosity and their ability to make the train compartment's two-foot-square folding table the center of an ongoing celebration, Victor and Eva provide the strongest echo of Boris's spirit I have yet found here. They insist we not go to the dining car and instead they press on us food from a bundle wrapped in newspaper. Earthy, aromatic black bread, thick slices of greasy sausage, and, on top of that, chunks of garlic Victor cuts up with his penknife. We mention that we had seen no fruit in Leningrad, and at the next station stop, Victor hops out and reappears with an armload of Moroccan oranges. More food comes from the bundle: pickles, onions, and gooseberries, which look like tiny, green- and white-striped grapes. Eva crowds us around the tiny table: "Come closer, come closer." Victor pours glass after glass of vodka, and we toast peace, our meeting, Russia, America, our children. . . . They ask if we need money. They impulsively open their suitcase and insist on giving us presents, which are obviously things they were bringing home to their children. For breakfast the next morning they offer us vodka and lard.

At intervals, when I run out of Russian words or while a snoring Victor sleeps off the breakfast vodka, I lie on the upper bunk with the rolled-up bedding for a pillow and reread *The Case of Comrade Tulayev*, Victor Serge's panoramic novel of the Great Purge. The birch forests of Byelorussia, then the black earth of the Ukraine, pass by outside the dusty window.

As the train takes us south, I wonder just why it is that I feel so drawn to Serge. Is it, as I have been telling friends, simply because he believed that free speech and democracy could be combined with some form of socialism? That seems incomplete; strong feelings are seldom so rational. Why am I trying to track down his roots, almost as if he were a relative, like Boris? I think in one sense I want him to be.

As I look back now, it seems to have happened like this. By the time I was twenty or so, affected by the upheavals of the 1960s, I felt myself to be on the political Left. But no sooner had I learned what the ruling class was than it dawned on me, to my dismay, that I was in it. I came from two generations of industrial capitalists. I spent some years trying to disguise that fact, but this proved difficult, as such escapes always do. What was to be done? Slowly, without seeing it quite clearly until now, I think I began to feel that I could transcend my background only if what I believed in carried the same force as ancestry, was something shared back over generations. The need for that kind of tie to the past runs far deeper than I—in the first flush of rebellion—had acknowledged. Not having all the real ancestors I wanted, I see now, I have come all this way to finish the process of adopting one.

.   .   .

Natasha, in Leningrad, had called herself a dinosaur. What about the other dinosaurs, Victor Serge's kind? Are there any revolutionaries left in the USSR? Anyone who still believes in the dreams that ignited the Russian Revolution, however much they have been betrayed since then? We probe repeatedly. With people we meet we talk about the movement against the Vietnam War and the other sorts of politics we have been involved with in the United States, although it all looks rather paltry from here, where any open challenge to party orthodoxy can land you in jail for years. Arlie, a sociologist who studies gender roles, asks about some of the obvious inequalities between Soviet men and women. But people we meet, even the editors of a *samizdat* underground journal, have no interest in talking about such issues. They despise the Soviet government, but are politely bewildered by anyone who would oppose a government in the West. The true-believer Soviet patriots—and we meet a few of those, too—are uncomfortable with the specter of people challenging the authorities and demonstrating in the streets, even in New York or San Francisco. For both groups, the red flame of October, in all its possible versions, has long since flickered out.

So far I have found no one who embodies what I'm looking for: the politics of Victor Serge, a belief in a utopia that is neither the totalitarianism of the Soviet Union nor the consumer society of the West. Is such a vision still relevant in the USSR today? Perhaps "relevant" is not the right word. Rather, is it within the scope of possibilities people here see spread before them? This it is not. Too much evil has been done here in the name of socialism for anyone to be interested in utopias of any variety. And to most Soviets, anything whatever from the West—ideas, books, music, blue jeans, electric razors—is the greatest allure, the forbidden fruit.

.   .   .

In Odessa, we go looking for the house where my uncle Boris spent most of his childhood. We find it at last, after a confusing search among winding alleys whose names have been changed once since the Revolution and again since Stalin. On a high cliff overlooking the Black Sea, the lovely, quiet street is bordered by rows of poplars. The house is subdivided into apartments now; a woman in the courtyard tells us that there are some twenty residents. Boris lived on the second floor, I know, for his parents walked a pony upstairs to give him for his fifth birthday. I fancy his room to have been on the side facing the water. There he would have had the same view that we have now: a score of ships at anchor, a long, curving breakwater.

It was in the waves beyond this breakwater that Boris, at the age of sixteen, performed his first act of heroism, diving into a stormy sea to rescue a drowning man. People stood on the breakwater making bets about whether the two would make it back to shore. Tsar Nicholas II awarded Boris a silver medal.

He gained other medals in battle later, winning the empire's highest decoration for leading his men, sword in hand, in the capture of a fortified mountaintop in World War I. His coat was ripped by an enemy bayonet. There were plenty of peacetime heroics too: in 1933, Boris piloted the filmmakers Martin and Osa Johnson across Africa, skirting fogbound, badly mapped mountain ranges and landing on lakes where no plane had ever landed before.

Again the question of relevance: How much does physical courage still matter? Boris's life would be quite different today. Test pilots have been largely replaced by computer simulation, and warfare no longer has the stylized, courtly dueling of his fighter pilot days when, if you shot down a German pilot on your side of the front, you later dropped a message over his airfield to say if he was alive or dead.

More of a problem is that unthinking bravery can serve any cause. Standing here, by his vine-covered house, I feel glad, almost relieved, that Boris was born in the late nineteenth century and not at some later time. Then he might well have been flying not at some proving ground in the 1930s, but in Vietnam in the 1960s. I can feel free to admire him only if I put such thoughts aside. To me now, a far better kind of courage seems that of Victor Serge—the ability to stick to your beliefs when the whole world is against you. Computers will never make that outdated. Nonetheless, I want a full share of Boris's spirit in my revolutionary utopia: space for individual boldness, for defiance of propriety, for landings on lakes unknown.

· · ·

Boris flew as long as he could, fifty-three years. The doctors made him stop, and he sold his beloved Grumman Mallard. With no battles to fight or planes to fly, he sat like a caged lion for long, quiet hours reading and napping, although he came to life instantly, eyes wide, nostrils flaring, head thrown back, if an attractive young woman entered the room. When he turned eighty there was a big party—champagne, dinner, and dancing.

Not long before, Boris had had an operation to implant an electronic pacemaker, and during the birthday party he showed it off to people between waltzes. His cheerful directness was unchanged. "It's good," he told me, as he tapped the metallic bulge under his shirt. "It will give me another two or three years."

He was right. That final time I saw him was two and a half years later. Shortly after that visit, I sent him a picture of me in a glider. When there was no thank-you letter—Boris's mother had passed on to him the manners she learned at the Smolny Institute—I knew he was dying.

Victor Serge's last years were more difficult. In 1933, Stalin exiled him to the remote city of Orenburg. People were starving; children clawed each other in the streets for a piece of bread. Serge became fast friends with the other political exiles there, a small group of men and women who shared their food, nursed one another, and kept each other alive.

In 1936, continuing protests by French intellectuals finally won Serge's release from Russia. Before he could leave, the secret police seized the manuscripts of two books he had written in exile, including the novel he thought his best.

Serge's politics made him an outsider in Europe. Neither the establishment nor the Communist press would publish his articles.

His primary forum was a small labor paper in Belgium. There, and in a series of new books, he railed against the Great Purge that was devouring the cream of Russian revolutionaries; he also defended the Spanish Republic and spoke out against the Western powers for accommodating Hitler. These ideas were not popular: to make ends meet, Serge had to work at his old trade as a typesetter and proofreader, sometimes correcting the galleys of newspapers that would not publish his writing.

Back in Russia, Serge's sister, mother-in-law, two brothers-in-law, and two sisters-in-law disappeared into the *gulag.* His Russian-born wife, Lyuba Russakova, became psychotic from the persecutions the couple had suffered, and was put in a Paris mental hospital. When the Germans invaded France, Serge had to flee. The United States refused him a visa. Just ahead of the Gestapo, he and his teenage son left Marseilles on a boat to Mexico. In France, the Germans burned his books. The texts of several survive today only because copies were preserved by the Resistance.

Even on this final flight of his exile-filled life, Serge never allowed himself to *feel* exiled. An internationalist always, he felt at home wherever there were people who shared his beliefs. He recorded the clenched-fist salute his shipload of anti-Nazi refugees got from Spanish fishermen; he organized even at sea: "Out in the Atlantic, past the Sahara coast, the stars pitch up and down above our heads. We hold a meeting on the upper deck, between the funnel and the lifeboats." In Mexico he stayed true to his vision of libertarian socialism, and again met resistance. Pressure from both the British and Soviet ambassadors cut off his access to the Mexican press. He turned again to books and wrote his two greatest, the novel *The Case of Comrade Tulayev,* and his *Memoirs of a Revolutionary 1901–1941.* They were written, as the Russians say, for the desk drawer; neither was published in his lifetime.

One day in 1947, writes Serge's British translator, Peter Sedgwick,

He met his friend Julián Gorkin [a Spanish Republican refugee] in the street; they talked for a while, and shook hands when they parted. . . . Not long after that, doubtless feeling ill, Serge hailed a taxi, sank back into the seat and died without telling the driver where to take him. His family found him stretched out on an old operating table in a dirty room inside a police station. Gorkin recounts what he looked like: "His upturned soles had holes in them, his suit was threadbare, his shirt coarse. Really he might have been some vagabond or other picked up from the streets." Victor Serge's face was stiffened in an expression of ironic protest, and, by means of a bandage of cloth, the State had at last closed his mouth.

.   .   .

Moscow. We have one day left in Russia. The journey feels somehow incomplete. There seems too great a gap between the numbing drabness of the Soviet Union today and the larger possibilities suggested by the lives of Boris Sergievsky and Victor Serge. Perhaps it is time to say good-bye to those heroic images, to acknowledge finally that life today, here or anywhere, proceeds on a less grand scale. And so, having run out of ancestors to trace, we start off in what appears—or so we think—a different direction entirely.

Until now we have seen few of the Soviet dissidents. Except for their courageous struggle for civil liberties, their dissent from the Soviet system seems quite different from that of someone like Victor Serge. Their dream is not of a revolutionary Russia in any sense, but of one like the West. Most idolize the United States. Nonetheless, these are some of the best and bravest people in this country, and we want to pay homage to one of them. We enter a Moscow apartment building and climb many floors up through the nighttime gloom, as if ascending a cathedral tower.

At the top, a door opens into warmth and light. The man who greets us has eyebrows that slope downward, giving his face a distinctive, angular look. He wears his sweater unbuttoned down the front and seems like a kindly, shy professor welcoming a group of graduate students.

Our host is Andrei Sakharov. In his kitchen some fifteen of us squeeze around a table built to seat eight. The phone and doorbell ring continually. More people keep entering. There are introductions, but I lose track. Sakharov, his country's premier scientist and the father of the Soviet H-bomb, now the subject of increasing repression, has used his enormous prestige to give what shelter he can to the community of other dissidents in Moscow. It turns out we phoned him on the right day: in the summer he is at his *dacha* outside the city, but returns every Tuesday evening to host an open house at his apartment.

Sakharov greets someone at the door, then brings him to the kitchen. "Here is someone for you," he tells the gathering. "Back only one week."

A young man strides into the room. He is tall and thin. He wears sunglasses even though it is night, suggesting eye trouble, but he sits down at the table with a brisk mien that is like bracing air in the packed kitchen. He has just returned from five years' imprisonment and another three of Siberian exile, and has come to pay his respects to Sakharov.

An older person at the table, an imposing, barrel-chested man with a big black beard, asks the newcomer what camps he had been in. This man must be a former prisoner also, for he calls the stranger by the familiar form *ti,* as do all prisoners in every language that makes the distinction.

The young man tells his story. He had been a lathe operator at an oil tanker shipyard on the Black Sea. Workers had not been paid as promised. He and some others printed up a leaflet protesting this (the first criminal action), and then got several dozen workers to go down to local Communist Party headquarters to complain (the second). The organizers were arrested and sent to labor camps. Ironically, the workers soon got their promised pay. In the Siberian camps, he says, he met other prisoners also convicted for labor organizing.

"It sounds to me," I say, "as if you and your friends were doing something like what the first Bolshevik organizers did seventy years ago. Did you ever discuss that?" A half-laugh, half-sigh runs around the table.

"Yes," says the returned prisoner, a bit sadly. "We did."

"But the difference today, my friend," adds the barrel-chested man at the table, in English, "is that the authorities are much stronger. The working class is much weaker."

I ask the young man if there is any single message he would most like people in the West to hear. His answer is unexpected.

"Yes, there is. In your radio broadcasts, the Voice of America, the BBC"—millions of Russians listen to these—"you do not say enough about workers, about what are trade unions in the West, about what workers get paid, about the right to organize, the right to strike."

His story is finished, and, abruptly, he is gone. A handshake for Sakharov, a firm nod to the rest of us, and he is out the door.

The sudden exit creates a momentary pause around the table, and I turn to the older, burly, bearded man who spoke before. He carries a rough-hewn walking stick and looks like Moses. I ask his name. He is Lev Kopelev. Writer, scholar, ten years in the prison camps, the model for the character of Rubin in Solzhenitsyn's *The First Circle*. We had hoped to meet him, but his telephone hadn't answered and we had given up. He too, it appears, has come into town just for this evening.

With Kopelev is his wife, Raisa Orlova, a prominent critic who writes on American literature. She has bright eyes that take in everything and a face at once warm and iron-willed. Although she and her husband eschew any labels that might lessen their solidarity with other dissidents, they are clearly, exhilaratingly different from everyone we have met so far. "What's happened to *Ramparts?* Is it still publishing?" Orlova asks eagerly. "What are all your antiwar movement people doing now?" She wants to hear about the time Arlie and I spent as civil-rights workers in the South. Alone, of all the people we've met in Russia, she has read Victor Serge. The other dinosaurs still live.

The phone rings in the next room; it is someone calling from abroad for Sakharov. As soon as he starts to speak, the line goes dead. Sakharov says this happens often. Another phone call, this one from Lithuania, with news of a new indictment in a nationalists' case there. The people here have been following this trial. Sakharov passes around the table a message he has just received from another prisoner whose case they know.

I ask: Do they think groups overseas such as Amnesty International are helpful to them? Sakharov nods. Orlova says, "I cannot say whether they have long-range political impact, but I can tell you it does incredible things for the spirits of the prisoners. I know a man who was a political prisoner for many years in Soviet Georgia. Somehow Amnesty got his name. One day at the prison he received a postcard from someone in Switzerland saying: We know about you, we are working for you. The man was stunned. 'It was—' he told me later, 'it was as if the doors of the prison had opened and I could see the sky.'"

I ask if anyone minds if I use people's real names in writing about this evening. Kopelev lets out a belly laugh. "My dear friend! They saw us when we came in"—he points out the window at the street—"they hear us as we speak"—he points to the ceiling—"so why should we worry?"

The hubbub at Sakharov's table continues. A German friend is with us tonight, and conversation is in English, German, and Russian, everybody talking at once. Whoever is listening in via hidden microphones for the KGB this evening must have a colossal headache. The center of attention now is Marya Slepak, wife of Vladimir Slepak, a leader of the Jewish emigration movement who was sentenced to five years in exile for hanging a banner from their apartment window. She shrugs off a sympathetic touch on the arm. "*Nichevo.*" It is nothing. It could be worse. She has sent her husband food and money but has no idea if it got there. Now she is leaving for Siberia to try to join him.

"I know the area," Orlova tells her encouragingly. "Our daughter and son-in-law were exiled there, I visited them." Elena Bonner, Sakharov's wife and herself a prominent dissident, stands on a chair, opens a high cupboard, and starts passing Marya Slepak cans of food for the trip. Other food, gifts, and supplies materialize and get passed across the table. One woman gives her American chewing gum (a great delicacy here), explaining to us, "That's for her to give the station ticket agent when he tells her there are no seats left."

When the evening ends, Sakharov apologizes that he never had time to answer some questions I had for him. "But I think it was more important for you to hear what that young man had to say." I ask if there is anything we can do for him when we get back to the West—phone calls, messages . . . He says, simply, "Write. Publish. Tell what you have found."

And what have I found? That you recapture the past at risk: time passes, issues change, no image of political heroism should be frozen. Perhaps I have been too narrow in conceiving what it means to be a radical in Russia—or anywhere—today. A vision of utopia, of that combination of individual freedom and economic justice not yet attained by either East or West is all very well. But usually you have to put utopia aside and engage in the battles at hand. And here, at the moment, those happen to be largely in defense of something most leftists, myself included, usually view with snobbish dismay, ethnic nationalism: Jews who want to immigrate to Israel, separatists in the Baltic states and the Caucasus. But if you care about justice, you have to defend those being persecuted. That, surely, is what Victor Serge did when he tried to intervene with the secret police on behalf of oppositionists of many sorts, often with opinions different from his own.

We know that we will not be able to sleep tonight. We walk back across half of Moscow to our hotel. We make our way through crooked, narrow streets, passing two-story, yellow stucco buildings, unchanged since Pushkin's time. Not far from Red Square, we pass the prison where Victor Serge was interrogated on his way to exile in 1933.

We are absolutely certain that if he were alive and in Moscow, he would have been at Sakharov's apartment tonight.

. . .

There is little left to tell, except of the time my two dinosaurs almost met.

Petrograd, October 1919. The city is under siege. Churchill has called on the West to strangle Bolshevism in its cradle. The White Army makes a bold, unexpected drive on the city from the south. Terrified Bolshevik soldiers flee before its British-supplied tanks. In Petrograd, bread is running out. Half-starved workers pilfer the factories.

The populace believes the city will fall, the old regime return. Jews are mocked in the streets. The situation seems hopeless. The Central Committee sends in Trotsky in his famous armored train, followed by Bashkir cavalry on small, long-haired horses from the steppes. Barricades go up. The White Army advances. Its troops reach Pulkovo Heights, site of an old observatory a few miles south of the city. A White soldier, legend has it, offers one of the generals a chance to look at Petrograd through his binoculars. The general laughingly declines, saying that the next day he will be walking on his beloved Nevsky Prospect.

Boris Sergievsky is an infantry officer with the attacking White Army. Victor Serge is in the Red trenches that block its path.

An Adirondack lake shimmers through trees outside the window. It is my last visit with Boris. He moves slowly, but thinks clearly and remembers well. "We were so close. We were so close, Adam, I could see the golden towers of St. Peter and St. Paul."

A puzzled cabdriver waits while we climb the hill at Pulkovo. A beech grove shades us from the hot sun. On one side, a peasant woman in a red kerchief walks slowly around the edge of a field, in search of something—wildflowers? mushrooms?—she does not find. From the hilltop you can see the distant city. Boris was right: on the horizon is a gleam of gold.

This hill is as far as the White Army got. It was here that the Reds met them. The Whites fought bravely, but fell back. The tide of the Civil War turned; the battles died away; and a Russia slowly took shape that was not the one that either Boris or Serge had risked their lives for.

It was on this hillside, on the evening of October 20, 1919, that Boris Sergievsky and Victor Serge, in the opposing armies, were probably only a few hundred yards apart, perhaps even closer. They did not know each other, of course; in the rest of their lives, each doubtless never even heard the other's name. They were both men of impulsive, improbable friendships, and I like to think that had they met anywhere but on a battlefield, they would have liked each other. But what they might have said to one another—about democracy and justice, sensuality and adventure—that conversation we can only imagine.

1979

From Hitler to Human Rights

Aryan Nations is a white supremacist group that combines Nazi ideology with a racist brand of biblical fundamentalism. Its members wear uniforms: light blue shirt, dark blue tie, and a sleeve patch with a Maltese cross. They are based in heavily armed compounds in Idaho, Utah, and Pennsylvania, with smaller outposts elsewhere. Some of these fortified compounds have stockpiles of food, water, and ammunition. Members or veterans of Aryan Nations have been linked to bombings in several Western states; they are a particularly bellicose part of a much larger extreme right-wing movement that has far more blood on its hands.

If you had recently been a journalist visiting Aryan Nations' Idaho headquarters to do a story, the first person to greet you at the compound gate would have been the organization's personable, articulate national spokesman, Floyd Cochran. Cochran brought something to Aryan Nations that few hate groups had before: media savvy and a shrewd sense of marketing. When reporters visited the Idaho compound, he served them coffee and doughnuts instead of chasing them away. Cochran was calm and smooth, and quickly realized that he would get more space in newspapers if he did not use racial epithets. Aryan Nations' chief, Rev. Richard Butler, proudly called him "the next Goebbels."

In his mid thirties, Cochran had avidly read Ku Klux Klan and Nazi literature since he was ten or eleven. Before moving to the Aryan Nations Idaho compound, he had spent time in jail in New York state for threatening to burn down a synagogue. When talking to the press, Cochran sometimes sported the group's blue uniform, but soon realized that when hunting new members, casual clothes worked better. Besides handling reporters, he became

Aryan Nations' chief recruiter, working in Tennessee, Ohio, Washington, Oregon, and elsewhere.

In a first for such far right groups, Cochran reached out to a new constituency: unemployed white loggers in the Pacific Northwest. He told them that they were being sacrificed to "an affirmative action program for the spotted owl." And in what was probably another first, he took the white supremacy message to young people with music videos. To the background music of the Guns & Roses song "Welcome to the Jungle," he filmed black pimps and prostitutes at work on Seattle streets, then young white mothers wheeling baby strollers through a park. The Aryan Nations address came on screen at the end.

One day in the spring of 1992, shortly before he was to be the featured speaker at Aryan Nations' annual Hitler Youth festival, Cochran was chatting with Wayne Jones, chief of security at the group's Idaho compound. Cochran mentioned a phone call he had just gotten from his former wife. Their younger son, who was four years old at the time, was about to go to the hospital for an operation to repair a cleft palate.

"He's a genetic defect," Jones replied. "When we come to power, he'll have to be euthanized." After all, hadn't the Nazis done just that?

Cochran was stunned. For the first time, he says, it dawned on him that the hate he was preaching could circle back to people close to him. Cochran found himself in great turmoil, for his entire life had been based on a belief in white supremacy and all that went with it.

Several months after this conversation, Cochran told his boss, Rev. Butler, that he felt he couldn't be Aryan Nations' public spokesman anymore. Butler gave him a hundred dollars and said, "You've got five minutes to get off the compound." Cochran did so, carrying little more than two changes of clothes. The inner turmoil continued, but within seven or eight months Cochran was speaking out against racism as forcefully as he had once spoken for it—on college campuses, before youth groups, and in prisons.

.   .   .

These are the outlines of Floyd Cochran's story as I first heard it. I was intrigued but skeptical. People drop out of hard-core hate groups all the time, and not always for good motives. For some, the thrill fades. Some are at risk of prosecution, and win safety by becoming FBI informants. Others are convinced that they can write a best-seller or sell their story to the movies. But, although surrounded by some extremely violent people at Aryan Nations, Cochran had not been under threat of arrest. And, since leaving, he had even turned away one or two publishers offering ghostwriters and money.

When I managed to track down Cochran by phone, there was a bottled-up tension in his voice. But one of the first things he said had the immediate ring of truth. "If ever anybody tries to tell you that a change like this happened overnight, don't believe them. It's a long business. For me it's still going on."

In the same phone conversation, Cochran went on to mention two names I knew. "If you write something about me, it's very important that you give a lot of credit to two people in particular, Leonard Zeskind and Loretta Ross. Human-rights workers in this country don't get much attention. The year after I left Aryan Nations was a tough one for me. I couldn't have made it if I hadn't been able to call these two all the time, even if it was the middle of the night. I owe them a lot."

So: the two people who had most helped this one-time neo-Nazi along his new path were a Jewish man and a black woman. I wanted to find out more.

.   .   .

Oxford, Mississippi, January 1994. The first image that pops into my mind when I finally see Cochran is that of the hollowed-out eyes and gaunt faces of the half-starved Jewish prisoners in the movie *Schindler's List*. Cochran is of medium height and extremely thin, almost emaciated. From time to time his bearded face crinkles into a warm smile, but at rest its expression is one of sadness. He always hunches forward slightly, as if he were perpetually walking against the wind.

We meet at the campus guest house of the University of Mississippi, where each room has two books: a picture history of Ole Miss football through the ages and a Bible. Cochran is spending several days on this campus. Although he is making some public appearances here, he has registered at the guest house under another name, for death threats and hate calls from his former comrades follow him wherever he goes.

This is an interesting spot for Cochran to be carrying his new message to, for Ole Miss was a major battleground in the struggle against segregation several decades ago. And a stark reminder of that era is unfolding at a nearby county courthouse the very week of Cochran's visit: the second trial of white supremacist Byron De La Beckwith for the 1963 murder of civil-rights leader Medgar Evers. In his days with Aryan Nations, Cochran wrote several articles praising Beckwith, for which he was given a banquet and plaque by Beckwith's family. But now he wants to visit the courthouse in solidarity with Medgar Evers's widow.

Over the next several days I follow Cochran day and night: a visit to a sociology class, lunch with several local ministers, dinner with faculty members and the campus newspaper editor, an interview at the student TV station, a speech. We also spend a good deal of time talking alone, some of it while driving to the courthouse and back.

Cochran smokes continually. He drinks about fifteen to twenty cups of coffee a day. In his days in the racist movement, he says, it was thirty-five or forty. "After you've had five or ten cups, you're not hungry." He has weighed 136 pounds for years. All his meals, I notice, he leaves half-finished.

Those who study the radical right usually estimate that there are roughly 25,000 hard-core activists in hate groups like Aryan Nations, the Ku Klux Klan, and the like in the United States today. Another 150,000 men and women are active sympathizers—people who attend the occasional meeting or rally, buy the literature, and so on.

"Armchair racists" is what Floyd Cochran calls the active sympathizers: he was one himself until, some four years ago, he headed west to the Aryan Nations compound near Coeur d'Alene, Idaho. The life he left behind in upstate New York, where he grew up near the Canadian border, had not been happy. His parents' marriage was stormy; as a child, Cochran repeatedly ran away. He spent several years in foster homes. As an adult, he got divorced, drank too much, and spent many months in county jails—bad checks, drunk driving, breaking and entering. When he was out of jail, Cochran made his living herding cows and shoveling snow on local dairy farms. During one spell behind bars, he earned a high school equivalency diploma. He never went to college, but was always an avid reader. "My ex-wife told the judge that she's probably got the only husband around who, when he doesn't come home at night, she's got to go down to the library to find him."

In being a social loser, Cochran was like many others attracted to extreme right-wing groups. Cochran understood this pattern and, once he became an Aryan Nations recruiter, consciously applied it to his work. "We used to send people into the cities to pick up homeless kids and bring them back to the compound and give them a place to live. You give a homeless kid some food and a place to stay and tell him that you love him, you can do a lot of things with that kid. One of the strongest recruiting tactics I had was to tell people, 'We are your family.' Or, if there was a single mother, I'd say, 'In an Aryan society, a man would take care of his children, not pack up and leave.'

"When young people came to Aryan Nations, we'd give them a hug, then give them responsibilities—to mow lawns, haul wood, mundane kinds of things. One of the paradoxes was that we would give you responsibility and hold you accountable for it, but at the same time if you couldn't find a job—hey, it's not your fault. It's the Jews who're stopping you, or it's because of affirmative action . . . even though northern Idaho is 98 percent white! I used to watch people who'd get up at noon and say, 'I can't find a job.' The number one thing is that nobody in the racist movement gets blamed for anything—myself included. My marriage didn't work? It's not my fault, it's because I was a racial activist and my wife couldn't stand it. I didn't graduate from high school? It's because my Jewish English teacher didn't like me."

While at the Aryan Nations compound, the lost souls Cochran recruited would also get a heavy dose of pageantry and ritual. Several times I watch as Cochran shows Ole Miss audiences slides and a videotape that reveal life on the inside: watchtowers; Nazi and Confederate flags (never the U.S. flag, which is regarded as the flag of ZOG, the Zionist Occupational Government); a meeting room named Aryan Hall; a ceremony called "Soldier's Ransom," where the faithful kiss a sword and pledge to uphold the honor of the white race and of white womanhood; a wedding, where a young couple marches down an arch of arms raised in "Heil Hitler!" salutes. The various Aryan Nations compounds can contain everything from firing ranges to printing presses to schools for the children. The women do all the cooking.

Cochran at first thrived on all this. Aryan Nations was the first close community he felt part of. The strict military discipline—no drinking, no drugs—was good for him. He also found his vocation as a publicist, instinctively sensing the lessons that corporate executives take expensive seminars to learn. "I realized that there were about twenty-five questions I was constantly asked by reporters, and so I developed the answers, and I constantly fine-tuned them." Cochran enjoyed a limelight he had never known before. "When I went to Aryan Nations, I'd milked cows all my life. Six months later, I'm on CBS News! I'm in *Newsweek!* I'm in a PBS special!"

It took some persuading before he could get his biblical fundamentalist superiors to approve his fondest dream: spreading the message with music videos. But finally he realized the button to push: "I said, 'We all admire the Führer. In his day, *he* was on the cutting edge of technology—he used radio, he used film, he used an airplane. *We* should be on the cutting edge of technology too.' Then they approved the idea."

. . .

Again and again during the next two days, his voice always filled with a compressed tension, Cochran returns to talking about the pivotal moment when he was told that his son deserved euthanasia. I asked him if he would still be in his old job if this had not happened. "I might have changed to another group," he says, "but I'd still be part of the white racist movement."

Cochran is too hard on himself in saying this, I think, for he has something that would have made it difficult for him to stay in any cult forever: a sense of irony.

"One night I was doing guard duty. It was 12:30 or 1:00 and a taxicab pulls up to the gate. Aryan Nations is ten miles from the nearest town, so it's not like taxis are cruising by all the time. A man gets out and says he wants to see Pastor Butler. I say, 'Hold on! We need to see some identification.' He unbuttons his shirt and pulls out his stomach, and on it is tattooed ARYAN WARRIOR. I tell him to stand there and I call up to Frank, the sergeant. Frank comes running down to the gate, dressed in nothing but his BVDs, and carrying a shotgun. So I've got this cab driver sitting there, it's midnight, and this guy with his gut hanging out, and Frank standing there with a shotgun and a pair of underpants on. And I'm thinking to myself: 'I'm saving the white race?'"

When Cochran finally did part ways with Aryan Nations, he

used his media know-how to call a press conference and apologize to the people of the Pacific Northwest. But then he found himself with no job, nowhere to live, and no money to leave the area. For some three months he lived in a tent in Coeur d'Alene, pitched first in a city park, and then in a public campground.

While living in his tent, totally uncertain what to do next, Cochran had a visitor one day, Larry Broadbent. Broadbent is the former undersheriff of Kootenai County, Idaho, where the Aryan Nations compound was. Although a veteran of nearly thirty years in law enforcement, Broadbent has a most unsherifflike passion for human rights. For years he raised hackles among his fellow lawmen by declaring that women should be hired as sheriff's deputies. He has also served two terms on the Idaho Human Rights Commission, and at one point was the target of an assassination plot for which a member of Aryan Nations was convicted. Broadbent and Cochran had tangled when Cochran was at Aryan Nations, but now Broadbent made sure Cochran had enough money for food and a shower, and invited him out to dinner. More important, he linked Cochran up with the Center for Democratic Renewal, an Atlanta-based civil-rights organization that monitors the radical right.

"Leonard Zeskind was the first person to contact me," says Cochran. "Leonard is Jewish. This was really an eye-opener for me. I mean, here's a person who a month earlier I was advocating killing. And he's the first person to call me up. And not to ask for anything. Other than: 'Do you want someone to talk to?'"

Not long after, Cochran and Zeskind had the first of many meetings. It was the first time as an adult that Cochran had spent any time with someone Jewish.

"In the racist movement, one of the things I would teach was that white people had positive electrons. But the Jewish people, the children of Satan, had negative electrons. And that if you walked into a room with them, those electrons would go off. The first time I was around Leonard, I kept walking around both sides of him. This was about a month after I got out of the movement. I didn't say a word. Finally Leonard said, 'I shut 'em off!'"

"I talked to him for four days straight," says Zeskind today. "I liked Floyd. He was a smart guy. He was struggling, both to find a way out of the movement and to make sense of the whole process. I wanted to find out if this was a hard-core hater, or someone who had joined for other reasons. A lot of people get involved in the white supremacist movement because of the lack of an attractive, viable alternative. Once Floyd found an alternative he was able to blossom."

The next new friend Cochran made was Loretta Ross, a black colleague of Zeskind. "In the summer of '92 I got this call," she says, "from Floyd Cochran. I took the call. 'You mean *the* Floyd Cochran?' I thought he was calling to deliver a death threat! Which is perfectly normal in organizations like this."

Several months later, Cochran and Ross finally met. She was the first black person he had talked to at length. "Loretta and I were having dinner one day. And she was talking about her son. About wanting him to have an education. Hoping things would go well for him. The same way I'd talk about my son. For me that was a big awakening. Because I still thought that black people have kids just to get on welfare."

Ross says she has learned a great deal from Cochran. "He's been on an incredible journey. The first time we met he was very guarded. He censored himself. But it's been fascinating for me to watch his growth, to watch the changes.

"I have to confess that my own feelings underwent some transformation. Until I had the experience of deprogramming racists, I have to admit that I felt towards them a lot of the things they felt towards me. But they're people with aches and pains and loves and hates just like me. Floyd has taught me as much as, hopefully, I've taught him. That's what this nonviolence business should be all about.

"I think most blacks in America, especially those in the middle class, don't get to see the face of white poverty. Or get to know marginalized whites like Floyd, who'd rather catch a Greyhound bus from New York to Seattle because the experience of catching a plane was so foreign to him.

"The thing that's impressive about Floyd is his sense of integrity. He has strong fears of being a pimp, of being someone who'll be in it for the money. We had to talk him into accepting a contract with a speaker's bureau. He thinks if you really believe, you should do it all for free."

. . .

Since Cochran left the movement, the speaker's bureau has been able to book one or two appearances for him each month on college campuses, which earn him a bare-bones living. But Cochran usually stays on or near each campus for up to a week, speaking for free to any churches, YMCAs, high schools, or jails willing to hear him. He has moved back to upstate New York and regularly sees his two sons. He lives in a trailer. He has turned down several offers to do a quick book, because he doesn't want to write "a pop culture book about see-what-a-wonderful-and-great-person-I-am." He is eager to get out his message, but is careful about the medium. When the *National Enquirer* called recently, he told them, "You've got the wrong Floyd Cochran."

Parents from around the country whose children have gotten caught up in the racist or skinhead movements call Cochran for advice. He has tried his hand at deprogramming, but admits that his efforts have not been too successful. Now when families contact him, he puts the distraught sets of parents in touch with each other. He worries that there is no organized support network for young people trying, as he did, to leave the movement.

Cochran's former comrades regard him, he says, as "a race traitor working for the Jews." While he was waiting at a New York TV studio recently before a talk show confrontation with some white racists, one pulled a gun out of a holster. "He didn't point it at me. But he made sure I saw it," says Cochran, who was too rattled to talk coherently on the air. About 90 percent of such threats are bluster, he says, but he worries some about the other 10 percent. In virtually every public speech, he makes a point of saying that he lives with a very large dog.

Much in Cochran's personal life seems unresolved. "I'm kinda friendly with women," he says, but with none, it appears, for too long. During his visit to Mississippi, he is juggling messages from two of them and is not at all sure where he will be living a month or two hence. He grew up in a family of fundamentalists, and still sprinkles his conversation with biblical references (he has an almost photographic memory for things like Bible verses and telephone numbers). But he feels he can't go back to any kind of Christian fundamentalism because of its animosity toward gays. He has not yet found a relationship to God he is comfortable with. "There is something missing inside."

Cochran also has to contend with some unfinished psychological business. A part of him, he confesses, still feels an emotional tug pulling against what he now believes. "I used to watch documentaries of World War II and Hitler. But I've found that I can't watch them any more because I almost feel . . . maybe he wasn't so bad, maybe he did do some good things . . ."

Last year, Cochran felt caught in the same kind of contradiction when he was asked to testify before the Montana state legislature in favor of bills decriminalizing homosexuality and strengthening protection for gays and lesbians. He did so, but "I had a real struggle with that. My stomach was in knots. I began to sweat. My mind was saying one thing but inside it was something else." Before the lawmakers, however, he was his usual articulate self, mocking those who feared these measures would lead to gay recruitment: "I've had Jehovah's Witnesses knocking on my door before, but I've never had a gay person knocking on my door to recruit me."

Another piece of unfinished business is Cochran's sense of guilt. "How do I apologize to someone that I've made to feel less than a man or woman? I told a whole roomful of black people that none of them were going to heaven." A teenage boy he knew, Jeremy Knesal, now faces up to forty-five years in prison on federal explosives and firearms charges in connection with the bombing of the NAACP office in Tacoma, Washington, and preparations for attacks on synagogues and black rap singers. Cochran worked closely with Knesal at the Aryan Nations compound. "I made sure he came to Bible study, to Race Eugenics class, to the Racial History class I taught. I pumped him up. So I'm indirectly as much responsible as if I'd thrown the bomb."

Cochran's politics today tend toward the libertarian. He is dubious about welfare. He doesn't like sales taxes. He's against gun control. He doesn't have a license for his dog. He doesn't have a driver's license. Yet at the same time, he has no truck with politicians who combine the appeal to self-reliance with any kind of racism. When he was in the white supremacist movement, he says, "George Bush reconfirmed for me everything I always thought about black people when he used the Willie Horton ad."

.   .   .

On his last night in Mississippi, on at least his fifteenth cup of coffee of the day, Floyd Cochran speaks before a multiracial audience at an Ole Miss auditorium. He looks more gaunt and hollow-eyed than ever, and is nervous beforehand: every structure on campus is labeled SMOKE FREE BUILDING. Wearing only a thin windbreaker, Cochran keeps dashing for a smoke outside—where it is ten degrees above zero.

Cochran begins this talk, as he always does, with an apology for his past. He then goes on to tell his story, and to show the slides and video: guards in fatigue uniforms, a flaming swastika, "the man who said my son should be killed," and, next to a church pulpit, a plowshare beaten into a sword.

He spends a lot of time parsing the complicated genealogy of the various right-wing sects, churches, and parties. They are so numerous, he says, because there are "so many people who want to be the Führer, and not enough followers!"

After about an hour and a half the speech and official question period are over; the M.C. thanks Cochran, the crowd applauds and begins drifting out. But Cochran, as a matter of principle, never leaves such an event until the last person wanting to talk to him has the chance to do so. This evening I see why.

For more than an hour he answers questions from a dwindling knot of students who have come up to the front of the auditorium, until finally, while janitors are turning off lights and packing up the video equipment, there are only two people left: a white couple in their early twenties, who seem to have been waiting until everyone else has left. The man speaks with a heavy Southern accent. His face is intelligent, intense; his forehead is knotted in worry. His story comes pouring out in a rush.

"I was a skinhead. For ten years. I'm out of it now. My best friend is black. He's going to be the best man at our wedding. But I'm having trouble getting rid of some of the attitudes. A lot of trouble. I got into an argument with a black student and I threatened to crack his skull. I feel *real* bad about it."

I've seldom seen anyone look so tormented. It's late and Cochran is tired. He offers to meet the couple for breakfast the next morning, before he has to leave for the airport.

At 7:30 A.M., we meet in a coffee shop near the campus. The young man, whom I will call Ben, is trembling so hard that when he leans against our table, it shakes. He grew up here in Mississippi, Ben says. At a young age, his parents told him, "We better not catch you playing with niggers on the playground." When a black family was looking at a house for sale in his neighborhood, "my dad saw this and went and bought the house, to keep them from moving in." Ben's uncle fears a coming racial Armageddon. "He's stockpiled three thousand guns and several million rounds of ammunition." But he loves his uncle, Ben says, a tremor in his voice.

"When I was in high school," Ben goes on, "we had race riots. I got in a lot of trouble. I was standing out in the school parking lot with an AK-47 and about two hundred people behind me. I was wearing a Nazi Youth uniform." After this, he hung out with skinheads. When he left the movement, his parents kicked him out of the house.

It appears that the argument Ben described last night is not the only one he has been in recently. He has trouble controlling his feelings. On one occasion, "I kicked someone so hard I thought I'd killed him. I snapped."

Ben's girlfriend is four months pregnant. He again mentions the black friend who will be best man at their wedding. But even that he is agonized about: "I don't know if I'm doing it because he's been a good friend to me who's been there when I needed him . . . or because it will throw my family into a complete culture shock."

And, it emerges, there's still another problem: Ben has an ex-wife and small child who are still "in the movement." He hasn't seen them since he left.

"I don't know how to deal with the things I've done," Ben says, still trembling. Under the table, his fiancée comfortingly holds his hand.

"We can't change any of the things we've done," says Cochran. The role of confessor does not come easily to him. He is more at ease describing his own sins than hearing an outpouring of some-one else's. But he tries his best. Searching for things to say, he tells Ben that he, too, found life hard after leaving the racist movement because of people in it whom he had come to care about, racism aside. And now he knows he can never talk to them again.

Ben nods, still miserable. He seems tormented by a sense of sin: "I'm not a perfect person. I still have racist thoughts." I sus-pect there may be more things he hasn't told us about, and that his journey onward may be much harder than Cochran's. Cochran invites him to come along on the ride to the airport, and I say good-bye.

. . .

What makes for transformational experiences? I have long col-lected such stories, and in one way, Cochran's resembles some of the others. Often, as when Cochran heard the remark about his son, there is a moment when someone is taken by surprise—and suddenly finds himself identifying with the objects of his hate.

John Newton was an eighteenth-century English preacher and an ardent Abolitionist. He wrote the hymn "Amazing Grace." Newton began his working life, however, as a slave trader. His turning point came when a tyrannical, suspicious slave-ship captain, whose crew he was on, held him as a virtual prisoner for a year. During this period Newton himself experienced something resembling slavery. It seems to have been this memory, festering within him, that later led to his great change.

In the 1960s and 1970s, Gordon Winter was a key informer and agent provocateur for the South African security police. Information he gave his superiors caused dozens of people to be arrested and tortured. Still living a double life, Winter married and had a child. One day in a store he saw a black father with a small child buying dog food. He asked why, and the man said it was the only meat he could afford. According to Winter, this was his transformational experience. He fled the country. At some risk to himself (for the South African authorities sometimes assassinated their enemies overseas), Winter wrote an extraordinarily damaging book detailing everything he knew about the security apparatus.

Floyd Cochran's transformation is less dramatic than these, but it is just as real. It is still under way. It may get harder. Soon his fifteen minutes of fame will be over; the speaking dates and talk-show invitations will dwindle. On bad days, he worries about whether he might relapse into old habits that could land him back in the county jail. And he worries whether his two children might somehow, perversely, find his time at Aryan Nations something exciting. But one thing he is quite sure of is that whatever happens, he will never again feel himself a defender of the master race. And for anyone who believes in the possibility of human change, that's a victory worth celebrating.

1994

Keep Up Pressure in All Directions

Joel Schatz has wire-rimmed glasses and an Old Testament-sized beard. He is six feet two inches, plus a few extra inches from a big mass of curly black hair flecked with gray. "This trip we're about to take," he says enthusiastically, "is so important that I've even gotten a haircut." Its effects are not noticeable.

Joel is sitting in the study of his San Francisco apartment, where most of the furniture consists of pillows on the floor. The largest object in sight is an enormous reflector telescope, which can be pivoted on its pedestal and aimed out a high window, Joel explains, "to remind me of my place in the cosmos. We're all voyagers out there. If I had millions of dollars I'd build neighborhood observatories all over the world. And at each one I'd also have good conga drums, so people could drum together."

The object of Joel's attention at this moment, however, as it is much of the time, is his four-pound, Radio Shack Tandy Model 100 portable computer, one of the first laptop computers made. "I bought this machine for $399. For $1.82 a minute—$1.82!—I can send a telex message to Moscow. Think what it will mean when you can get thousands of Americans and Soviets on the same computer network. Once scientists in both countries begin talking to each other on these machines *they won't be able to stop.*

"I'm not a scientist," Joel adds. "I've only owned a computer for four months. I don't understand how they work. I'll leave that to other people. I'm just interested in how they can improve communication on this planet."

Defying the deep freeze in relations with the Soviet Union, Joel has already made three trips to Russia to work on other types of electronic exchanges. One has been large-screen two-way TV broadcasts, known as "space-bridges." Another has been a link between a Moscow apartment and a southern California radio studio, in which an odd assortment of people ranging from TV mogul Ted Turner to an Oakland, California, fire captain to poet Yevgeny Yevtushenko to a Moscow faith healer have talked to one another live, over U.S. radio stations. In a few days, Joel is leaving for Moscow again. Intrigued by the novelty of his various private peace missions, at a moment when the cold war seems as fierce as ever, when President Reagan wants tens of billions of dollars for his Star Wars scheme, and when the two superpowers are locked in the biggest peacetime arms race in history, I have invited myself along.

·   ·   ·

A day or two before our departure, I stop in at Joel's apartment again, and find him staring at the display screen of the Radio Shack computer. The Soviets so far have nothing so sophisticated or politically uncontrollable as electronic mail, but through his e-mail service, Joel can receive messages from half-century-old telex machines in Russia.

Joel is stumped, however, by the latest telex message from Moscow: LOOKING FORWARD TO SEEING YOU. PLEASE BRING SLOW-SCAN TV EQUIPMENT AND TECHNICIAN.

"Slow-scan television!" says Joel. "Jesus! Where are we going to get one of those?"

Slow-scan television is an inexpensive technology that has been used by American scientists since the 1960s. Basically it allows you to send a still picture over a telephone line, to an ordinary TV set.

"Well," Joel scratches his head, "if they want slow-scan, we better give them slow-scan."

During the next day Joel arranges to borrow a slow-scan TV from a Colorado manufacturer who is interested in world peace (and who would also doubtless like to sell some of his machines to the Soviet Union). The man assures Joel that the equipment is simple to operate and that all the instructions are in the box.

"If the Soviets want a technician," says Joel, "we're going to have to bring him in by TV."

The slow-scan apparatus is sealed in a waist-high cardboard carton. We are to change planes in London; at the San Francisco airport, Joel checks the box directly through to Moscow. On the flight to England I ask Joel, who is forty-eight years old, about his life before he started doing U.S.-Soviet electronic exchanges.

"I was energy adviser to the governor of Oregon for five years. Before that, one job I had was at a mental health center in Colorado. Once I handed out a questionnaire to all the psychiatrists there asking them what they did to cope with being depressed. There were a variety of answers: they listened to music, they had love affairs, they took a few days off, they went camping. I pointed out that none of these services—absolutely none!—did we offer to depressed patients coming to us for treatment. We just offered them talk. The psychiatrists didn't like my attitude *at all.*

"How did I get into the peace movement? I'm not in it. The peace movement is mostly people who sit around and talk about how terrible it is that the U.S. and the Soviet Union aren't talking to each other. That's a waste of time. What you've got to do is to *do* it: to go out and start talking to the Russians. That's what I'm going to do this week, with the help of people like Joseph."

"Who's Joseph?"

"Joseph Goldin is our key Soviet contact. If I accomplish anything on this trip, it'll be because of him. You'll see."

.   .   .

On a chilly night in April 1985, after changing planes in London, we land in Moscow. On his landing card, in the space for "occupation," Joel puts "Futurist." On his visa application, he has listed himself as "Cultural Repairman."

At the baggage-claim area, Joel's suitcase and mine are there, but no slow-scan TV. Furthermore, the British Airways people seem to have gone home for the night. "It will come next plane maybe," a Soviet official suggests doubtfully.

We are met at the exit from customs by a stocky, smiling, round-faced man in a black wool cap. "Joseph!" Joel calls out, embracing him. "My cosmic brother!"

That night we have dinner at our hotel, the Metropol, a marvelous relic of prerevolutionary times. Under a high stained-glass roof, Joel and Joseph, who have worked together now for nearly two years, talk about space-bridges, global town meetings, and other electronic schemes. Joseph has no official connection to any institution, a most unusual status in the Soviet Union, and one that has gotten him in trouble with the authorities. But clearly he is Joel's Soviet counterpart, another cultural repairman.

After dinner Joseph rises to head home to his apartment and says, "O.K. I go back to my headquarters now. I see you in the morning."

Later, in his hotel room, Joel considers what to do about the missing slow-scan box. It is now Friday evening. Joel has a guidebook to Moscow with five phone numbers listed for British Airways, including, allegedly, the home numbers of the resident manager and his assistant. But four numbers don't answer and at the fifth a Russian voice vigorously denies any connection to any airline.

"Obviously we're not going to find this thing over the weekend," says Joel. "Well, that will give you a chance to get to know Joseph."

· · ·

Most Americans who have been to the Soviet Union during the cold war have ended up meeting certain types of Russians: Intourist guides with their grammatically perfect English; well-dressed smiling officials at the Soviet Peace Committee who sit across a green baize table laden with mineral water and explain how much their country wants peace; young people who come up to you on the street and want to buy your blue jeans; Jewish "refuseniks" who have been denied permission to emigrate.

Joseph Goldin fits none of these categories. At all times he wears his skull-fitting black wool cap, nondescript corduroy pants, and a thick blue denim work shirt. A thin fringe of beard surrounds his face. In his lapel is a tiny silver pin in the shape of a dolphin—a token of his friendship with Igor Charkovsky, a Moscow mystic who believes in human communication with dolphins and whose followers practice underwater childbirth. In a country where all professionals have business cards in the same format—last name, first name and patronymic, academic degree, title, institution—Joseph has stationery showing a drawing of a man's head: the lower half is a face gazing at you, the top half is a partly completed, many-floored Tower of Babel. Around the edge of this head scrolls an inscription in Russian: EXPEDITION TO HIDDEN HUMAN RESERVES.

"The thing you have to understand about Joseph," says Joel, as we wait on Saturday morning in Joel's closet-sized hotel room for Joseph to arrive, "is that Joseph is single-minded. Everything he does is aimed at bringing into being one great plan."

"What's the plan?"

"Better let him explain it to you."

Joseph arrives, with a brisk, purposeful stride that has successfully carried him past the *dezhurnaya,* the vigilant woman who sits at the stair landing of every floor of every Soviet hotel and resolutely shoos away nonguests. About the missing slow-scan box he says, "I will get my people working on this problem."

We go down to the hotel restaurant for lunch, and Joel and Joseph plan the week's activities. Although the slow-scan exchange is at the top of their agenda, they are also juggling a dizzying variety of other U.S.-Soviet exchange projects ranging from computer networks to children's books.

But all this is prologue, in Joseph's mind, to Joseph's central project, an idea he calls Mirror for Humanity. When he and Joel are finished their scheduling, I ask him about it.

"Humanity—sense all peoples share that they belong to same humanity—does not exist. Yet! That we must create. How? Use radical new means of communications: large-screen TV."

These giant TV screens, some as large as a three-story building, cost several million dollars each. So far they have been installed mainly in U.S. and European sports arenas. Joseph's Mirror for Humanity plan is to create a network of such screens in cities everywhere. The screens would be placed in squares and parks; people in each city would be able to see and talk to people in the others. And, Joseph explains, because you could place TV cameras to take in each screen and the people watching it, people watching elsewhere would be able to see their faces on the screen *in* other cities.

"This is what I mean by creating humanity," he concludes. "The kingdom of words is dead. Atomic weapons have created a new kind of silence. We must *see* each other. The last times we looked at the earth, we discovered great things—whole continents, geography. Now we must reach new level of consciousness. When you see yourself in the other city, we no longer have just exchanges of representatives of populations, but of entire populations themselves."

.   .   .

Saturday evening a friend of Joel's takes us for dinner and the night to the house of a Russian couple who live in the countryside an hour's drive from Moscow. The Russians speak no English, and Joel no Russian, but he is not the least bit handicapped. I know a little Russian, and translate their questions over the dinner table to Joel.

"You are a follower of Reagan?"

Joel shakes his head and frowns: "Absolutely not."

"You are therefore a Democrat?"

"No. Completely independent."

"Ah . . . there was a man named Anderson who ran for president in your country several years ago. An independent also. You are a follower of Anderson?"

Joel shakes his head again, and points at his place setting. "Reagan—here," he points at the knife; "Anderson—here," he moves his finger a few inches to the plate; "Democrats—here," he moves his finger a few inches more to the fork; "me—*there*, he raises his whole arm and points at the ceiling.

.   .   .

The evening of the next day, we are with Joseph again, walking in central Moscow on a street of old buildings that is being made into a pedestrian mall. "Come. This way," Joseph says. "I want to show you. Now. Stop. Right here. This is where we will have big screen for Moscow.

"Very important to have screens where there is no traffic," says Joseph. "You know, on certain holidays, Gorky Street, our main street, is closed to traffic. It is incredible experience! To see people moving. A flow, a flood of bodies, a *liquid* of bodies! Feeling themselves liberated to go where traffic is expected to be. So screens must be where there are no cars."

I ask how he envisions people communicating with one another, city-to-city, on these giant screens.

"You will be able to come up to the screen, see somebody, say, 'Hello! How are you? This is my child—look! Will you write letter to me?'"

Joseph's enthusiasm is so infectious that I haven't the heart to ask why he thinks the Soviet government, which now even makes it difficult for people to make international phone calls, would ever permit such a thing. Joel also has little concern for such obstacles. "You know," he says, gazing down the empty street, "you could even use these screens to have a teleconference banquet. Seattle and Tashkent sit down to have dinner together. Why not?"

Joseph is forty-four. In his youth, he says, he studied music, then biophysics. He also wrote movie scripts, was a sailor on Arctic Ocean freighters, and worked with a Bulgarian psychologist who believes that if people *act* the role of Russians, Americans, or whatever, they can learn a totally new foreign language in three weeks.

"But I always felt not complete. That this was not me. I knew all the time: real musicians should be a little different from me. Real scientists should be a little different from me. It was only when I met people in your human potential movement that I heard people say: 'Trust your vision. Follow your instincts.' This is explanation of my strange way of life.

"I want to do such things here, to explore our hidden human reserves. All the time people are telling me: 'Joseph! You have forgotten in what country you are living. You cannot do that here. You should leave for America.' I know the difficulties. And of course I had bad time—they put me twice in psychiatric hospital. But this is my country. I went to Academy of Sciences. Finally they let me set up a committee to study hidden human reserves. I said to them 'Look! There are waves of interest, curiosity, love moving to us from seashore of America but nobody here can receive such signals. We must make instruments to receive these waves and send reflections back.'"

.   .   .

On Monday morning, the two electronic prophets are hard at work in Joel's room at the Metropol Hotel, planning the first U.S.-Soviet slow-scan TV exchange, which is to happen on Friday. Overnight several telexes have come in from people Joel is working with at the Ark Communications Institute in San Francisco, an offbeat foundation that is financing this whole project.

"Tremendous," says Joel, passing the telexes to Joseph. "Look, they've lined up two Nobel Prize winners to appear, Don Glaser and Glenn Seaborg, who used to be head of the Atomic Energy Commission—he's a real catch. And Gerard Piel at *Scientific Ameri-*

can. Now all we have to do is get that damned box here. Time to call British Airways."

Joel plugs in another piece of electronic equipment he has brought along, a portable speakerphone—a small, battery-powered loudspeaker that fastens onto a telephone receiver.

Out of this gadget comes the calm, very British voice of John Burley, Moscow station manager of British Airways. He says that he is terribly sorry to hear of the lost slow-scan. He will work on the problem.

"Please hurry," says Joel. "We've *got* to find that box. There's a lot riding on this. We've got two Nobel Prize winners ready to go on the air Friday!"

"Jolly good," says Burley, sounding politely baffled. "I'll do what I can." He says good-bye.

Joseph pulls out some papers for me from his briefcase. "About Mirror for Humanity. I brought for you. Read."

The typed manuscript, in English, is headed HOW TO ADDRESS ONE BILLION PEOPLE. It is an outline for a grand-opening ceremony for Mirror for Humanity, on Hiroshima Day.

> As the Sun rises above the horizon the montage film crew will take the Sun up over the Earth through the network of space bridges, switching the image from one enormous video-screen to another in a smooth glissando, changing with the land-scapes and different populations. In some countries we see yesterday's twilight, in others the dark of night . . .
>
> People in the seven countries will see seven "wonders of the world," *sakura* (flowering cherry) in Japan at the foot of Mount Fuji, the Bronze Age observatory at Stonehenge in England, the Sistine Chapel in Italy, a view of the Moscow Kremlin from the Moskva River, the Zwinger in Dresden and the dolphinarium in Hawaii.

When I finish reading, Joseph adds: "The sunrise we will show from megalithic observatory on the island of Malta. They have ancient sunrise ritual there, at Hagar Qim, one of oldest observatories in the world. People watched sunrise there thousands of years ago. This we must use to show humanity we can watch sunrise thousands of years from now."

.   .   .

Tuesday morning Joseph is not successful in getting past the *dezhurnaya* on our hotel floor, who sternly marches him down to the front desk. Only after twenty minutes of arguing is he allowed upstairs again. The little loudspeaker is still attached to Joel's phone; the room is now strewn with papers, notebooks, a nearly empty bottle of lemon-flavored vodka, and several collages of sketches and photographs just brought by Joseph. Without pausing to take off his ever-present black wool cap, he explains.

"This is what we are preparing for the slow-scan conference Friday. This," he gestures at one of the photos, "is Academician Raushenbakh. Famous Soviet scientist. He designed equipment that photographed dark side of the moon, twenty-five years ago. And here," he points to some sketching beside the picture, showing lines receding to a horizon, like a diagram of how to draw in perspective, "is where we are showing how Raushenbakh, like every scientist, must create his own space in which to work. These are images that represent his space. It is like Cézanne had his own conception of space. The geniuses of every culture distort space, which is why all artists at all times are always right.

"Music can be involved also. And three screens can be used, not only one! Also we can split this image, and make many Raushenbakhs." Joseph points to different corners of the room. "He will be here! There! Maybe over there!"

The phone rings. Over the loudspeaker box comes the voice of Rick Lukens, a collaborator of Joel's in California.

"We think we've got a vice president of AT&T to be on the hookup. We're going to have people in four different cities at this end: Berkeley, New York, Washington, and Boulder."

"Rick, that's tremendous," says Joel. "But we can't do anything if we don't get the damned box. Any word on that?"

"We're working on it. British Airways can't find it anywhere."

Joseph gets on the phone: "Rick! Each of the scientists participating must bring images to transmit that show creation of his own space. His space in which to work. We will create space for Raushenbakh. We will create space for Goldansky, who discovered molecules in cosmic rays. We will do it!"

Joel takes the receiver back. "But this whole thing's irrelevant if we can't get the box. We have to get the box!"

The irony of all this is that neither Joel nor Joseph cares much about slow-scan television. Joel's dream project is a U.S.-Soviet computer-conferencing network. Joseph's is his giant-screen Mirror for Humanity. But—it has taken me several days to figure this out—the Soviet Academy of Sciences has given permission only for a slow-scan TV test, while officialdom here is still wary of the other projects, which threaten to unleash too much communication beyond the control of censors. And so Joseph has maneuvered to get Joel officially invited to demonstrate slow-scan TV. The two of them, who share a sixth sense of how bureaucracies work, have decided to go all out with this slow-scan project to get their feet in the official door. Thus, each hopes, their grander visions will be brought closer. Heading out the door, Joseph turns back with one final burst of inspiration.

"We must do slow-scan in color! We must find ways of making it three-dimensional! And we must call it something special, this new link. When film was invented, they called it motion pictures. Here we have no movement, so why don't we call this motionless pictures? First motionless-picture link between U.S. and Soviet Union!"

.   .   .

Joel is proceeding on the assumption that the slow-scan equipment will get here by Friday. Therefore he must secure a location for the Soviet end of this performance. He is now striding purposefully down a long corridor in a Moscow office building. Joel's pace accelerates as he approaches the office he is aiming at, a Soviet agency that provides conference facilities for foreign businesses. The Academy of Sciences supposedly has asked this agency to find a suitable place for the slow-scan demonstration. Joel comes through the door practically at a run. The Soviet receptionist is startled by the sight of this big, bearded, hairy American in a purple shirt, carrying his portable computer in a purple cloth case.

She scurries off and reappears in a moment with a frowning man in a brown suit. He listens in increasing bewilderment to Joel's talk about AT&T, slow-scan TV, *Scientific American,* ". . . and two Nobel Prize winners ready to go on the air!"

"Low scan?" he asks. The proper message obviously has not gotten here from the Academy of Sciences.

Joel explains everything anew. "This event is vital for the

planet! We're set to go on Friday. We're going to need two open phone lines to the U.S., a TV set, a video technician, a good audio amplifier, and facilities for the press."

At this strategic moment in the conversation, Joel pulls out his card. The Soviet Union is very big on business cards. Joel's reads:

ARK COMMUNICATIONS INSTITUTE
U.S.-Soviet Special Projects Division
Joel Schatz, Director

The "Director" looks impressive, even if Joel himself is the entire Special Projects Division.

"Wait a minute. Please!" The official is agitated. He is probably trying to decide whether this crazy American was let into the country by accident, or if there is some $50 million computer deal riding on his being treated properly. "Please. Wait here."

He takes us to a conference room in the same suite of offices. He shoos out three Russians having a meeting there, then heads off to make some phone calls, trying to figure out who we are.

"There are two rules for dealing with bureaucracies," says Joel, while we wait. "One is to come in fast, faster than anyone can see, like an unguided missile. The second is to give *them* credit for the results."

The bureaucrats in this office are now conferring. They do not seem able to decide what to do with us. They tell us to come back tomorrow.

.   .   .

That evening I question Joseph.

"What about those times they put you in the psychiatric hospital? What happened?"

"Well," says Joseph, "January 1983 came big campaign for everyone to be at his job. January 22d I was invited to police—local police, not KGB. They ask me to bring documents showing I am employed somewhere. 'Well,' I explain, 'I am doing my business. Space-bridges. Hidden human reserves. What is problem?'

"'Joseph,' they say, 'it is new time and new reality. We are just doing our job. We give you a month. If you need facilitation to find a job, we help. But on 22d of February, you can expect us.'

"So, a month later police knock on my door. 'Month passed,' they say. 'Where is document that you are working?'

" 'I am working,' I say to them.

" 'Where?'

" 'I take part in two international competitions. With Mirror for Humanity project. One is international architects' contest for new communications center in Paris. I design space-bridge terminal.'

" 'But Joseph,' they say, 'Where you paid?'

" 'Easy to explain,' I tell them. 'Look, here is list of prizes. If I win, I paid by jury.'

" 'But if you not win?'

" 'That's my problem. I try next time.'

" 'Joseph,' they say, 'Why you making trouble for us? Why you not working?'

" 'I am fully employed,' I say, 'by myself!'

"Then they put me in hospital. For examination. Anyone who is not employed, you see, they think he is psychiatrically sick. Finally they take me to court.

" 'What are you doing?' the judge asks.

" 'Are you really interested?' I ask. 'I am making researches about hidden human reserves.' I make this testimony into one-hour lecture.

"Finally judge opens the court door to me. 'I wish you good luck, sir,' he says, 'but please bring to court all documents proving you are working.'

"Then again they come to put me in hospital. This time psychiatric hospital, much worse. First time was only psychiatric ward of regular hospital. Twelve days I was in second hospital. I was working all time, writing draft of Mirror for Humanity proposal. I write letters to people, to Central Committee, to America, to Academician Velikhov [vice president of the Soviet Academy of Sciences], all from hospital as if it were my headquarters. Other patients very interested. Academician Velikhov was out of country; when he got back, he call up to somebody, explain that I am doing major work, and they let me out of hospital. Nurse said: 'This has never happened before.' "

The patrons who have now several times rescued Joseph from his run-ins with the authorities are two powerful scientists: Boris Raushenbakh, the dark-side-of-the-moon man, and Yevgeny Velikhov, who heads the drive to widen the use of computers in the

USSR. Joseph claims he was not mistreated in the hospital, or forced to take drugs—the usual Soviet routine with forcibly hospitalized dissidents. But friends who saw him after he was released said he was deeply shaken and that it took him some months to recover his energy.

Never mentioned by Joseph, but probably a further source of his repression by Soviet authorities is something else. For Joseph and Joel, with their influential friends, their electronic leaping of national frontiers, and their enthusiastic subversion of the established order, are the unmistakable embodiment of something Russia's rulers have feared for several centuries: the International Jewish Conspiracy.

"Joseph," I ask finally, "are you sure it won't get you in trouble, my writing about how they put you in the hospital?"

"My friend," says Joseph, "only one thing gets me in trouble, big trouble. Atomic war. That I work to prevent." He places his palms together and shoots his hands forward, like a diver. "I am like a bird with single destination."

.   .   .

Wednesday. In his tiny room at the Metropol Hotel, which now looks as cluttered as a political campaign office, Joel is elated. A telex from California says: BOX LOCATED AT ISTANBUL AIRPORT. THEY WILL SHIP TO YOU SOONEST.

"Istanbul!" says Joel. "How the *hell* did it get there? They must have put it on the wrong plane at Heathrow."

The phone rings. The voice of John Burley at British Airways is talking to Joel on the speakerphone, sounding disturbed.

"Mr. Schatz. Do you . . . uh . . . have any influence with the Turkish government?"

"Nobody's ever asked me that before. Why?"

"Well, uh . . . it seems that Turkish customs has impounded your equipment. Our chap there says he can't get it released."

Joel holds a council of war. How can he get the box sprung?

He first considers calling the American embassy here in Moscow: surely they could put pressure on the Turks? Then we reject this idea: the U.S. government doesn't know about this whole venture, and, if it did, might not like it. Joseph remembers that he knows an American correspondent here who knows the Turkish ambassador. He reaches for the phone.

Joel fires off a telegram to the United States: BOX IMPOUNDED BY TURKISH CUSTOMS ISTANBUL AIRPORT. BRING MAXIMUM PRESSURE TO BEAR. URGENT.

There are more phone calls, all fruitless. Joel looks ever more disheveled. In precisely forty-eight hours' time, two Nobel Prize winners, one prominent editor, a vice president of AT&T, and several of the most famous scientists in the Soviet Union are scheduled to be electronically linked together by a box of TV equipment now under lock and key in Istanbul.

"They can't *do* this," Joel says in despair. "They have no *right* to. That box wasn't even going to Turkey."

Again the phone rings, and the voice on the speaker is John Burley's. This time he is more cheerful: he has just had a telex from his man in Istanbul, saying the box is freed and will be put on the first plane to Moscow.

Joel and Joseph drink a vodka toast and make plans.

.   .   .

Thursday. With about eighteen hours to go before the demonstration with the Nobel Prize winners, we are in a conference room in downtown Moscow. We eagerly take the slow-scan parts out of the box. Reportorial objectivity has vanished: I have somehow become part of this madcap venture and am trying to plug cables into sockets and to study diagrams to see where wire A attaches to input B.

While Joel and I are trying to figure out how this unfamiliar equipment works, Joseph, who can never stay still for a moment, is searching for photos of great moments in human communication to transmit on the slow-scan link. He is now on the phone to friends at a Moscow film studio, asking for pictures of Watson and Bell. Meanwhile, several bewildered-looking Soviet officials who have just arrived have noticed Joel's Radio Shack computer. They've clearly never seen a laptop computer before. Joel cannot resist showing it to them. It is not even clear if the men understand English, but that doesn't stop him.

"Three hundred ninety-nine dollars! And for $1.82, I can send a message to the United States. See this outlet here? Through this I can talk to any city in the world. With only four AA batteries! This is going to revolutionize communication on the planet!"

The Russians cluster about and play with the computer while Joel resumes trying to assemble the slow-scan.

Joel is hoping to test the equipment tonight, and has ordered two phone lines to the United States. But after five hours of waiting, the phone connections never materialize. Has the KGB put a stop to this project? The test is postponed until tomorrow.

Joseph drops us off at the hotel in the early hours of the morning. "I go back to my headquarters," he says. "Call me any time of night if there are developments. Don't hesitate."

.   .   .

Friday at midday (midnight in California), we reassemble in the conference room we were in last night. This is our last day in Moscow but our first chance to even test the slow-scan equipment.

There are some twenty people in the room now. Joel has gotten his two telephone lines to the United States at last. One of them is soldered to the TV set, the other is for a phone Joel is holding. He walks back and forth across one end of the room, shouting into the phone: "Rick! Can you hear me?" Finally, out of Joel's speakerphone attachment comes the voice of Rick Lukens in Berkeley, California, eleven time zones away. A troubleshooter from the slow-scan factory in Boulder was supposed to be on the line too, but has evidently gone to bed. The TV screen is blank.

"We're transmitting again, Joel," says the disembodied voice from Berkeley. "Can you see anything?"

An image now begins to appear on the TV set, formed by a rapidly moving dot traveling from left to right across the screen.

Joel is ecstatic. "This is a great moment for the planet!"

The picture leaves much to be desired, however. Although vaguely recognizable as a human figure sitting in a chair, it looks as if black icicles were dripping down from the top of the screen, and as if the whole thing were viewed through a web of herringbones.

Joel explains the problem on the phone, and then says, "O.K., now I'm going to send *you* something." He aims a video camera at a painting on the wall, and pushes a button. "Can you recognize this guy?"

Thirty seconds later comes a voice from Berkeley: "Lenin!" A buzz of excited whispering in Russian runs around the room. A visual image from this room has just traveled almost halfway 'round the world. Several of the Soviets stand up, to get a better view of the TV.

"We're still getting all that black stuff, Joel," says the increasingly sleepy voice from Berkeley. "And the herringbones. Send us another picture and we'll try sending the same picture back to you."

"O.K., Rick," says Joel, "I'm going to send you Joseph."

He points the camera at Joseph. With his blue denim shirt, wool cap, and silver dolphin pin, Joseph is the only man in the room not wearing a coat and tie. A minute later, with a double row of black icicles, one acquired going and one coming, a barely recognizable picture of Joseph's round, beard-fringed face appears on the Soviet TV screen.

"Aha!" says Joseph, who has never been allowed to travel to the West. He beams triumphantly at the roomful of Soviet bureaucrats: "I have been to America and back!"

However, after two and a half hours, the black icicles are still there. The people in Berkeley, where it is now 2:30 A.M., sound groggy, and say they're going to have to do some research on this problem. The link-up with the Nobel Prize winners is postponed. Joel regretfully puts the slow-scan equipment back into its box. We head back to our hotel to pack.

On the drive to the airport the next morning, however, Joel is again ebullient. "Look what we've accomplished! We made the first-ever link between the U.S. and the Soviet Union with this technology. And we've got their commitment to go ahead. This will be catching. You know, there's a guy named Sheldrake, an Englishman, who postulates that the universe doesn't have laws; it only has habits. That's the approach I take. We've got to change those habits, shift the paradigm. I think we made a start."

At the airport, Joseph accompanies us to the head of the customs line. A guard puts out an arm to prevent him from going farther.

"Remember!" Joseph calls across the space between us, his briefcase in hand and the black woolen cap on his head. "Age of religion is over! Age of politics is over! Age of communication has begun!"

. . .

Do electronic exchanges between the United States and the Soviet Union do any good? It is so much fun being around Joel Schatz and Joseph Goldin that one hesitates to spoil the party by even asking. Nonetheless, a skeptic might point out that technology alone does not decide what gets communicated between peoples; governments do. So far, for some seventy years of their troubled coexistence, Americans and Soviets have had the use of the two great communication technologies of modern times: the mail and the telephone. But each nation has at times interfered with the delivery of mail from the other, and the USSR has cut off the direct dialing of international phone calls. If two-way TV and other such exotica begin to carry anything less bland than the messages they have conveyed up to now, the Soviet authorities could cut them off as well.

"O.K.," says Joel impatiently to such arguments, "but why do people get transformed when they participate in a space-bridge? Why do people who go to the Soviet Union for the first time come back on a high, even when they see refuseniks and the KGB and all the rest of it? It's because they've seen that there are *human beings* over there. That's a revolutionary thought today. Do you see it in *Rambo?* Tell me that."

Some three months after our trip together, Joel goes to the Soviet Union again. A blizzard of telexes from him pours back to San Francisco: a birthday telex to his son, love telexes to his wife, messages to a wide variety of electronic coconspirators.

After he gets back home, I go to Joel's apartment. Sitar music drones on the record player. Piles of telexes are stacked on the floor. Joel proudly demonstrates his latest electronic gadget, a tape recording of holophonic sound: "It's three dimensional!—A quantum leap beyond conventional stereo." He is full of new plans. Over the weeks that follow, however, Joel begins to be worried that his messages to Joseph Goldin are unanswered.

"I bet they want him out of circulation during the Youth Festival that's going on now," says Joel. "They're locking a lot of people up. Too many foreigners around."

Joel sends urgent telexes to two foreign correspondent friends in Moscow, and the next day one replies. JOSEPH WAS PICKED UP BY LOCAL POLICE ON WEDNESDAY . . . AND TAKEN TO A PSYCHIATRIC CLINIC. . . . A MOVE HAS BEEN LAUNCHED MAINLY BY RAUSHENBAKH TO GET HIM RELEASED.

Two days later comes another message. JOSEPH IS STILL NOT FREE. WE ARE DOING ALL WE CAN. . . . UNFORTUNATELY, ALL THE TOP PEOPLE CONNECTED WITH JOSEPH ARE ALSO OUT OF TOWN.

"Dacha time," says Joel. "Velikhov and all Joseph's supporters are away. That's why the police were able to put him in the clink now. He'll be there until they're back from vacation."

Meanwhile, Joel has been able to launch the project dearest to his heart, computer conferencing between U.S. and Soviet scientists. He shows me some of the transcripts. After several months in which the participants talk to one another mainly about hardware, software, and the prospect of conferencing bilingually, Joel suddenly calls me up, alarmed and indignant.

"They've done a computerectomy on us!"

"What? How?"

He explains: "The Department of Commerce told the New Jersey Institute of Technology [site of the mainframe computer on which the U.S. and Soviet scientists have been talking to one another] this may be illegal. So the conference has stopped. This is insane! We're not breaking any laws. I'm getting the ACLU into the act. This is free speech! Planetary communication among consenting adults!"

A week or two later he reports: "It seems that since there's no regulation saying that you *can* do this kind of computer conference with Russians, they're saying we *can't.*"

Finally, with Joel on the phone as well, his lawyer manages to get through to the right person at the Department of Commerce. The man has something to do with export licenses. "This was unreal," says Joel, describing the phone call. "'Export!' we told him. 'We're not exporting anything except words! The same things you export in a book or a magazine article or a first-class letter. Are there laws against that?'"

This argument wins the day, and, after a three-week interruption, Joel and his collaborators get a written go-ahead from the Commerce Department, setting a precedent for future U.S.-Soviet computer links.

.   .   .

At the end of 1985, Joel decides to go public. To celebrate the past year's activities, he and Joseph plan "Midnight in Moscow" parties in San Francisco and Moscow for New Year's Eve. Because of the time difference, the new year will arrive in Moscow when it is lunchtime in San Francisco.

"Now we'll *really* put the slow-scan to work!" Joel explains to me. "We've ironed out the bugs now: no more black icicles. Joseph's going to get his scientist friends, Arkady Raikin—the great

Soviet comedian, some folk dancers, and maybe Yevtushenko. We'll get some equivalent people at this end."

At last, it seems, there will be an event like the one Joel was trying to arrange in Moscow, the long-delayed, fitting climax to the saga of the slow-scan. This time I'll be watching it from the American end. A sympathetic San Francisco businessman has loaned Joel his office, and on New Year's Eve about a hundred people assemble there for a buffet lunch. A TV set sits on a pedestal, waiting for the call from Moscow. Joel steps before a microphone and explains to the crowd that Joseph and his friends are already now assembling with a slow-scan in a Moscow café. Everyone applauds.

The room grows more crowded. The appointed hour comes and goes. A phone rings, and there is a sudden hush.

Joel picks up the receiver with a booming "Hello!" Then he grimaces and tells the audience: "Wrong number."

A few minutes later there is a buzz of excitement from Joel's end of the room. Eight different TV crews from local stations and the networks are surrounding Joel, jostling for position, pointing microphone booms at his beard. He is talking on the phone. A few minutes later he takes the microphone again to tell the crowd— which by now has swollen to 150 or so—"We can't even get through to the international operator in Pittsburgh. And if *we* can't get through, the Russians can't. It's electronic gridlock!"

Reporters scribble down the phrase in their notebooks; they know a headline when they hear it. The crowd applauds. Joel sits down with his Radio Shack computer on his lap and fires off some telexes to Moscow. One after another, the various people who were scheduled to send slow-scan images to Moscow perform for the crowd, to ever-greater applause. Poet Michael McClure reads a poem, "partly in English and partly in an invented language, so there's no translation problem." He reads another poem, about gravity, "something universal for all of us." Someone else takes the microphone to introduce an audiotape of whale calls. A videotape shows Eskimos doing a peace dance on the ice of the frozen Bering Sea, where the United States and the Soviet Union almost touch. Astronaut Rusty Schweickart speaks about how he has seen the earth from space and it's all one planet. The mayor of San Francisco phones in. Jazz singer Bobby McFerrin does a few songs. At the side of the room, august but tapping his foot in time with the music, is Glenn Seaborg, Nobel laureate and former Atomic Energy Commission chair. When his turn at the mike comes, he makes an impassioned plea for a comprehensive nuclear test ban treaty.

Joel is on the phone again. He shrugs helplessly.

"Try Sprint!" someone calls, to great hilarity.

The press, however, is happy: they've got good food, free drinks, a Nobel Prize winner, an astronaut, the quote about electronic gridlock, singers, poets, and even a live visiting Russian, a journalist who cheerfully gives interviews to all comers. Furthermore, members of the press have one another: the presence of so many reporters and cameras is tangible proof that this is a certified news event. After two or three more hours of drinking champagne, everyone seems to have forgotten that the TV screen is blank and that no calls from Moscow have gotten through.

The next day, astonishingly, the party is on the front page of the *Los Angeles Times*: U.S.-SOVIET NEW YEAR'S EVE PARTY GETS SIGNALS CROSSED. BUSY SIGNAL FOR PEACE CALL reads the headline of an equally friendly story in the *San Francisco Chronicle*. SCHMOOZING BETWEEN SUPERPOWERS says another paper. "The revelers sipped wine, nibbled on hors d'oeuvres and talked of peace" reports Reuters to its subscribers worldwide. Joel is delighted: "Fantastic! I think we're even more successful when we don't get through."

.　.　.

Meanwhile, the various exchanges continue. A recent telex from Joseph urges Joel: KEEP UP PRESSURE IN ALL DIRECTIONS.

Joel adds: "You know, there's only one problem in what we're doing, tying the world together electronically. We're still missing one billion people. I need to find a Joseph Goldin in China. I have some feelers out."

1986

PART TWO

*To the Navel of the World
and Other Journeys*

World on a Hilltop

On the night Mel Bancroft was expelled, most of Pomfret School was up past midnight. In a school of only some two hundred boys, you got to know each other well, and we all knew Mel—or thought we did. He was a superb athlete, and at Pomfret this was important: he earned his letters early in soccer and hockey and he danced agilely across the tennis court in a white Pomfret shirt and Bermuda shorts. Mel was popular, but there was an uneasiness in his eyes, and he talked a little too fast. He wore the madras jacket, white socks, chinos, and brown loafers that were the unofficial uniform of New England prep schools in the late 1950s. He let the word get around about how he continued his athletic exploits during vacations: skiing in Europe, rock-climbing expeditions, scuba diving—all trips he was ferried to in his family's limousine and private planes. "No, not plane, *planes,*" insisted one boy who had it straight from Mel, the horse's mouth.

One spring day, when the leaves were out on the elms and the crack of baseballs echoed across the school's green lawns and ivy-covered buildings, this whole picture of Mel's life cracked down the middle. Mel Bancroft was found to be embezzling money from the Tuck Shop, the small student-run candy-and-stationery store in the school basement. The same day it was discovered that the sizable array of skis, climbing boots, tennis rackets, and the like in Mel's closet, and some of the cash in his wallet, had been stolen from other boys. Mel Bancroft, it turned out to the astonishment of the entire student body, was not from a wealthy family after all. He was on scholarship. A solemn-faced Mel was interrogated by the headmaster and several teachers. Late that night—in a modest sedan, not a limousine—his parents arrived to pick him up, and his Pomfret career was over.

Mel Bancroft is not his real name, but all other details about him here are unchanged; he went on, incidentally, to became the CEO of a highly successful corporation. Pomfret School is still in business, on a beautiful rural hilltop in northeastern Connecticut. Now, as then, it is basically a school for the rich. Until the day Mel's world collapsed, I never realized how difficult life there must have been for a student whose family did not have money. Since then, I've often wondered what Mel Bancroft must have felt, for it takes vast emotional energy to keep up a façade with all your friends year upon year. Mel felt driven to steal not just ski boots, but an entire biography for himself. Behind his anxious darting eyes lay a desperation. He must have felt like a light-skinned black person who successfully "passes" for white in a Southern town, and who is at last found out.

.   .   .

Pomfret is one of the many boarding schools that were built, mostly between 1850 and 1900, as New England copies of the British model. Both Pomfret's official language and slang were redolent of British class distinctions: teachers were "masters"; freshmen were "weenies." Until the early 1950s, new boys still underwent hazing from the older ones, that ritualistic preparation for distinctions of class and rank in the world outside. At Pomfret, entering freshmen were herded on some pretext into a squash court, then pelted with wet tennis balls by seniors in the spectators' gallery above.

Depending on how far in the air your nose is when you name them, there are one to two dozen American schools like Pomfret. I do not mean private schools in general, or even private boarding schools, whose number is at least in the hundreds. Rather, I mean that select group of well-established schools, mostly in Connecticut and Massachusetts, all a century old or more, with names as familiar as those of the powerful families whose children they educate, so that, in ruling-class circles when somebody asks a mother what her son is doing now, she need only say, "Oh, Danny? He's at Pomfret." And no further explanation is needed. As Danny's life goes on, he will find that the world is laced by a network of other prep school alumni, and that by little signs—a stray reference, a phrase, a touch of accent—they can recognize each other. I have often found this happening to me, particularly when I least expect it, and in those moments of mutual recognition I suddenly see myself as part of a tribe and subtribe to which, however unwillingly, I belong.

Even before I could articulate the feeling, I always thought that my four years at Pomfret were pivotal in my life and in my awareness of the world, or at least of the narrow slice of it into which I was born. I found myself thinking about the school even more once my children grew old enough to be curious. You mean you *lived* there? And there were no blacks? And no *girls?* Today it more and more strikes me how bizarre and unjust is the entire world of prep schools. And yet a significant percentage of the people who run this country are among their graduates. These schools cannot, like monasteries, be dismissed as irrelevant.

I arrived at Pomfret at the age of thirteen, on a crisp fall day at the height of the cold war. Eisenhower was in the White House, God was an Episcopalian, and I was miserably homesick at being away from my parents for the first time. The school was a cluster of red-brick buildings with white trim and a commanding view of the surrounding countryside. The window of my room looked across a football field, down into a wooded valley, and up to the top of a hill on the other side, where an old farmhouse and barn stood out against the horizon. The dormitories had a distinct musty smell, a smell of sweat and steam heat and decades of sunlight seeping into wooden walls. I occasionally catch a whiff of that smell in an old, sun-warmed paneled room that hasn't been dusted, and it brings everything back.

Although I was too nervous to notice it, any other American arriving at Pomfret that day would have been struck by how, side-by-side with only a modest library and science labs, this school for a mere two hundred boys had amazingly lavish sports facilities. Squash courts; tennis courts; football, baseball, and soccer fields; a track; a gym with an indoor track and rowing machines; rifles for target shooting; a ski jump on one hill and a slope with a rope tow on another. Today the school also has an indoor hockey rink and four indoor, year-round tennis courts.

The teachers were almost all men. Classes were small, seldom more than fifteen students and often fewer. Three times a day, we donned coats and ties and gathered in the Common Room next to the dining hall. Each night while we were waiting there for the dining hall doors to open for dinner, the same student always played the piano, well enough to draw a little coterie of hovering admirers. He knew only one tune—"Has Anybody Seen My Girl?"—but no one seemed to mind.

We did a great deal of talking at school: announcements to the daily assembly, reports in class, speeches and panel discussions at weekend conferences on current events, meetings of various student-faculty committees, readings at the daily chapel service. Each student ate his three meals a day with half a dozen other boys at a dining table headed by a teacher and his wife—and then was rotated weekly, by roster, to another teacher's table. Years later, a friend asked me if we had had any special training in how to do well in corporate job interviews. No, I replied. But after I had described the daily routine, she said, "Adam, don't you see? The *whole thing* was a practice interview!"

.   .   .

If there is any single thing that stands out in my memory of Pomfret from my first timid weeks at the school, it is the impression that by being there I was somehow beginning a certain path in life, a path whose destination I did not know, but whose existence was as clear as if there had been signposts along my way to class each day.

In fact there were signs everywhere, usually engraved in wood or marble or stone. Plaques in the chapel honoring Pomfret boys who had fallen in the two World Wars. Wooden tablets in the gym listing baseball and football captains back to the 1890s. Signs above the doors to all buildings, naming them after the alumni who had donated money for them. Even the many years' worth of initials carved in the wood-topped desks, spreading across each classroom like a sea of alphabet soup. Often these names were familiar, when there was a son or grandson of the same family just up the dormitory corridor or next to you at soccer practice. It gave you the feeling of entering a web that stretched backward and forward in time, connected both to the past and to the secure future awaiting you as a Pomfret graduate.

No ticket to the future is completely secure, especially today, but a prep school diploma helps. One study of people listed in *Who's Who* found that a graduate of one of the top ten prep schools was thirty-nine times more likely to end up listed in the book than a graduate of the average high school. The twentieth century has seen three prep school alumni as president—George Bush (Andover), John F. Kennedy (Choate), and Franklin Roosevelt (Groton)—and many more among those who tried: Adlai Stevenson (Choate), Robert F. Kennedy (Milton), and Averell Harriman (Groton), to name but a few. Ruling-class families in this country often send their children to the same prep school over the generations: Cabots have usually gone to St. Mark's, Fords to Hotchkiss, Mellons to Choate, Vanderbilts to St. Paul's, DuPonts to Pomfret. When we found names like these among our classmates, or found somebody's father in the newspaper headlines, it did not seem odd. We expected it. That was part of being at Pomfret.

.   .   .

From the Pomfret newsletter over the years, giving news of alumni in each graduating class:

> 1909—*John A. Morris* . . . is a special partner in the New York Stock Exchange member firm of Prescott, Ball and Turben. His interest, aside from that, is thoroughbred racing.

> 1935—*Thibaut de Saint Phalle* is a director of the Export-Import Bank in Washington.

> 1938—*Maxwell Marston, Jr.* is now living in Hilton Head Island, S.C. He reports that the second green of the Dolphin Head Golf Course is about 200 feet from his living room. He is still active in real-estate investment and construction.

> 1964—*Peter Kelsey* writes that after more than eight years practicing environmental law and energy law for the U.S. Department of the Interior, he has decided to get an industry perspective on these issues. He is now assistant general counsel at the Edison Electric Institute [the lobbying arm of the nation's private power companies] "looking for mutual respect and understanding of conflicting priorities."

.   .   .

The segregation that reserves schools like Pomfret mainly for the rich is enforced not by rules but by cost. The percentage is higher at some better-endowed prep schools, but at the time I was there, little more than 10 percent of Pomfret students got any scholarship aid. To send your child to any of the top prep schools as a boarder approaches the cost of tuition at a good private college, something most American families simply can't afford. The total tuition and other charges my parents paid to send me to Pomfret each year was higher than some Pomfret faculty salaries.

From this class gap between students and teachers came some tension. My teachers had generally gone to public high schools themselves; most had worked their way through college or had gone on the G.I. Bill. To make ends meet, they often took summer jobs—two of mine worked in a local lumber yard, for instance. But the students they taught were summering on Martha's Vineyard or visiting Europe. When the teachers saw how boys at the school lived—the style of life Mel Bancroft tried so pitifully hard to mimic—they were appalled. I vividly remember a teacher telling me that one day he had found a boy throwing away a brand new pair of pants, right out of the package, into a dormitory trash barrel. Why? the horrified teacher asked. "Oh," the boy said, "I ordered this suit because I wanted the coat. I don't need the pants." Little incidents like this, confided by teachers, made a deep impression on me, because it was the first time I saw my own social class through the eyes of another.

Some scholars of U.S. ruling circles say that it is precisely to learn those upper-class habits that elite families send their sons to schools like Pomfret. Not so, I think. Pomfret boys learned their values by being born to well-off parents, ranging from doctors and corporate lawyers to people who owned banks or newspapers or the inherited fortunes derived from them. The boys were sent to Pomfret to learn, instead, the middle-class virtues: ambition, hard work, good study habits—those things that the ruling class finds useful to help it keep ruling.

Many boys sorely needed such training. To make big money, especially during an entrepreneurial era like that of the robber barons, requires shrewdness and initiative. But being born into wealth three or four generations later does not engender these qualities. Often, the opposite. One boy during my time at Pomfret, a grandson of a famed turn-of-the-century sugar baron, had to repeat a year. Another, one of the DuPont clan, simply failed to do his homework and—the headmaster gravely announced in the school assembly one day—was put on the train to go home for several weeks until he got it done.

Looking back on it now, I think the school offered something you could call the Pomfret Bargain. From the point of view of parents, the bargain was: I'll pay that astronomical tuition if you'll get my kid into a decent college. From the point of view of Pomfret's teachers, the bargain was: I'll put up with those outrageously low wages so I can teach classes one-third the size of those in a public school. The role of the school administration was to make sure all parts of the bargain were kept and to provide the gloss of uplift and high purpose that covered the bargain's everyday workings. There were prayers in chapel asking God's blessing on "those who teach and those who learn." And there were speeches about the pursuit of excellence and about something called the Pomfret System, which was a lofty way of saying we had a student government.

Everything at Pomfret was covered with that gloss. Instead of saying "Hedley Skeffles gave $100,000 so we'd name the new squash courts after him," the speech at the ribbon-cutting ceremony would thank "Hed Skeffles, who has had the foresight, the courage, and the vision to understand Pomfret's needs in the decades ahead. Especially the needs of our athletic program." It still goes on: at an alumni gathering the last time I was back at school, I heard the headmaster refer to "the many privileges of teaching here at Pomfret and the advantages to us all of being without the *bureaucracy* of public schools." It soon became clear he was talking about the absence of teachers' unions.

.   .   .

The terms of a hidden bargain show more clearly when the bargain breaks down. This began to happen while I was at Pomfret, and it revealed something about changes in America's elite at that time. For the first half of the twentieth century, the Pomfret Bargain had worked: the school did the job it was contracted to do. Unless you were somewhat thickheaded, a Pomfret diploma could get you into an Ivy League college. Then, in the 1950s, several things started to happen. The U.S. population was growing rapidly, while the number of Ivy League and elite colleges, of course, stayed the same. The balance of American economic power began shifting toward the Southwest—people in previously unfashionable places like Phoenix and Houston had the nerve to want to send their kids to Harvard. And high-quality public schools, their curricula as good as any New England prep school's, appeared in well-to-do suburbs, particularly in the mid-West and Far West.

The result was that fairly suddenly the top Eastern colleges had so many qualified applicants that they could pick and choose. Grades and test scores rapidly came to mean a great deal. When I graduated in 1960, 30 percent of my Pomfret class went on to Harvard or Yale; during the following decade, that percentage plummeted, in some years, to zero.

During the years I was at Pomfret, this historic sea change was just beginning. Particularly for fathers, confident that their sons would go on to an Ivy League college just as they had done, it was an unexpected shock. Parents panicked and visited the school for long, anguished conferences with the headmaster: You mean I paid all this money and the best place you can get Johnny into is *Cincinnati?* During the decade or so after I graduated, with the bargain threatened, Pomfret fell into the academic equivalent of an economic depression. Desperate fund-raising appeals went out to alumni in the late sixties and early seventies. Pomfret had never quite been in the topmost rank of New England boarding schools, and so it was hit worse than most. One year it failed to fill all the places in its entering class. Faculty members had to take a temporary 10 percent pay cut, thereby seeing the terms of their part of the Pomfret Bargain eroded. There was even talk of closing down. For college admission purposes, was a Pomfret education still worth anything? Above a sheaf of toilet paper in one of the school men's rooms appeared some graffiti: "Pomfret diplomas. Take one." A *Newsweek* headline in 1972 asked CAN PREP SCHOOLS SURVIVE?

Today, however, prep schools are riding high again. The major reason is that public schools are hard hit. First came state tax-slashing measures like California's Proposition 13, then the Reagan era's cuts in federal aid to public schools. Those families who can afford it are looking for education elsewhere. Private schools all over the country are experiencing a big surge in the number of people trying to get in, the elite New England prep schools most of all. Don't worry, *Newsweek:* privilege endures.

·   ·   ·

Candidates for Board of Trustees, one to be elected:
Lewis Turner, Jr., '66. In 1973 he . . . began working for Bankers Trust Company in New York. . . . Today [he] is a vice president in Bankers Trust Petroleum Division. He and his wife Beth have one child and live in New York City.
Charles Baker Wheeler II, '40. Charlie Wheeler attended Wil-

liams College and served in the U.S. Army. . . . He subsequently worked for the Central Intelligence Agency, from which he retired in 1976. . . . His son Gordon graduated from Pomfret in 1969.

. . .

The Pomfret chapel is the same: the worn stone steps and dark wooden pews, the grandeur of Bach and stained glass and the Episcopal *Book of Common Prayer.* But something is different this weekend. Many of the students filing into chapel are wearing black arm bands. It is May 1970, the tenth reunion of my Pomfret class and the first time I've been back to the school in almost as many years. Several days ago the United States invaded Cambodia.

The country is swept by student strikes. A hundred thousand angry protesters march in Washington, D.C. At Pomfret, things are more decorous: all that is visible are the black arm bands and solemn knots of students, gathered here and there around the campus, listening to radios reporting body counts from armored columns plunging across the Vietnam-Cambodia border. On the other side of college, everyone knows, lies the draft. For the first time, I'm seeing Pomfret students aware that events in the outside world could affect their own lives.

All this is totally ignored by the returning alumni. On Saturday morning some of them attend panel discussions with guest speakers on subjects like "Does the Independent School Have a Role to Play?" (Surprise conclusion: Yes! The independent school *does* have a role to play.) In the evening the alumni gather for an array of class cocktail parties at a hotel some miles away from school, the nearest that can accommodate everyone. They float from one function to another on a wave of alcohol and reminiscence. Eyes flit furtively to name tags, to refresh rusty memories; hands clap on shoulders; one classmate opens the back of his station wagon to reveal a portable bar, with refrigerator. "Tim, you still at the bank?" "When we were here, sex was dirty and the air was clean. But now it's the other way 'round!" "Adam, I'd like you to meet Candy . . . Penny . . . Muffie . . ." New threads are revealed in the old networks: one alumnus has married another's sister, another has a nephew at school now, a third has come back to teach at Pomfret—an embarrassing come-down, in social-class terms: did he fail in business?

Much of the weekend is spent at this hotel. Despite the navy blue Pomfret School blazers many of them have brought out of the closet for this occasion, the alumni are far more comfortable mingling with each other than with students at the school. The president of Yale addresses us at a banquet. Later in the evening, when most people are watching old Pomfret football movies, several of us slip off to find a TV. Nixon assures the nation the invasion of Cambodia is only to find the secret, elusive communist military headquarters for all of South Vietnam. Four students have been shot dead by the National Guard at Kent State.

The alumni newsletter now reflects the escalation of the war. One schoolmate has flown some fifty missions in Phantom jets. Another, a former Pomfret ski-jump champion, has been killed under enigmatic circumstances in the navy, "in a scuba-diving accident at Guantanamo Bay." Two members of a class just older than mine write that they have run into each other in Saigon: one is working for the State Department and one for Brown and Root, the huge Texas construction firm that does work for the Pentagon. They write of how, over cool drinks on a Saigon villa's patio, they talked about all that had happened "since the class of '58 was loosed upon the world."

.   .   .

Loosed upon the world. The image of that Saigon patio conversation has echoed in my mind ever since. It sums up something important about the school, its ambitions, its arrogance.

The roots of those attitudes go far back. The English schools on which Pomfret and its American counterparts were modeled trained the British Empire's officials. In their mythology, even the school rebels serve king and country in the end. The classic boarding school novel is Rudyard Kipling's *Stalky & Co.,* a high-spirited tale of pranksters always in trouble with the straitlaced school authorities. But in the final chapter Stalky is an army officer in India, heroically fighting another kind of rebel—Himalayan tribesmen resisting the Crown. In the midst of battle, Stalky rallies his troops and officers (who include a few of the old school gang) by playing a song from school days on a bugle.

Most Pomfret graduates went into the more mundane areas of imperial administration: business, banking, or corporate law. Our board of trustees even held most of its meetings at a New York bank. Yet for some students, Pomfret's faculty and administrators had more glamorous aspirations. The school had graduated one secretary of state (Edward Stettinius) and an ambassador or two; teachers always implied that this was a highly desirable type of career. During my time at Pomfret, international relations became something of a theme: there were weekend conferences on the subject and frequent speakers—government officials, foreign students at nearby colleges. A prize catch, the son of the prime minister of Togo, a dapper man speaking Parisian French, once stayed in my room.

I was particularly encouraged to take part in these programs and to give little talks in the daily assembly on the crisis in Kashmir or whatever. One day in my senior year the headmaster was talking to me. "For every boy here," he said, "I like to imagine that we're helping him go in a particular direction, a direction *he* is best suited for. For you, I've always thought it would be something in the realm of foreign affairs, the State Department, something like that."

Suddenly, in a blinding flash of revelation that was one of the turning points of my life, I knew with absolute certainty that whatever I did, it would *not* be in that "realm." So: beneath all the rhetoric about the freedom to make one's choices in life, *they* still had a plan for me after all. Their plans were no doubt hazier and less sinister than I thought then, but it was an important lesson.

Another major lesson I learned at school, and this was a more complicated one, was that *they* had serious divisions in their ranks. The typical Pomfret trustee was a Hartford insurance executive or a Philadelphia banker, large of paunch and gold of watch chain, whose definition of a good school was the one that most closely resembled the dear old Pomfret he had attended forty years before. But during my time the headmaster, like many of the teachers, was in some ways an admirable and progressive man. He wanted to make the school coed, to admit blacks, and to put less emphasis on athletics. To the pinstriped trustees these hopes seemed positively Bolshevik. The crowning insult came when he hired a school chaplain who was not an ordained Episcopalian. The long-simmering conflict finally exploded, and the headmaster resigned. These battles seem antiquated now; almost all these changes have long since been made. But at the time the issues seemed very large

indeed. It was my introduction to politics: for the first time I saw
that the adult world did not have a united front. Through the
cracks in that facade I began for the first time to see the way to
some new choices of my own.

. . .

A spring day of brilliant sunshine, with bright yellow buttercups
bubbling up across the lawns and the scent of fresh-cut grass on
the breeze. On the hillcrest opposite the school is still the weathered old farmhouse and barn, home of unknown neighbors from a
different world. Returning to Pomfret after another ten years' absence, I would like to feel unsentimental, superior, but despite
everything, part of me still loves this place. I notice many familiar
buildings are now replaced or rebuilt, and briefly I catch myself
feeling, to my amazement, angry: how could they change things
so?

I walk along the path with my alumni name tag, nodded at
vaguely by young and unfamiliar teachers, perpetrating the great
fraud that I have become a grown-up. In the center of the school
grounds is a tall flagpole where we used to run up a string of
brooms when the football team had an undefeated season: a clean
sweep. But today this pole's American flag is at half-mast. It is
May 1980, my twenty-year reunion. Several days ago a helicopter
crash killed eight commandos in a failed attempt to rescue U.S.
hostages in Iran.

Despite this perfunctory acknowledgment of troubles in the
outside world, the campus mood is one of celebration. Many students are wearing a pin of crossed hockey sticks; the team won
some sort of championship and next winter will play in Finland
and Sweden. The sports action today is at the crew regatta. Along
the lakeshore are ranged Mercedes, Audis, BMWs with New York,
Connecticut, Massachusetts plates. One alumnus, wearing his old
letter sweater, stands with a stopwatch and calls out how many
strokes a minute a boat is making.

In chapel today prayers ask God's blessing on the work of the
school. The chaplain, resplendent in white robes, leads the singing
in a strong baritone, then reads the roll of Pomfret alumni who
have died in the past year and prays for the welfare of their souls,
"these Thy humble servants, whom Thou has called to Thee." But
with names like William Ross Proctor, Standish Bourne Taber, and

Charles Leo Abry IV, it is a hard to imagine them being humble servants of anyone.

Later I'm back in a familiar classroom. A year of chemistry I studied here: into what hidden recess of my mind did that vanish? And a year of trigonometry: what *was* trigonometry, anyway? Something about angles. Today I'm here talking with a group of students interested in careers in journalism. But I also get the chance to question them. One thing I ask about is that tension between middle-class faculty and upper-class students. Is this still as strong as when I was at school?

A young woman in the back row sits up and says with great feeling, "Yes, I know *just* what you mean." I had taken her to be a senior, perhaps, but she turns out to be a new teacher. "It's still the same way," she goes on. "I'll tell you something I don't think the students here know. There has always been a yearly ritual here at Pomfret. When the students go home in June, they're always told to take all their stuff with them; the school isn't responsible for anything left in their rooms. On that last day, we—the faculty— go through all the dorms collecting for ourselves things that the kids have left behind. It's just incredible: brand-new tennis rackets, bicycles, skates, stereo equipment—I'd say about 90 percent of the kids here have better stereos than I could afford. Last year I got a wonderful long wool cape for myself—somebody just didn't want to bother to pack it away during the summer."

.   .   .

That night it is moonless and warm; the stars are out. A teacher's house stands on the other side of a football field. A car drives up; a figure gets out to open the garage door, and for a moment, a woman's body is silhouetted in the light. Back in these familiar surroundings, I feel automatically, for the first time in two decades, the emotion I felt here constantly: the wracking ache of desire and of outrage at this sexless environment. And of envy of those privileged teachers: *they're doing it every night.*

Did those Pomfret faculty wives ever know how much they were lusted after, how often their every attribute was discussed, by two hundred boys? Distant and unattainable, they were the only women we saw. It was only after I graduated that it fully dawned on me how perverse it is to keep someone for four years almost totally isolated from the other sex. You could invite a girl to the school for only one Dance Weekend each term—two days tightly packed with chaperoned activities, during which, legend had it, the school authorities put saltpeter in the milk. Sometimes we had to vacate a dormitory to make room for the girls to stay; afterward, we would go through our rooms carefully to see if we could find anything feminine accidentally left behind—a hairpin, a lipstick, a whiff of perfume. If we did, there was a lot of raucous joshing, but underlying it an unspoken loneliness.

The only other occasion we got to mingle with girls also came only once or twice a term: joint glee-club concerts and dances held with Pomfret's counterparts among girls' boarding schools. You were assigned a blind date for dinner and the evening. The busload of girls from Miss Porter's School, or wherever, would arrive in the afternoon, pulling into a parking lot below the huge bay windows of the dining hall. Thirty or forty boys would stand in the windows, leaning on each other's shoulders, leering and ogling down at the girls as they filed off the bus. But all I felt was total terror. What would I *say* to my date, whom I had never seen before and whom, after five tongue-tied hours, I would likely never see again?

Perhaps only the women who live with male prep school graduates can be the ultimate judges, but my guess is that no man comes out of such an adolescence without some emotional crippling. It was not that we looked on women only as sex objects; it was that they were no kind of object at all. They weren't there. They didn't exist. Except on these rare weekends. Talking to a girl your own age was an *event,* like shaking hands with the president; it was analyzed and discussed and agonized over for months afterward. Should I have said this? Asked her that? To go from such an atmosphere to one in which you live, study, or work with women as equals each day requires a major adjustment, and I think some prep school graduates never made it.

I went to Pomfret about a decade too early. Today it and almost all the other major prep schools are coed. Why did they hold out so long? Even longer, in fact, than it took most of them to become racially integrated? Ultimately these schools were set up with the same hope that is behind all institutions that are by design for men only, from infantry battalions to the Catholic priesthood: the hope that sexuality will be sublimated into zeal for achievement. The appalling thing about this is that it works. I studied harder at Pomfret—sometimes six, seven hours a day, after classes—than I ever have elsewhere, before or since. But the price was too high, and I wish I had never had to pay it. I don't just mean the price in the dammed-up sexuality of those years, but in all the unexperienced gentleness, laughter, and, for want of a better word, roundedness of life, which cannot exist to the full where one half of the human race is kept separate from the other.

.   .   .

I wish I could say that I saw all these problems with prep school while I was there, but I have to admit that my four years at Pomfret were one of the sunniest stretches of my life. Yes, it was the place where I first came to understand something about social class in America. But my experience there had many other layers as well. In traditional classroom terms, I got a superb education. I learned for the first time that words could mean more than their surfaces. I learned that music could say things words could not. I entered as a boy who did his homework; I left as one who read books and, in some rudimentary way, thought about them. I had private tutorials in subjects I was especially interested in. As part of its international affairs focus, Pomfret organized summer seminars involving trips to Asia, Africa, and Latin America; I went on one of these and saw the Third World through nontourist eyes for the first time. Our seminar had three Pomfret boys and seven students from other schools; we studied race relations in the American South and in Africa. For a group of sixteen- and seventeen-year-olds this was an overwhelming, life-changing experience. More than half of us eventually returned to the South as civil-rights workers, or to Africa to work or study.

There you have it: the paradox. Only by being in an elite, able to go to a place like Pomfret, did I gain access to so broadening an opportunity. The real injustice about prep school was not in the content of what we learned in the classroom or in occasional outside ventures like that trip, but in the fact that all that wealth of experience was available, with rare exceptions, only to the few who could pay. For those rich enough to afford them, schools like Pomfret are the greatest affirmative action program in the land.

However, despite occasional windows onto the outside world like that trip to Africa, the school was a little minisociety quite far from the democratic ideal. Of course, American society as a whole falls far short of that ideal also. But certain key parts of it have usually been *socially* democratic: the draft-era military, for example, and many public high schools. There, for at least one portion of their lives, Americans of all classes and colors must rub shoulders with each other, learn to speak with each other, learn that we all share the same country. On our hilltop at Pomfret there was none of this. We knew that poor and black and working-class people existed out there somewhere, but, as if we were vacationers on a yacht, they were invisible.

To spend twenty-four hours a day exclusively with members of your own class from the age of fourteen through eighteen is a recipe for complacency, for conservatism, and, above all, for identifying the welfare of yourself and your friends with that of society in general. In fact, many New England prep schools began precisely because upper-class families did not want their sons and daughters going to school with the children of society in general. The rise and fall in the number of elite boarding schools founded in each decade in the late nineteenth and early twentieth centuries correlates very closely with the rise and fall in the number of immigrants entering the United States.

Certain historical photographs have the power to move us in a particular way: Queen Victoria is proclaimed Empress of India; Tsar Nicholas II reviews his troops. The picture affects us because it captures the arrogance of those who thought they and their descendants would rule forever. I think of New England prep schools in the 1950s as being caught in such a picture. Of my class posing for its group portrait on the chapel steps, where other classes had posed for sixty years before us and where, of course, future classes would pose for decades to come. Everybody line up now. Smile for the camera. Now freeze . . .

But the analogy is not complete. For most prep school graduates of my generation and older, the world still *is* that way, and they are still part of its upper reaches. The upheavals of the 1960s washed over Pomfret and its alumni but caused only a few defections and casualties. The school trained its graduates to master a certain world—a world with definite, unspoken borders. And it is that island world they still inhabit, however much it may have changed for their children and grandchildren. On one of those reunion visits, I ran into an old schoolmate. He introduced his wife (Candy or Penny or Muffie) and asked me what I'd been up to. Then I asked him.

"Well," he said cheerfully, "after college and the army, I went into investment banking. First Boston. But now . . ."—he threw his hands wide in a gesture of benign, tolerant acceptance of his own rashness—"I've gone *clear* to the other end of the spectrum. I'm a stockbroker."

1982

Summer of Violence

In the summer of 1964, nearly a thousand volunteers, mostly white college students, traveled to Mississippi as civil-rights workers. The South had already been in turmoil for nearly a decade, ever since Rosa Parks had refused to move to the back of the bus. But Freedom Summer of 1964 was something new. Never had activists so forcefully targeted the state where racism was at its worst: the author of a book comparing black people to chimpanzees, caterpillars, and cockroaches had just been made a justice of the Mississippi Supreme Court. And never had it been so absolutely certain that, within a few months, some of the civil-rights workers would be dead. People came to view those months, wrote the author Sally Belfrage, a volunteer, "almost as if it were our generation's Spanish Civil War."

At least six people did die from racial violence in Mississippi in 1964. To three who were black Mississippians, the national press and the Justice Department paid little attention. But when Andrew Goodman, Michael Schwerner, and James Chaney—two white New Yorkers and a local black activist—disappeared from a country road in Neshoba County, the state leapt onto the nation's front pages and stayed there. The FBI got into the act. Reporters flooded the county. President Lyndon B. Johnson sent navy sailors to join the search. During the six weeks it took to find the bodies of the missing three civil-rights workers, searchers turned up *nine* other corpses, all of black men, whom authorities had never bothered to look for before. Most were believed to have been victims of the same notorious county sheriff's department responsible for the deaths of Chaney, Schwerner, and Goodman.

Mississippi's whites took out their wrath that summer in other ways as well. No one kept count of the thousands of threatening

140

phone calls, or of the hundreds of times pick-up trucks full of jeering whites tried to run Freedom Summer workers' cars off the road. But in the state in 1964, more than a thousand civil-rights workers were arrested. Eighty were attacked and beaten. There were thirty-five shootings. Sixty-five churches, homes, and offices were burned or bombed.

One of those buildings was a dilapidated white frame house in a tree-shaded black neighborhood in Vicksburg, Mississippi. In the middle of one October night, it was partly destroyed by a large mass of explosives someone had slipped underneath it. The building was the town's Freedom House—a dormitory for activists, a black history "Freedom School," the headquarters for a new black community newspaper and for a drive to register black voters, and a library for which Northern sympathizers had sent several thousand books. The books helped. In boxes on the Freedom House ground floor, they absorbed most of the blast, preventing deaths or serious injuries.

A few weeks before the bombing, I was one of the civil-rights workers living in that house. And so it was with more than academic interest that I followed the various ways people marked the thirtieth anniversary of Freedom Summer in 1994: books, radio and TV programs, a remarkable film, and finally a conference and reunion, in Mississippi, of many of us who were there three decades earlier.

.   .   .

In 1964, the rhetoric that fueled Freedom Summer often stressed one theme: Mississippi was so benighted a place that it was hardly part of the United States. The state, for example, spent several times as much on the education of a white child as a black child, something that resembled nowhere so much as South Africa. Also like apartheid was the fact that any black Mississippian trying to register to vote was likely to get ridiculed, beaten, or jailed. There were other outrages on every side. When a white state legislator coveted some land a black woman refused to sell him, he had her committed for a year to a state insane asylum. A Mississippi newspaper that had mistakenly identified someone as Negro was found guilty of libel. And Mississippi had censorship: black faces seldom showed up in the newspapers, and when a young civil-rights attorney named Thurgood Marshall appeared on the "Today" show to talk about school desegregation, people watching the NBC affiliate in Jackson, the state capital, suddenly found themselves looking at a placard that said CABLE DIFFICULTY. What did this jamming of broadcasts from the outside world resemble if not the Soviet Union?

The black civil-rights activists who had been working bravely and quietly in Mississippi for years surely knew better, but I think for us white volunteers a major lesson of 1964 was that Mississippi both wasn't and *was* part of the United States. We learned that those in power in Washington were no more eager for change in Mississippi than those in power in Jackson. I arrived in the state in midsummer, and for me the end of innocence came only a few weeks later. Since the Mississippi state Democratic Party in effect barred blacks, Freedom Summer organizers had formed an alternative, open-to-all Mississippi Freedom Democratic Party. A long, painstaking, scrupulously democratic series of county and state-wide meetings had elected an integrated delegation that tried to take seats at the 1964 Democratic National Convention. It was not allowed to. The effort to bar it from all but an insulting token two seats was led by a man once famous as a civil-rights crusader, Senator Hubert Humphrey. President Johnson rewarded him for this job by choosing Humphrey as candidate for vice president. One member of the MFDP delegation was a great heroine of the movement, Fannie Lou Hamer, a former sharecropper on a cotton plantation, with a sixth-grade education. When she began making a heartfelt, eloquent appeal to the convention, President Johnson called a snap White House press conference to force her off the country's TV screens.

Washington also put the brakes on change in Mississippi in ways we didn't see at the time. I learned about one from John Dittmer's *Local People: The Struggle for Civil Rights in Mississippi,* published during the thirtieth anniversary year. Dittmer shows how the president of Brown University, Barnaby Keeney, used behind-the-scenes influence and the threat of canceled foundation grants to cut off crucial support that Mississippi civil-rights activists were getting from a black college there. Keeney was on the CIA payroll at the time.

·   ·   ·

There are always two histories: the history that happened, and the history that gets crystallized into an image, a song, a painting, a legend. For a time it seemed that the public memory of Freedom Summer of 1964 would be that contained in the 1988 Hollywood film *Mississippi Burning.* In this cops-and-robbers movie the villains are the murderers of Chaney, Schwerner, and Goodman. But, in an appalling travesty, black people in Mississippi, and the civil-rights movement in general, barely appear. The film's heroes are agents of J. Edgar Hoover's FBI. True, the FBI did help find the killers, but only when national outrage over the murders forced President Johnson to order it into action. Until then, FBI agents—who at that time included virtually no blacks—had for years simply stood by and watched, again and again, as voter registration workers in the South were beaten before their eyes.

It is refreshing, therefore, to find that 1994's finest look back at the Mississippi of thirty years earlier is another film. It will not be as widely seen as *Mississippi Burning,* but the documentary *Freedom on My Mind* rescues the memory of that time with quiet integrity. The film is a gem: understated, moving, and politically sophisticated, its scenes are threaded through with the freedom songs of the time and the haunting harmonica and guitar sounds of the rural South. Filmmakers Connie Field and Marilyn Mulford interview blacks and whites who were civil-rights workers in Mississippi, and gracefully interweave their stories with film footage and still photographs of three decades ago—often of the same people.

The effect is stunning. Endesha Ida Mae Holland describes how she was raped at the age of eleven by a white man, then dropped out of school and became a prostitute. When civil-rights workers came to town, she says with a smile, she hoped for some new business. Instead, they put her to work. Through the movement, she says, she gained a sense of worth and dignity. She organized, demonstrated, went to jail, and faced down the local sheriff—and suddenly we are seeing old, black-and-white newsreel footage of this very confrontation on the screen. At the end, we learn that she is now a college professor and playwright. If you ever have a chance to see this film, bring your handkerchief.

The movie's images sear: burning crosses; bombed-out homes; integrated groups of crewcut young freedom riders sitting-in at lunch counters while white toughs punch them; long lines of blacks waiting in the hot sun to try to register to vote. Chaney, Schwerner, and Goodman disappeared just as the summer began. Several former volunteers describe how, on the last night of their preparatory training at a college campus in Ohio, they heard the news from Bob Moses, the quietly charismatic, self-effacing teacher who was Freedom Summer's moving spirit. In great torment, he told the group of volunteers he was certain that the missing three were dead, and that anyone else going into the state risked death as well. We see a still picture of him speaking. Under the shadow of this knowledge, the next morning everyone left for Mississippi. We see their somber faces, black and white, roll slowly by at the windows of a bus heading south.

There was a kind of moral clarity about the movement of that time that seems tragically elusive today. "I wish it were possible," says Curtis Hayes, a black former civil-rights worker interviewed in *Freedom on My Mind,* "for young people now, even if it were just for a day, to experience the kind of camaraderie and the kind of commitment that we were a part of: to hear of someone in danger, and see people run to that danger as a hungry man would run to food, to give a hand, to give help. There are not words to explain it."

·   ·   ·

What I remember most from that summer is the fear. It was greater at night, less in the day, sometimes looming, sometimes in the background, like a traffic hum that never goes away. Never, ever, we were told again and again, go somewhere alone. Always be with others. If attacked, maybe one of you can run for help.

I know things have changed, but it's still a shock, arriving in Jackson for the first time in thirty years, to see a big banner in the airport, WELCOME MISSISSIPPI HOMECOMING. And can it really be that our gathering of several hundred people is greeted by proclamations from the mayor and the governor, and, in person, by a black member of Congress from Mississippi? And that one of our buses is escorted by a black sergeant from the state highway patrol?

Some of the former civil-rights workers, of both races, have brought their children, now in their teens and twenties. One session of the conference is given over to this younger generation. Many pay tribute, sometimes in tears, to their parents. Some are working in a nationwide collection of youth projects called Freedom Summer '94, everything from literacy teaching to neighborhood clean-ups to mediating gang warfare. This is not Generation

X. For me the most moving moment comes when a white woman, perhaps eighteen or twenty, stands up from the floor where most of the young people are sitting and says, "I live in a multiracial family. And that would not be possible if it were not for what happened here in 1964." She then reaches down, clasps, and holds up the hands of two siblings in an apparently adoptive family: one hand is olive, one black. Standing at the side the room, their middle-aged father looks on, with a smile so proud it almost soars off his face.

The adult faces at the conference are a reminder of how much that summer in Mississippi was a turning point in people's lives. So many of the now-graying former volunteers here went on to make their mark in the upheavals that followed 1964: the feminist writer Susan Brownmiller; activist and politician Tom Hayden; veteran community organizer Heather Booth.

The same is true of black staff members of the Student Non-violent Coordinating Committee (SNCC), the key group in the Freedom Summer coalition. These survivors of countless beatings and jailings worked in the South long before that summer and long after most of the white volunteers had left. In those days they always wore the SNCC uniform of T-shirt and one-piece blue denim overalls. Today John Lewis represents Georgia in Congress. Now a college professor, Julian Bond became one of the first black state legislators in the Deep South. Bob Moses runs a national demonstration project that teaches math to inner city children. (Not everyone came out so nobly, however: at one point during the conference former SNCC leader and Washington, D.C., Mayor Marion Barry, uninvited, gets up on stage.)

Throughout the weekend, waves of emotion come easily, especially when we sing—"Come by Here, Lord, Come by Here," "Guide My Feet, Lord, While I Run This Race," "This Little Light of Mine,"—sometimes led by the golden-voiced Bernice Reagon of the a cappella group Sweet Honey in the Rock. One day a busload of people, including the widow of Michael Schwerner and the mother of Andrew Goodman, goes to visit the grave of James Chaney, third in the murdered trio. They relight an eternal flame on Chaney's tomb. All is not yet at peace in Mississippi, for vandals have repeatedly attacked the grave.

In one session of the conference, a man of twenty-nine, holding a small child, announces that he was adopted, and that he has come to this meeting hoping to find his birth parents. One was white, one black, and they met in Mississippi Freedom Summer. He knows little more than this. If he cannot find them, he says, he at least wants to feel part of something they were part of.

He is not the only person here trying to recover something lost. Half a dozen times during the weekend I hear people say the same thing: that it has been decades in this country since so many black people and so many white people looked so glad to see each other. Sadly, Freedom Summer came near the end of an era. By the late 1960s, talk of black power had begun; whites were forced out of SNCC and many other civil-rights organizations; sharp hostility had erupted between blacks and Jews; and a kind of voluntary social segregation took hold in places like Northern universities and has remained ever since.

It is not that there were no black-white tensions within Freedom Summer. I saw them where I worked in Vicksburg, and they existed throughout the state. The white Northern students, many from elite schools, knew little of the South and were often arrogant. The black SNCC staff, many from poor or rural backgrounds, were veteran community organizers but often defensive. In a strange way, each group envied parts of the other's experience. There were clashes, uneasiness, cliquishness. Women of both colors were often shunted to menial positions. (Topics that might stir up some of these resentments all over again, such as the role of women in the movement, are not on the official conference agenda.) But despite the tensions, 1964 was still a moment in American history when it was possible for millions of people of different races to feel part of the same moral crusade. I hope such a time will come again. Today it feels far off.

.   .   .

Until the bombing of the Freedom House in October 1964, which happened after we summer volunteers had left, Vicksburg had had the reputation of being unusually peaceful. The local sheriff was unctuously polite to us. Miraculously, a tiny number of blacks in town were even allowed to vote. When I wrote home that summer, I assured my worried parents that I was in the safest place in Mississippi.

On the last day of the 1994 reunion in Jackson, three other participants and I, who had all worked in Vicksburg thirty years ago, drive there for the day. The town looks much the same. We drive past the Catholic rectory where a priest once brought black and white workers from the Freedom House together with a small group of local white college students. Feeling guilty, agonized, and profoundly frightened, they would meet us only in secret. When we went back for another meeting the next week, none of them showed up.

But Vicksburg in 1994 has changed a great deal. In recent years it has had a black mayor for a time. One of the local black men who worked out of the Freedom House is now on the county board of supervisors. Another, Eddie Thomas, sixty-nine, we find in his Palace Barber Shop, and we gather around and talk to him for several hours while he trims his customers' hair. He pulls out newspaper clippings and mementos, and seems delighted to see us, although in the corner of his shop I notice on sale a pile of *Muhammed Speaks*.

A more ominous change, I think, is that the barber shop and each of the black homes we revisit this day has something seldom seen in a black Mississippi house three decades ago: a large, blaring, color television set. As Eddie Thomas cuts hair, behind his elbow endlessly flicker white riders in black coats and hats, soaring elegantly over the jumps of a steeplechase. Could a great social movement, demanding sacrifice by its members and justice as its goal, a movement where people run to help someone in danger "as a hungry man would run to food," ever arise today amid the all-saturating, anesthetizing background noise of TV?

The most haunting experience that day in Vicksburg comes as we go to the neighborhood of the Freedom House where we worked and stayed. And from it I learn that the history I remember—which includes Vicksburg being a mercifully peaceful place, at least until the bombing—was in fact more complicated.

One of the other returning volunteers today is Fran O'Brien, a quiet white woman who is now a schoolteacher in southern California. As we slowly drive past the spot where the Freedom House used to be, suddenly she begins describing an experience she had on this street, that summer thirty years ago. Her story takes the rest of us totally by surprise.

It was evening, and starting to get dark—the most dangerous time. The Freedom House was at the top of a small hill, and cars could not make it up the muddy driveway after a rain. At the entrance to the driveway, therefore, several women volunteers were waiting for the ride that was to take them to the black homes where they were staying. (Male volunteers lived mostly in the Freedom House itself.) The car came, but there wasn't room for all of the women, and the driver told Fran O'Brien to wait: another car would be along in a moment to pick her up.

A few minutes later a car did pull up out of the dusk, and, relieved, O'Brien ran up to it. But inside were four men in white robes and hoods. One of them leapt out, clapped a hand over her mouth, and pulled her into the car. From their talk, it appeared that they were on their way to a Ku Klux Klan meeting, and were delighted to find one of these Northern troublemakers without even having to go looking. Terrified, O'Brien was driven to what seemed to be a vacant lot or empty field. The men then forced her to bend over the hood of the car. Two of them took pieces of rubber garden hose out of the trunk, beat her until they were exhausted, then passed the hoses to the other two.

O'Brien passed out, and does not know what happened next. When she came to, she was lying in the driveway of the Freedom House, where the Klansmen had evidently dumped her. She staggered uphill to the house, under the impression that she had been gone for many hours. It turned out to have only been thirty or forty minutes. The other civil-rights workers in the house could see that something had happened, and crowded around, questioning her. She could not speak coherently, she was traumatized, and her whole body hurt from the beating. An older black woman who lived in the house took her aside, comforted her, told her that everyone knew terrible things happened in Mississippi, and that it was O.K. if O'Brien didn't want to talk right now, and saw that she got safely home.

For twenty-five years, O'Brien never told anyone what had happened. At the time, she was frightened the story would get into the newspapers and that her family would be alarmed. Both then and later, she felt she had brought this horror on herself by violating the instructions so often repeated to us: never be alone. The episode left a major mark on her life. When she finally did talk about it at a gathering of former civil-rights workers in California in 1989, someone said: What about the people who told you to wait by the side of the road? How could they just drive off and leave you alone? For the first time it occurred to O'Brien that perhaps she was not the one to blame.

Hearing her story is a shock. I had gone through my weeks in Vicksburg in 1964 thinking that, in this murderous state, I had landed in an oasis of relative peace. It is even possible, although I have no memory of it, that I was one of the people in the house when Fran O'Brien came limping up the driveway, unable to talk about what had happened to her. Hearing her story made me rethink my time in Vicksburg in a different light. How much other violence went on around us that summer that I was naively ignorant of? How much other racist terror in the South got kept secret because the victims blamed themselves? And how much violence and pain close to us at any time are we blithely unaware of?

·   ·   ·

Making public the state's hidden violence and pain was, of course, what Mississippi Freedom Summer was all about. And in that it succeeded, even though its very success depended on a racism of perception. The organizers hoped that when white middle-class Northerners shared for a few weeks or months the daily insults and brutality that Southern blacks had endured all their lives, Congress would at last pay attention and do something. It did.

The national outcry over the murder of the three young civil-rights workers helped win quick passage of the Civil Rights Act of 1964. Continuing marches and sit-ins led directly to the Voting Rights Act of the following year. This at last won blacks entry to the Deep South polling booths from which they had been largely turned away for nearly a century. Even in Neshoba County, where they murdered Chaney, Goodman, and Schwerner, everyone can now vote. Today Mississippi has more than eight hundred black elected officials, more than any other state. When a black face appears on a national TV show, Mississippi's screens no longer go blank.

Racial violence itself has by no means disappeared from the state: black churches have been burned at night, and a number of young black men have died mysteriously in the state's jails and prisons. But now, in public at least, racism is usually coded as talk about crime and welfare. In that sense, Mississippi has finally joined the Union.

The movement was far less successful at uprooting economic injustice. When it comes to issues like jobs, it has been much, much harder to rally people to a national movement that has the same undeniable moral force as asserting the right of every man and woman to vote. In the last few decades, new farm machinery has thrown hundreds of thousands of black Mississippi workers off the land and into towns where there are no jobs for them. Except for the omnipresent TV antennas, the run-down shacks where they live look like Dorothea Lange's photographs of the Great Depression. Progress has been minuscule. In 1990, the black unemployment rate in the state was more than double the white rate—and more than double the rate for blacks thirty years before. In 1989, the median black family income was only 56.1 percent of the state average, a mere 6 percent advance over thirty years earlier. (In several counties, black families earned an even *smaller* percentage of white family income than they did thirty years earlier.) The comparative figures on black and white ownership of land, business, and industry in Mississippi are even more lopsided.

Fostered by high, seemingly permanent unemployment, there are now other troubles in black Mississippi as well, things that once were mainly big-city ills in the North: Gangs. Drugs. Crime. A soaring rate of teen pregnancy and single motherhood. The black neighborhood in Jackson where the Freedom Summer state headquarters used to be is beset by all of these things. When a volunteer returning to the 1994 reunion went to take a picture of the building, two men, apparently drug dealers who thought she had come to photograph them, pulled guns on her. Here, too, Mississippi has joined the Union. And the problems that brings will take far more than a summer to solve.

1994

We Are Not in Switzerland

The first unexpected event happens as soon as we come through customs at the San Salvador airport. Waiting at the exit is a young man from the U.S. embassy. He quickly buttonholes one member of our group, Representative Edward Feighan of Ohio, and takes him outside, where a bulletproof van is waiting.

There are some eighteen of us who have just arrived in the capital of an El Salvador torn apart by a civil war between government troops and leftist guerrillas. We are a delegation from the Commission on United States–Central American Relations, a Washington group dedicated to getting the United States to support justice instead of repression in Central America. The commission wants to raise the question: why is the Reagan administration spending several hundred million dollars a year to arm, supply, and train soldiers of one of the hemisphere's most brutal governments?

Our delegation has a shrewdly chosen cast of characters. These include representatives of business, labor, the church, Hispanic-Americans, and so on. But there are also two members of Congress, one of whom is coming on a later plane. Both sit on the House Foreign Affairs Committee, which sets the ceiling on aid to El Salvador. This guarantees that the Salvadoran government will give us red-carpet access to anything we want to see—a rare experience for those of us used to being in the opposition.

Also, three members of our group are known to the media: singer Mary Travers, of Peter, Paul and Mary; actor Mike Farrell; and Patricia Derian, who was President Jimmy Carter's assistant secretary of state for human rights and humanitarian affairs. This ensures that the U.S. press may notice what we say and do here: we will be investigating and protesting in the same breath. Already there are TV cameras here at the airport.

151

While we wait for our bags, the U.S. diplomat whisks Representative Feighan off to the embassy for "private briefings." These, Feighan tells us later, consist in part of his being urged to stay at an embassy residence, not at the Camino Real Hotel with the rest of us. Feighan wins us all as future campaign workers by choosing to join us at the hotel nonetheless.

We have dinner that night with some American reporters covering the war. I ask one if he feels safe working here. "Relatively," he says. "The U.S. embassy has told the guys who run the death squads: 'There are two kinds of people you have to lay off, or else there's big trouble in Washington—our journalists and your Jesuits.'" There are some lapses, but generally these instructions are obeyed. Despite the fact that the military looted and closed the country's main university and massacred some of its students, we find the Jesuit university still open; U.S. correspondents work in relative freedom.

.   .   .

Our first stop the next morning is in the suburb of Ilopango, at a complex of low buildings surrounded by palm trees and by hibiscus and oleander in bloom. Among the buildings, laundry is hung up to dry, dirt paths are neatly lined with bricks, religious posters are on the walls, small children are pulling toy trucks on strings. Improbably, this is the Cárcel de Mujeres, the women's prison.

There are few prisons in El Salvador. The authorities don't feel the need. Particularly in rural areas, most people kidnapped by the security forces simply vanish. Sometimes their bodies are found later, in dumps where vultures swirl overhead; sometimes not. The remainder of those seized, especially those arrested here in San Salvador, the capital, get delivered to one of the prisons after torture and interrogation.

Once in prison, it seems, they are left pretty much alone. There are 140 women here at Ilopango, 82 of them "politicals." The politicals are in a separate section of their own, so that their ideals will not spread to the other prisoners. None of the 82 has been formally charged.

Ana Margarita Gasteazoro is thirty-two; before her arrest she was an English teacher. She has black hair and wears jeans, sandals, and a crucifix. She is a member of the MNR, a legal party associated with Social Democratic parties of Western Europe. Two years ago she was arrested. "They came at about five o'clock in the morning with about fifty uniformed men," she says. "They searched the house and looted it completely. As soon as they got there, they tied us and blindfolded my husband. They threw him on the couch and took his shoes off. After beating him hard with rifles, they put wires in a socket and then tied them to his toes and gave him electric shocks." She and her husband were then thrown into car trunks and taken to the headquarters of the Salvadoran National Guard. "We were there for fourteen days," she says in matter-of-fact, almost accentless English. "I was put near where he was, where I could hear him scream while he was being tortured. I was beaten up. I was tied to a bed with handcuffs. I was sexually abused."

The prisoners seem well organized. Gasteazoro tells us there is a medical committee, a small co-op that makes crocheted and embroidered items that can be sold, committees for job assignments, finances, and entertainment, and a commissary. Like many other prisoners we speak to, she says she feels relatively safe here. Prisons in El Salvador house people whom, for inscrutable reasons of their own, the security forces wish to keep alive. It's outside, she tells us, that people get "disappeared." "People don't disappear out of prison. Perhaps the day I leave something will happen."

Gasteazoro translates the stories of other prisoners. When speaking of rape and torture, some break down in sobs and can go no further, but Gasteazoro's voice remains calm. She gives us a tour of the prisoners' sleeping quarters—rooms of bunks like an army barracks. Openings in a wall of concrete latticework are stuffed with crumpled newspaper in a vain attempt to keep out the winter wind. The women have kept their surroundings very orderly and clean. One prisoner, a schizophrenic, runs up to us and begs money for baby formula—she is convinced that this will make her well again.

Amid cots and cribs in the prison's nursery, we stop to talk with Eva Perez de Franco, forty-one. She is dressing her baby, who was only three days old when de Franco was arrested a few months ago. She is the former mayor of the town of Oratorio de Concepción; her crime, as far as she can tell, is to have been a Christian Democrat. This centrist party is actually part of the government. But it is disliked by the right-wingers who run the security apparatus: they have killed dozens of Christian Democratic activists and elected officials.

About three weeks ago, de Franco's twenty-year-old nephew came to visit her here at the prison. As he left, he was met outside the gate by some uniformed men, beaten, thrown into the back of a pickup truck, and driven off. He has not been heard from since.

As we prepare to leave, Ana Margarita Gasteazoro asks where we are going next, and I tell her it is to an interview with the foreign minister. "Say hello to him," she says. "He knows me well." It is a small country.

At the last moment, the prisoners discover that Mary Travers is a famous performer. They ask her to sing. And this she does shyly, almost in a whisper, sitting on a concrete bench in the courtyard with the women prisoners gathered around:

> How many years must a man look up
> Before he can see the sky?

For the first time all morning, Gasteazoro begins to weep.

.   .   .

Afternoon. The men's prison, La Esperanza—"the hope"—holds 576 political prisoners, from age fifteen up. This prison is more crowded than the women's, and dirtier; trash lies about on the walkways and under the stairs. The corridor walls and ceilings are a tangle of home-rigged wiring that brings electricity to light bulbs in the cells. No guards patrol the "political" section, for fear the prisoners might influence them. On the walls are slogans, a poster of Che Guevara, a bulletin board of political news, and even a large map of the country showing what territory is now controlled by the rebels.

Many prisoners crowd after us into a small cinder-block room, standing against the walls, sitting, crouching on the floor or climbing up the bars of a cell door across the corridor in an attempt to hear. Again the same stories. A small, older, bearded man has been beaten so severely that he has had to have his testicles amputated. There are other such cases, they tell us.

One of the prisoners wears an American T-shirt that says "Yosemite National Park." Another's bears the name of a chain of stores: "The Athlete's Foot." The man with this shirt is a former public school teacher, Rafael Antonio Carrias, once active in the teacher's union, arrested and tortured by the National Guard. He takes off his T-shirt to show us garish, ridged scars that cross his chest and back like long purple ruts gouged in his skin: the effects, he says, of hydrochloric acid burns at the hands of his interrogators.

The prisoners give us a set of documents to take with us, copied by hand in neat, almost microscopic printing, the writing of a scribe in a society without typewriters or copying machines. These documents are a tabulation of all the political prisoners held here, written out afresh for anyone allowed to visit who might be able to get this information to the outside world: name of prisoner, occupation, age, place of capture, date, branch of armed services involved. At the end there are neatly ruled charts summarizing data from the list, just as statistical tables might accompany a scientific article. One table lists the abuses and what percentage of prisoners have suffered them. TORTURAS: *Fracturas por golpes* [broken bones], 3 percent; *Asfixia* [suffocation], 8 percent; *Colgados* [suspending or hanging], 14 percent; *Choques eléctricos* [electric shock], 32 percent; *Golpes en al cuerpo* [beatings], 96 percent.

Finally, in some bewilderment, we ask the prisoners: Why has the government let us see you? We have come up with several possible explanations ourselves: (1) No one stopped to think; (2) someone is trying to embarrass the Department of Justice, which runs the prisons; (3) the Department of Justice is trying to embarrass the armed forces, which do the torturing; or (4) the government considers it a human-rights advance that it bothers to keep prisoners at all. The inmates here at La Esperanza believe the last explanation. "They want to demonstrate to the world," says one, "that not *everyone* who is captured is assassinated."

I pose the same question later to a veteran American correspondent stationed here. He says: "This country has a very strange sense of P.R."

.   .   .

Under current U.S. foreign aid law, the Reagan administration must "certify" every six months that El Salvador is making an effort to comply with international standards of human rights. Thus certification time is when delegations like ours visit. For dealing with them, the U.S. embassy has things down to a routine.

Officials talk to us in an auditorium deep inside the embassy: past armed police outside, fortresslike watchtowers, marine guards, iron grills and heavy doors that resemble watertight bulkheads on an ocean liner, as if this little colony of Americans were all equipped in case of shipwreck to float away to safety over a hostile sea. The ambassador is back in Washington this week, doubtless lobbying for more guns and planes for the Salvadoran armed forces, so we are received by his second in command, Deputy Chief of Mission Kenneth Bleakley, a buoyant, forceful man with a closely cropped black beard. He begins by saying something about the ominous thousands of Cubans working in Nicaragua. When challenged about the relevance of this to El Salvador, he immediately says, "O.K., you don't like that," and smoothly switches to what he probably thinks of as the human-rights briefing.

It is a masterful performance. His very language signals: we're all progressives here. He talks of the local "oligarchy," of El Salvador as a "sick society," of the vital importance of land reform. Despite everything, he declares, we're making progress. After all, they held elections, didn't they?

He does not mention that each Salvadoran voter signed for the receipt of a *numbered* ballot, to be deposited in a transparent plastic ballot box. Or that one reason opposition parties refused to participate was that each was required to submit the names and address of three thousand members—convenient hit lists for the death squads.

An indication of progress, Bleakley says, is that the last batch of Salvadoran soldiers trained in the United States got a full week of instruction in human rights and in the Geneva Convention on treatment of prisoners. A full week! He admits that there are all these unfortunate death-squad killings and disappearings, but says the numbers are down sharply.

Bleakley does not mention that the embassy compiles these figures from the local press, which is far from bold or thorough on the subject. One of the last newspapers critical of the government ceased publishing a while back when its editor and one of its photographers were found by a roadside one morning, their bodies chopped into pieces.

·   ·   ·

Late one afternoon, as dusk is falling, we walk up several flights of stairs in a rundown office building to meet with members of the Popular Democratic Union, a coalition of moderate labor and professional groups. This organization was highly touted by the U.S. embassy a few months ago as part of the "emerging democratic center" in El Salvador that our government is supposedly trying to encourage. There are eleven men and one woman in this room, several of the men in sombreros, most in workers' clothes, and one, from an association of accountants, in a suit and tie. But they do not play the upbeat role assigned to them.

As they talk, the reason becomes clear: in the past year the military death squads—having finished off just about everybody openly identified with El Salvador's Left—have begun working on the center. The people here give us the names of 160 trade unionists who have been "disappeared" since 1980. A man from the municipal employees union says that in the past six months alone, nine of his members have been imprisoned, ten killed, four disappeared. Darkness falls over the city as we talk; the room is wanly lit by a couple of bare bulbs. There is a palpable, quiet despair here in the room. These are people who have not thrown in their lot with the guerrillas, but instead are dutifully playing by the rules in a society where the rules mean nothing. Unspoken, but in the minds of us all as the numbers of the dead and vanished are reeled off, is the knowledge that if another American delegation tries to meet with these same dozen people six months from now, at least one or two of them will be dead.

.   .   .

That evening we meet more Americans and Salvadorans at a reception. I talk with two young U.S. embassy staff members, said to be the most liberal here. Both, it turns out, have renewed their stay for a second tour, because this country is where the action is. "Here," says one, "I can take a visiting senator to see a cabinet minister, just like that." He snaps his fingers. "Somewhere else in the Foreign Service I might have to wait twenty years."

One of the two members of Congress in our group, Robert Torricelli of New Jersey, has a special mission. Besides seeing the country, he wants to bring home the body of a young man from his district, a free-lance journalist named John Sullivan, Jr., who was ambushed and killed in El Salvador some two years ago. There are many problems, however, among them the fact that Sullivan's dead body, like that of many death-squad victims, was blown apart with explosives.

Later, an aide traveling with Torricelli tells me that a Salvadoran took him aside at the reception and offered to sell him a piece of Sullivan's body.

. . .

"In El Salvador the order to kill you doesn't have to go out as an order," says Leonel Gómez, who spoke to our group before we left the United States. Gómez is the former deputy director of his country's Agrarian Reform Institute. Ever since the regime stalled further land reform and gunmen killed his closest colleague, he has lived in Washington. "The mechanism to kill people is very sophisticated. The military that run the country—if you become a threat to them, they will float your name. They will call a meeting of military commanders; they will say, 'You know, this man David ——— is getting to be a threat to us.' Then the commanders themselves will float his name when they have their meetings with their own officers. They'll say, 'You know, today we heard of this man who's making a lot of trouble for us.' Then when those officers meet with the sergeants, his name will be floated again. And you can assume David ——— will be dead." Only occasionally, Gómez says, do any names get written down. "There is a list of 138 names, of official enemies of the country. You get a lot of macho points for being on it."

More than thirty thousand noncombatant civilians have been killed in El Salvador since the country's civil war began. The soldiers who, in or out of uniform, are responsible for most of these deaths are drawn from many branches of the police and army. At the top of the pyramid, officially in command of every uniformed man in the government forces of El Salvador, sits the country's most powerful man, the minister of defense. During our visit, this post is held by Gen. José Guillermo García. García gained his job through a renowned mastery of the Salvadoran military's Byzantine internal politics. But the United States has decided he is not fighting the war briskly enough and is trying to oust him. Until recently, though, it praised him as a moderate.

Some of García's reformism apparently consists of proclaiming that all abuses have stopped. "In terms of the torture, I would say that it has been *eliminated* from our system," he says as he receives us one morning at the Defense Ministry. A large man in an olive fatigue uniform, he sits behind a semicircular table, flanked on one hand by Bleakley, the U.S. embassy's deputy chief of mission, who is always at the side of any top Salvadoran official we interview, and on the other by an unidentified Salvadoran wearing sunglasses and earphones.

Patt Derian and Mike Farrell tell García: Look, we've seen the scars of people who've been tortured. That means that either the torture is a matter of policy or the armed forces are out of your control. Which is it?

García replies: "There are many who would desire that the armed forces of El Salvador have a greater degree of control than any armed forces in the world."

He goes on to deny that the death-squad killings are carried out by soldiers: after all, you people yourselves say these captures are always done by men in civilian clothes.

But why, we then ask, do some people taken away by these same "civilians" turn up in government prisons?

There are more critical questions, and García, increasingly impatient, finally bursts out, "We are not in Switzerland!"

Midway through our meeting, the Salvadoran at García's side leaves and is replaced by a uniformed colonel, who puts on the earphones in his stead. He pulls something out from under the table: the earphones, it turns out, are connected to a Sony Walkman. García is known for his love of technological gadgetry; every once in a while he borrows the earphones himself, to make sure everything is being properly recorded. Exactly why he should bother is unclear, because the room is awash with some half-dozen TV crews. Camera operators, people holding overhead microphone booms, technicians with bulky shoulder bags of equipment all keep bumping into each other as they maneuver around, trying to aim their cameras and mikes at whoever is talking.

The interview goes on most of the morning. For our delegation, which by now shares an unspoken understanding of how best to conduct such meetings, this is a chance to air our outrage on U.S. television: we let Derian and Farrell, who are most likely to get airtime, do much of the questioning. For Representative Torricelli, the meeting is a chance to talk to his district about "the disappearance of one of *my* constituents, John Sullivan . . ."

Only later do we see that García is playing to yet a different audience. That night, virtually the entire meeting is broadcast on El Salvador's national television. We calculate that García figured that any embarrassment over our barrage of questions on human rights was outweighed by the fact that his face preempted other shows and was on the nation's TV screens for nearly two hours. It shows who's boss.

.   .   .

Today five of us fly into the war zone. We are joined by a four-person CBS crew. We are heading for Morazán province, where government soldiers are fighting the guerrillas. As we set off in a small chartered plane, a Midwestern voice crackles over the cockpit radio asking for takeoff clearance. Twice weekly there is a U.S. military ferry flight to an air force base in Panama, a Salvadoran on board informs us cryptically, "so the officers can go buy tape recorders."

We fly a half hour to the southeast, over farmland intermittently pockmarked with shell craters and past the blue-green forested slopes of a huge volcano, to the city of San Miguel. There we go to the headquarters of the army commander in this region, Colonel Jaime Ernesto Flores. Flores has repeatedly been touted by American military advisers as one of the few Salvadoran field commanders who wages proper counterguerrilla warfare—ambushes, constant small-unit patrols, night attacks. Other senior officers tend to stop fighting after dark. Like many other top commanders, however, on weekends Flores usually goes back to the capital, where he is rumored to have lucrative business interests.

Flores is a colossally fat man with a black mustache. He greets us warmly, having evidently been told only that a delegation was coming from Washington. He begins by saying how grateful he is for American military aid, and how useful it is in combating the *subversivos.* He complains, however, that his most recent shopping list, which included more trucks and backpack radios, has not yet been filled. He draws circles with a black grease pencil on a plastic map overlay: his troops, it seems, are chasing the rebels out of one town after another. We ask if we can go see some of these newly reoccupied towns. Of course, says the colonel, let's go.

Flores wears a pearl-handled revolver and a knife about fourteen inches long, sheathed in black leather. As we leave his headquarters, he picks up an Israeli submachine gun. Outside he climbs into a maroon Wagoneer station wagon with no military markings. The CBS crew follows in a pickup truck, and the rest of us bring up the rear in a taxi.

Our little caravan winds north. Dry brown hills are swathed in black, where weeds have been burned off. We pass a refugee camp with pitiful walls of thatch and cardboard. An extraordinary number of soldiers stand along the roadside, in small clusters, every mile or two.

For the first time, we hear the deep boom of 105 mm cannon shelling rebel positions. Finally, at the end of a dirt road is a small mountain village incongruously named Delicias de Concepción, our final stop in the chain of villages under Salvadoran army control. Beyond here, a bridge has been blown up, and guerrilla territory begins. Five soldiers were killed and ten wounded in fighting near this town yesterday, a captain tells us. No prisoners were taken by either side, he says, which may or may not be true. (The guerrillas periodically release prisoners to the International Red Cross; government troops seldom admit to having any, and are believed to shoot most guerrillas they capture.)

In the village, the CBS crew interviews Colonel Flores. By this point it has dawned on him that the North Americans with him today are not the kind who can get him more backpack radios. So he switches gears easily: "The highest command we are under is the command to respect justice! Human rights are very important. The people here know the army is fighting to protect their rights. Ask any of them! Just ask them." He gestures at the several dozen peasants, mostly children, impassively observing this strange gaggle of officers, TV people, and notebook-laden foreigners who have temporarily taken over the main street of their village. But, with twenty or so heavily armed soldiers also standing about, it does not seem a promising atmosphere for us to engage them in free political discussion.

The CBS reporter asks Flores a final question: "Are you winning the war in Morazán?"

"*Sí!*" says the colonel emphatically. The camera crew pack up their equipment swiftly and with smiles of great satisfaction. The day before, I find out later, they had been with the rebels less than ten miles from here, and the local guerrilla leader had answered the same question with the same word. Back to back, the two answers are a sure shot for the evening news.

As we drive back, many nearby hilltops, as well as the roadsides, are dotted with more small groups of soldiers. Flores points out the obvious: the road is safe; we have not been fired on. Therefore, he says, the many claims we have heard about rebel threats to the highways are false. Suddenly it occurs to me: there are so many soldiers guarding the forty miles or so of road we've driven on, how can there be any left to fight the guerrillas? Flores says he has sixteen hundred men under his command, yet we've seen well over half that number along the highway. Furthermore, in this region of heavy fighting, the commander has taken the whole afternoon off to lead our group of visiting gringos on tour. Has he also redeployed all his men to guard the road? It may be strategically more valuable to impress a few visitors from Washington than to kill a few more guerrillas. Flores has, in effect, stopped the war for a day to show us around.

.   .   .

The government of El Salvador has, with much fanfare, appointed a Peace Commission. And did you say human rights was a problem? Lo, there is now a Human Rights Commission.

We visit some of its members one morning in their spacious, pleasant, paneled offices. Sunlight streams through floor-to-ceiling windows; bustling clerks give us packets of documents to show how the commission's investigators have promptly looked into various cases. Among the commission's members here today are a lawyer, a trade unionist who says virtually nothing, and a priest. When we describe the acid burns we saw on a prisoner's body two days ago, the priest, Monsignor Delgado, asks: Can we be sure these wounds were not sustained in a gun battle with government forces?

Another member of the commission, absent today, is the chief of the National Police. Last December, in one of the first cases the commission solved, a young man who had disappeared was found, after seven days of investigation, in a cell at the National Police. When asked at the time whether this adversely reflected on his fellow commissioner, Monsignor Delgado replied: "A father doesn't always know what all his children are doing."

.   .   .

This morning in Washington, the Reagan administration officially certifies to Congress that El Salvador is making "progress" in human rights. This afternoon in the capital city of San Salvador, several of us meet under some trees in a dusty yard with some women from a group called the Mothers of the Disappeared.

They will be brief, they say; they are afraid to go home on the streets after dark. The first to speak is a thin, intense woman wearing a blue apron. She says she is illiterate. She is forty-eight years old but looks many years older.

"I'd like to tell you what has happened to my family.

"In 1979, they captured my first brother. Eight days later, his body was found, on a mountain, with thirty-two other corpses. He had been taken by the National Guard. Then the National Guard captured me as well. They broke all my teeth. They hit me in the head. Because of the blow on the head my eyes have given me problems since.

"On March 2, 1981, they took away my daughter. She was pregnant. They captured her in the middle of the city, in a park by the marketplace. I am left with her orphaned children.

"On May 21, 1982, the Treasury Police came to get me because I didn't have my identity card—the first time I was taken away, they had taken my identity card and they never gave it back. They tortured me for three days. They hung me up, pulled my hair and beat me.

"On October 13, 1982, my second brother was taken from the house, at 10:30 at night, and found the next day at 11:00 A.M. He had been disemboweled. We found the body only because my mother was trying to buy fish that day and heard someone in the market say that there were so many bodies in the river that the fish were contaminated."

But that is not all. "When the National Guard captured me," she says, her voice rising, "they raped me. And they did this to me." She pulls down her dress top to show a two-foot-long red scar that crosses her body diagonally, like one leg of an X, from neck to lower ribs, over where her right breast had been.

After this interview, we return in silence to our hotel. Westin International Hotels. Partners in Travel with United Airlines. Beach Towels Available at Poolside. Plastic packets of shampoo, chrome Kleenex box holder in the bathroom, little wrapped packages of soap. Can I really be sitting here, having heard what I have just heard? I stare at my notes numbly.

It is not until a month later, while traveling, using some spare time in another hotel room to work, when I listen to the tape recording of this interview for the first time, and hear the woman break down sobbing at the end, hear the *whoosh-whoosh* of a military helicopter that flew overhead at that moment, and hear her final cry: "I want you to take my testimony back! And tell Señor Reagan that what he's sending here is making us all orphans!" that the full horror of her experience overwhelms me. No one in Dante's Inferno could have suffered more. As nearly as I am ever likely to in my life, I looked that day into that abyss.

·   ·   ·

The same evening, an hour or two later, an American embassy van with driver, two-way radio and armed guard calls for us at the hotel. Outside the van's windows the sights of this teeming Third World city press in from all sides: sidewalks overflowing with children, open-air markets, dogs, pigs, and chickens, buses with people packed on the roofs, women carrying goods on their heads, trucks and motorcycles belching gray-black smoke. Yet strangely, all is quiet. It is as if we are watching a movie with the sound off. For on the inside of each window is a layer of bulletproof plastic about an inch thick. Lead shields, the guard tells us, are inside the doors and underneath the van. We glide on toward dinner, encased in silence.

Of the various branches of El Salvador's armed forces, one of the most brutal is the National Guard. It was National Guard soldiers who murdered the American nuns in 1980; who tortured with electricity the husband of Ana Margarita Gasteazoro, whom we met at the women's prison; who poured acid on Rafael Antonio Carrias, whom we met at the men's prison; and who sliced off the breast of the woman we met this afternoon. This van is now taking us to a dinner party at a large U.S. embassy residence. The guest of honor is General Carlos Eugenio Vides Casanova, commander of the National Guard.

The general is a stocky, unsmiling man of medium height. Tonight he wears no uniform, merely a *guayabera,* a Salvadoran embroidered shirt. Other military guests—two Salvadoran colonels; Colonel John Waghelstein, the chief U.S. military adviser here; and another U.S. officer—are similarly in *guayaberas.* They look indistinguishable from any dinner party of middle-class Salvadorans. So: is this, too, what the Inferno is like? Will its proprietor dress normally, give briefings, express his concern for civil liberties?

General Vides Casanova is a neighbor, says our host Kenneth

Bleakley, the embassy deputy chief of mission; he lives a few doors away. And, he adds, the general is very concerned about human rights. "Why, look here . . ." and he takes from a table an impressively thick, black, ring-binder notebook with dozens of loose-leaf pages. Each page is a list—name, date, serial number, and so forth—of National Guard soldiers suspended or disciplined for various offenses. Somehow, though, none of this disciplining has ever resulted in a single Salvadoran security man ever being convicted of killing a civilian. When I start to raise this point, the general says, "These matters are now in the hands of the judiciary. There is nothing I can do."

Several streams of visiting Americans have converged here for dinner tonight: our delegation, a former Senate aide, a visiting academic, a group of congressional staffers who have been traveling around Latin America inspecting something or other. Much Washington gossip is traded over drinks.

A high wall topped with barbed wire surrounds a lawn and a crescent-shaped swimming pool. We sit down to eat at two tables on the covered patio, under a vaulted A-frame ceiling of stained and varnished wood. At my table are, among others, Colonel Waghelstein, who is a big, blunt man with a cigar; and a Salvadoran, Lieutenant Colonel Ricardo Cienfuegos, who is slightly tipsy. I ask Cienfuegos his job. He describes his position in the military hierarchy, then adds, "But my real job is to talk to the gringos."

I ask him how the war is going. He wants to talk instead about human rights, he says. For unclear reasons, he asks that it all be off the record. So be it. He launches into a long and impassioned spiel about law, social justice, and democracy. When he is finished, he turns to Waghelstein and asks, "Did I do all right?"

"You did just fine, my boy, just fine!" Waghelstein booms and slaps Cienfuegos on the back.

Cienfuegos's name appears on a list of conspirators caught in a failed 1980 attempt to install rightist leader Roberto D'Aubuisson in power.

(Some two years after that evening, Cienfuegos was shot and killed next to the tennis court of his posh country club. His assassins covered his body with a rebel flag. They had gotten into the club by dressing in tennis clothes.)

Over dinner, Colonel Waghelstein, whom the American embassy people call "Wag," talks abut his service as a counterinsurgency expert all over the world: Vietnam, Bolivia, the Dominican Republic, the Philippines, and Venezuela, which he seemed to have liked best. "The Vennies," he says, "the Vennies really knew how to do things right." You have to back up your antiguerrilla actions with "ag reform," he explains. Without paying attention to "the social side of this thing," you'll never get anywhere.

Waghelstein is sad that the U .S. Army is slighting his specialty, antiguerrilla warfare, which now goes under the name of "low-intensity conflict." At the U.S. Army staff college at Fort Leavenworth, they have cut the number of low-intensity-conflict hours in the curriculum way down, and he's trying to get it raised again. Despite everything, there is something likably direct about the man, in contrast to so many other officials we've met. He is visibly impatient with the rhetoric he has been ordered to use, most of it crafted to avoid reminding anyone of Vietnam: "You get your advisers in there . . . uh . . . we're not allowed to call them advisers: now they're *trainers* . . ."

Meanwhile, at the next table, two voices are rising steadily higher. One is General Vides Casanova's. The other belongs to Gino Lofredo, the organizer of our delegation. For a week now, with little rest, he has been our travel agent, tour guide, nursemaid, chief translator; for a week before our arrival he was here, carefully planning and setting up our tightly packed schedule. Now, the last night of our stay, he has little patience left. When Vides Casanova denies that troops under his command ever torture prisoners, Lofredo calls him "a liar and a murderer."

Vides Casanova hotly begins a tirade about American slavery, racism, Hiroshima, and Vietnam: after all that, how can Americans have the nerve to accuse Salvadorans of anything? Then he says, "Step outside, and let's settle this *hombre a hombre.*" Our host, Kenneth Bleakley, looks alarmed.

Since on the street outside are seven or eight men with submachine guns (at least three appear assigned to this house, and the Salvadoran officers have brought their own bodyguards), Lofredo wisely declines.

Bleakley then tries to keep the conversation under control by calling on people to speak, by name, like a teacher in class. When this does not work and the glares continue, he rises, clinks his knife on a glass, and makes a little speech saying that he has always found the military men present to be fully cooperative in dealing with human-rights matters, and that frank exchanges of ideas are valuable, and that now it is time for everyone to go home.

.   .   .

The morning after this encounter, everyone in the delegation is uneasy on the long drive out to the airport. Salvadoran soldiers lounge near the vacant tollbooths on the highway, but none of them stop us.

To the puzzlement of the other passengers, our group breaks into a cheer as the plane lifts off. Later, as we wait between flights at the Miami airport, Mary Travers gathers us around a cassette player and plays a new song by her singing partner Paul Stookey.

> And if 60 million seems too much to spend
>   in El Salvador,
> They say for half a billion they could get it right:
> Bomb all day and burn all night
> Until there's not a living thing upright
>   in El Salvador.
> They'll continue training troops in the U.S.A.
> Catch the nuns that got away
> And teach the military hands to play
>   "South of the Border"
> And kill the people to set them free:
> Who put this price on their liberty?
> Don't you think it's time to leave
>   El Salvador?

1983

Isle of Flowers, House of Slaves

These days few spots are purely in the Third World or the First. In Dakar, Senegal, the sun-drenched, crumbling one-time colonial capital of French West Africa, bits of Europe are scattered through surrounding Africa like an archipelago. The First World islands are sleek, high-rise resort hotels, where the temperature drops twenty degrees as soon as you step into their aggressively air-conditioned interiors. Virtually all the guests are white, mostly from France. In the lobbies are newsstands, boutiques, travel agencies, and bars where a liter bottle of Vittel mineral water costs the equivalent of several days' wages for a Senegalese laborer. Many hotels have their own beaches. One of the biggest, the Teranga, is separated from its beach but has its own private bridge across an intervening road filled with packed buses and black pedestrians. And so the European visitor can go direct from hotel to beach without setting foot in Africa along the way.

Farther down that road, iron fences have gaps in them; coils of barbed wire on top have half rusted away. A defunct lighthouse holds a giant rusted lamp fixture. As I jog along the road early one morning, men are urinating in the street, getting up after sleeping the night in the ruins of buildings, underneath roadside bushes or on the seawall. The tens of thousands of people in Dakar without homes are not only from inland Senegal but also from other countries of West Africa. They have come to this port city in a desperate search for work. Dakar's population has ballooned from eighty thousand in 1945 to well over a million today.

A sign on a dilapidated gate facing the seaside road says AMBASSADE DE FRANCE—PRIVÉE. But the embassy clearly moved elsewhere long ago, for through the open gate is visible a half-disintegrated building where people living as squatters in the basement are now emerging to do their morning washing at an outside faucet. A mile or two away, in the center of town, a public fountain is dry, because of a long drought. Homeless migrants sleep in squares and parks. Some of these grand squares still have monuments celebrating long-departed French officials. One statue is of André Maginot, who was minister of colonies before building his ill-fated Line.

The hope that pulls migrants to Dakar comes from the city's status as a regional as well as a national capital. Many offices that once housed French colonial administrators now are the West African headquarters for various international bureaucracies—United Nations agencies, the World Bank, and private aid organizations—trying with little success to heal Africa's economic wounds. Partly because so many thousands of aid officials live here, driving cars with special green license plates, Senegal has gotten a large share of assistance funds. However, a sense of despair lurks outside the hotel terraces and beaches and casinos: there is talk of AIDS, which is working its way westward across the continent, and of cholera, and each day crowded trains and buses bring more people from the continent's interior, seeking jobs that aren't there.

.   .   .

Almost anywhere in the Third World a white American tourist feels conspicuous, but nowhere more so than in Africa. Your skin so immediately brands you as a possible source of tips, handouts, purchases. My family and I try to avoid all this, traveling light so that we can decline the services of the vast flock of porters at the airport. But there is no disguise, for anybody with a white skin here is rich beyond measure: the price of a fish dinner at a beach-front restaurant could feed one of those homeless people by the roadside for several weeks. You cannot walk anywhere without people immediately falling into step beside you, thrusting items at you, speeding up or slowing down as you do: *D'où venez-vous?* Where you stay? *Guten Tag!* You like buy masks? Carvings? *Mon frère, il est à New York!*

Our hotel is not one of the skyscraper islands, but our room has a powerful air conditioner nonetheless. We turn it off and open the window to let in the sea air; each day when we come back after the room is cleaned, the window is shut and the air conditioner on. Something else evidently happens during these room-cleaning sessions: one day we find an embroidered belt and several pairs of earrings missing from my wife Arlie's suitcase. It is a curious theft, for none of these things were worth more than a few dollars; we had brought the earrings along to give away as presents. And several far more valuable items—my portable tape recorder and electric razor—are untouched. We are puzzled. Despite the country's poverty, whoever stole these things was obviously motivated more by beauty than money. Was it a woman?

We decide we ought to complain, but not too stridently. We don't want to be Ugly Americans.

That evening, as we are waiting in the corridor for our children to come out of their room, the hotel manager walks by: a smiling Senegalese man, exuding briskness and energy.

"You are having a good time?" he asks, "The hotel is good? Everything is all right?"

The hotel is fine, we say, except some things that were taken.

"That's terrible!" he exclaims, "That must not happen! You must get them back! I will see to it."

·   ·   ·

From *Dakar: Outpost of Two Hemispheres,* by Emil Lengyel (New York, 1941):

"Facing Dakar is the island of Gorée, surprisingly similar in location to Governor's Island in the port of New York. . . . Even though small, its strategic importance is great, and it is heavily fortified, in anticipation of grave events. It was the principal settlement of the French along this coast for many generations . . . and because of its sturdy cannon it kept the troublesome natives at a distance at a time when they were less placid than they are now."

Gorée was strategic indeed, not just for the French but also for the English, Dutch, and Portuguese, all of whom controlled the island and defended it against "troublesome natives" at one time or another. For this small island some two miles offshore from Dakar was a major transshipment point for the slave trade. Of the 12 to 15 million Africans shipped in chains to the New World over the centuries, an estimated 1.2 million of them passed through Gorée. The island's location in a sheltered bay, at the start of the route across the Atlantic, made it a convenient spot for slaves to be sold from coastal dealer to trans-Atlantic trader, to be inspected, weighed, and sorted, then branded on the shoulder and shipped on to the New World.

Of those slaves who embarked on the rough, sweltering Middle Passage, perhaps 20 percent or more died on the journey. A still higher percentage, historians say, died in captivity before even leaving Africa, some of them in holding cells in places like Gorée. And so we take the twenty-minute ferry ride to the island one day; it seems as important a place to visit as the infamous railway platform at Auschwitz where Dr. Mengele made his selections.

Unexpectedly, though, a somber mood is difficult to maintain. Gorée turns out to be a lovely spot. There is a festive air on the rusty boat that crosses the sparkling water from Dakar. At the beach near the ferry dock, the children of French tourists swim together with Senegalese youngsters. Bold teenage swimmers exuberantly clamber up the moving ship's sides and use the top deck as a diving platform.

The island is stunningly beautiful: gentle surf washes all sides; there are no cars; narrow lanes wind between sun-faded pink, yellow, and ocher stucco buildings with terra-cotta roofs. These pastel houses have wrought-iron balconies, columned porticoes, walls covered with brilliant red bougainvillea. The breeze billows a white curtain from a window. These are the old slave-traders' homes, many with holding cells in the basement. The people now living in them commute to Dakar on the ferry, and include a few Europeans and Americans, drawn by the island's haunting beauty. Scrawny goats, chickens, and sheep wander the lanes. The women on the streets here, as in Dakar, are strikingly beautiful: very tall, with smooth black skin and slightly Semitic features. The island has a restaurant, a few cafés serving beer and fresh seafood, a school or two, a church, a mosque perched next to the surf. The sandy streets are shaded by coconut palms and baobab trees; the Rue des Gourmets runs parallel to the Rue des Donjons. Can those slaves have passed through here? It is hard to believe.

The Maison des Esclaves is a stone building on the water's edge. From a courtyard, twin semicircular stairways climb to a second floor. The ground floor is a series of interconnected cells that could hold up to two hundred slaves waiting to be loaded onto trans-Atlantic ships. They have elongated slit windows only a few inches wide. Passageways connect all the cells with a small stone doorway, no bigger than the front door of an average home. This was called the Door of No Return. It led to the wharf where the slave ships docked, and through it passed those departing on the deadly journey. In 1787, the year of our Constitution, twenty-two packed shiploads of slaves left Gorée for the Americas.

The House of Slaves has a longtime curator, Boubacar Joseph N'Diaye. In a forceful, booming voice, he tells all who visit about the horrors of the slave trade. There is no money for exhibits; the only signs are in N'Diaye's bold handwriting, in French, written with felt-tipped pen on paper and taped to the whitewashed walls. The signs are more moralistic than informative, but perhaps that's appropriate. On the second floor, where the slave merchants had their offices in airy, high-ceilinged rooms that open onto a veranda, N'Diaye's sign reads: HOW COULD THEY LIVE ABOVE, WITH WHAT WAS HAPPENING BELOW?

· · ·

The friend we have come to Dakar to visit, the Ghanaian-born novelist Ayi Kwei Armah, who now lives here, asks about my visit to the House of Slaves. I tell him I was moved by that sign in the merchant's quarters.

"Yes," he says, "but you could write the same thing about people here today: 'How can they live above, with what is happening below?'" I see what he means, for this is the subject of most of his novels, which are widely read in Africa.

In those air-conditioned islands of Europe that dot this city, the buildings that are now government ministries, corporate offices, and international aid agencies, the officials are often Africans as well as Europeans—people earning French or American manager's wages in a society where the per capita income is $330 a year. The gap between this tiny elite and the rest of the population is vast, and has widened far more since Senegal became independent. Among its signs are Peugeots and BMWs on potholed streets, elegant homes with VCRs and walled gardens, fenced-off and guarded suburban housing developments.

Ayi Kwei tells us that the old colonial distinctions between *blancs* and *noirs* and *petits blancs* (French skilled workers) has been further subdivided: Europeans are now known as *blanc blancs* and Africans with European wage levels as *blanc noirs*. Another ramification of the vogue for things white is a current fad among

Senegalese women for skin lightening. This often is disastrous: doctors here now must frequently treat scars and blotches, sometimes permanent, caused by the acids used in skin-lightening creams.

.   .   .

When we return to our hotel room that evening, the earrings and belt have miraculously reappeared. What happened? Is there a maid, known for her love of such things, but who is always forgiven? Or were the objects only borrowed for an evening, to be worn, shown off, and returned?

.   .   .

No one on a brief tourist visit can fully understand Africa's current misery, but certainly what one sees in a few days bears out the common diagnoses. Those hotel-islands of Europe are mostly European-owned as well; the profits from visitors like ourselves mostly leave the country rather than stay. And Senegal is reeling from the same basic problem confronting most of Africa: its economy, as in colonial days, is geared to producing raw materials for Europe and America. For hundreds of years the raw materials were humans; today they are crops. Worldwide the price of raw materials is going down. This has been good for multinational corporations, but disastrous for the Senegalese villager. Senegal's principal crop is peanuts, which provide over half the rural population's income. But in real terms, the price of peanuts today has fallen to less than one-third of what it was when Senegal gained independence in 1960. No amount of foreign-aid bandaging can fix that. During the African famine of the 1970s, aid agencies were sending grain to starving Senegalese; giant farms near Dakar controlled by the California-based Bud Antle Inc. were shipping planeloads of melons, tomatoes, and eggplants to Paris.

The upshot of all this is that more money flows out of Africa each year than flows in. Even the very money itself seems stricken: the French-speaking African countries, who share a common currency, cannot afford to even print enough bills to replace those that wear out. These bills are like no others I've seen anywhere: rumpled, torn, faded to the point of being almost illegible, the texture of fragile, threadbare silk.

The grand plaza in the center of Dakar is called the Place de

L'Indépendance. But one day the newspaper carries a story that a committee of two hundred prominent local citizens has been formed, to plan how the city will celebrate next year's bicentenary—of the *French* Revolution. Before leaving Dakar, I go to the office of Air Afrique to try to confirm our tickets home. A big crowd of Senegalese presses up against the counter; there will clearly be a wait of hours. An airline official beckons me aside and sends me to an upstairs office. Because—it dawns on me as I'm halfway up the stairs—I am white. Independence for this part of Africa has yet to arrive.

1988

Empire's End

A MOSCOW JOURNAL

Arrival, January 1991

Our plane lands after dark. Sitting in the front seat of a taxi, I start to put on the seat belt. "*Ne nada!*" [you don't have to] says the driver. Russians are very macho about driving. We tear into Moscow at frighteningly high speed. On the snowy, slippery road, cars zoom back and forth between lanes without signaling. Oncoming cars and trucks appear as faint, paired points of yellow light: a crust of sandy snow has splashed up from the street and frozen to their headlights.

The Apartment

At last, after many months of long-distance arrangements, we arrive at the apartment where Arlie, our fourteen-year-old Gabriel, and I will live for some six months while I do the research for my book.* Our building is an enormous relic of the Stalin era: eight stories high, extending around all four sides of a large city block. The entryway is filthy, dark, strewn with cigarette butts and apple cores. The tiny elevator sounds like a meat grinder. But in the apartment itself, thick walls and sturdy double-paned windows keep out the cold. We are the only foreigners in the building.

The only thing missing is most of the furniture we were promised, such as beds and desks. "The workmen were too drunk to bring it today," explains the friend of a friend who has arranged all

---

The Unquiet Ghost: Russians Remember Stalin (New York: Viking Penguin, 1994).

this. The apartment has a chain-pull toilet, exposed pipes everywhere, and a plug that doesn't quite fit the bathtub. But we were prepared for that, bringing a flat, one-size-fits-all rubber disk from home. We feel like explorers on safari, pleased at carrying the right equipment.

In preparation for us, the apartment has just been repainted. Thick light green paint covers some of the cracks where windows meet frames, making them impossible to open. On the other hand, if the windows *did* open, Arctic-temperature air would come through, so perhaps it's just as well. Soviet economic shortages include whatever is the ingredient that makes paint dry: our newly painted doors stay sticky for days.

The window of my deskless study looks across the street to a vacant lot with two snow-covered piles of pipe. Something is being built—or perhaps demolished.

A Party

Most of the guests are from the network of people who found and fixed up the apartment for us. This is an ad hoc business venture that technically is not quite legal, for the country is in a twilight period when the old state-controlled economy is collapsing but rules for a new one are not in place.

One of these people I've known for four days; the others I've never met before this evening. But within an hour we are talking about the meaning of good and evil. These people lost three close friends in an auto accident six months ago, and they talk about their belief that the spirits of the dead live on among those who loved them. One woman, Lena, whose fiancé died in the accident, says she believes you can cure yourself of grief by doing good. There are more good people in the world than bad, she says, and if you treat people as if they were good, it will bring out the goodness in them. Is there anywhere else in the world where I would be talking so quickly of such things with people I had never known before?

There is also much talk of the supernatural. Andrei, a computer specialist, is a firm believer. *Extrasyense* is the Russian word they use. He says his mother, a gynecologist, can touch a woman's stomach and reliably predict the sex of an unborn child. A friend of his can run his hand over a computer circuit board and tell where the problem chip is; he can *feel* electricity flowing. "Many people like that in this country," says Andrei.

At midnight, they turn down the lights and light a candle. It is a feast day of the Orthodox Church.

Accreditation

Foreign journalists working in the fast-crumbling Soviet Union must be accredited. For this I go to the Foreign Ministry's sleek, modern press center. The man responsible for my case is a dapper young diplomat, speaking excellent English, wearing an elegant suit and the only well-shined shoes I've seen after a week in snowy, muddy Moscow.

Despite his suave exterior, his world is collapsing around him. "You must report all your movements outside Moscow to me beforehand," he says, mechanically reciting a prepared spiel, "twenty-four hours in advance when you go to major cities or republic capitals, forty-eight hours in advance when you go to other cities. You are required to report the names of the hotels where you will be staying, and your Aeroflot flight numbers . . . but . . . I know Aeroflot reservations are not too definite these days.

"Certain areas of the country are strictly off-limits to foreigners. They are marked on the map on the wall over there . . . hmmmm—at least the map used to be over there, but someone seems to have taken it down."

"Do you have another copy?" I ask.

"Try the news kiosk downstairs," he shrugs. "They might have it."

Bureaucracy I

I find that we can get the *International Herald Tribune* delivered to our mailbox each day. So I go to the agency that handles this, give the people our address, and take out my wallet to pay. Can I pay in dollars? Not possible, says the secretary. In rubles? Also not possible. By credit card? Not possible. By check? Absolutely not possible (personal checks are still unknown here).

Instead, she tells me, the bill can only be paid in cash at a certain bank. I trudge some blocks through the snow to the bank. After I stand in line for a while, unsmiling clerks behind the counter go to work on the task of accepting my money. They fill out forms, make entries in ledgers, take papers to be checked by a supervisor in a back room, stamp documents, separate carbon copies from originals, scrutinize my passport and visa, and finally give me a form to be presented, with my money, to a cashier at the other end of the bank counter.

Various other people are waiting for the cashier as well. We foreigners—German students, Scottish businessmen, Sri Lankan diplomats—roll our eyes in silent solidarity. The waiting Russians are resigned and expressionless. A take-a-number system, a startling innovation for Russia, allows us all to sit down and wait in front of a TV. It shows a rousing Japanese samurai movie with a Russian voice-over—watched, with total absorption, by the bank guards as well. Perhaps also with waiting customers in mind, a Ping-Pong table stands in a corner of the bank lobby. No paddles or balls are in sight.

Finally, the cashier takes my money and sends me back to the other end of the bank counter to collect a receipt. I then trudge back through the snow to take this receipt to the newspaper agency to certify that I have paid. Paying this bill has taken an entire morning.

Winter

At 8:00 A.M., it is still almost completely dark. One night a terrific gust of wind blows open our bedroom windows. I nail them as far shut as they will go, then fill up the cracks with strips of torn newspaper, and put wide tape over that. In the morning the outer pane of glass is frosted over. The wind carries great whorls of snow down from the roof.

At the end of January, Moscow has the coldest weather in a dozen years: −35 F. every night for about ten days. As I'm doing an interview in the unheated waiting room of a notary's office, the ink freezes in my pen. Another day I walk through a large pedestrian underpass. The crowd of people in this confined space heats and moistens the air: when it meets the still colder street air, it condenses. Coming out of the underpass, we are all wreathed in fog, as if emerging from an underground cloud chamber.

Steam comes out of gratings around buildings, and the trees above them are covered with hoarfrost. During the cold snap, forty-two people in the city are hospitalized with frostbite, according to the newspaper. I've bought myself a good Russian fur hat, but often I'm the only man on the street with the ear flaps down. Occasionally I see men with no gloves.

Indoors, strangely, it sometimes gets too hot. There are no knobs on the radiators. The heat is piped into the building from a giant plant that heats this whole part of town. It's either on or off, and this time of year it's on, full blast, day and night. When a room gets too warm, we have to open a window.

The cold does not deter people from having fun. One Sunday, with the outdoor temperature risen to a near-tropical + 20 F., we join thousands of Muscovites taking the Metro to Gorky Park, to see an exhibition of ice sculptures. Nearby, a troupe puts on a variety show on an open-air platform: clowns, costumed folk dancers, Father Christmas, the Snow Queen, and three dancing bears. Just as we rejoice in having found something so Russian, one of the bears is led on stage and dances to "Rock Around the Clock."

At the Novodevichy Monastery another weekend, we find people skiing across a frozen pond. Someone has chopped a hole in the ice, and a man in a bathing suit scoops out a few chunks of floating slush, jumps in, and vanishes underwater. He reappears, calls out, "Very pleasant! Good for the health!" to us, then climbs out and stands in his bathing suit, hands on hips, calmly watching the skiers.

Meanwhile, through all this winter weather, a mystery endures: the two piles of pipe in the snow-covered vacant lot across the street from our apartment. One pile is twisted, rusted old pipe; one pile is new pipe. What are they building? Are they waiting for spring? Occasionally one or two people trudge over the snowdrifts and poke through the piles, looking for something to salvage.

Telephones I

Our phone sometimes gives a feeble, abbreviated chirp—the beginning of a ring. I race to pick up the receiver, but all I hear is a busy signal. That's what whoever is trying to call us is also hearing, it turns out.

"Your line is weak," says Andrei, the computer expert. Try

calling a strong number: the time, the weather. Maybe that will help give your line strength."

The "American Settlement"

Just as Sturbridge Village reproduces a nineteenth-century town in present-day Massachusetts, so there is a reproduction of an American town in the center of Moscow. I sometimes hear Russians refer to it, in a tone that suggests the mystery of unimaginable luxuries, as *amerikanski posyolok,* "the American settlement."

What they are talking about is the U.S. embassy compound, surrounded by an eight-foot-high red-brick wall on all sides. The compound is perhaps a hundred yards wide and a quarter of a mile long. Inside the walls is the new, unused embassy building, mired in an endless controversy about Soviet microphones embedded in the beams. But far more striking is the remainder of the compound, which is very much in use. Fifty or sixty American-style town houses, with cars parked in front, house diplomats and their families. There is a large school, gym, and basketball court, swimming pool, weights room, sauna, bowling alley, airline ticket office, cafeteria, TV room, bar, barbershop, and a grocery store about the size of a 7-11. Most of these facilities have their entrances on a wide walkway, like an indoor shopping mall.

All of this is designed so that Americans in the embassy will do their socializing, drinking, eating, and mating with each other and not with Soviets—who are, with extremely rare and closely chaperoned exceptions, not allowed into the compound. Gabriel tells us that some students at the school, where he goes, say they often don't go "off compound" for days at a time. The father of one of his classmates tells us sadly about the embassy's "no-frat" policy: no American with a security clearance is allowed into a Soviet home without another, cleared American being present, and even that is discouraged.

Food I

Like the other Westerners in Moscow, we are the beneficiaries of monetary apartheid, for we can shop at the several dozen stores that take foreign currency. We use the small new Finnish supermarket, whose only drawback is that the labels are all in Finnish. We read them aloud at dinner: is *avastuupulanenaa* really that mustard we wanted, or is it yellow shoe polish? We eat a lot of what we call Baltic Mystery Fish: frozen fillets, with indecipherable text and a fishing boat on the package. Another American tells us he recently bought a bottle of what he thought was apple juice, for the label showed an apple. He took a big swallow and found it was vinegar.

The Soviet state food stores are crowded and dimly lit. Several near us always have long lines of people waiting for stubby carrots, wilted cabbages, and occasional fatty cuts of beef. On a rare day, there are a few gaunt, emaciated chickens, that look as if they had collapsed after staggering across the finish line of a triathlon. The clerks are rude, grumble at the customers, and walk off for unannounced breaks. A pleasant exception is a bread store in our building, where we buy delicious Russian black bread, with a touch of something (molasses?) that gives it a wonderful aroma.

Because the ruble is almost worthless when converted to dollars, a loaf of bread costs us the equivalent of about one American cent. On the other hand, in a hard-currency store near us, Kleenex goes for $4.50 a box.

Sometimes we shop at one of the city's open markets, where middlemen sell farm products for rubles, but at free-floating prices. An enormous array of fruits, nuts, vegetables, and dried fruit is on display; every kind of meat, from a goose to tiny suckling pigs, lies freshly slaughtered and bloody on newspapers that are spread on a table or on the sidewalk. Unlike the state store clerks, the traders here *want* you to buy. "Sir, try this! A small piece, just for you!" The prices, however, are five to ten times what they are in the state stores, so the average Soviet can only come here for special occasions—or if he or she has some source of extra income.

Most of these food merchants are from the Caucasus. The same is true of the two men who one snowy day drive an enormous trailer truck up to our local Metro stop and quickly begin selling fresh melons out the back of it. Muscovites make many racist remarks about these merchants, who seem to be profiting so much from the changing economy. (Those making the really big money, high Soviet bureaucrats siphoning riches from the publicly owned resources into their own pockets, are more likely to be ethnic Russians. But they are out of sight, not behind the counter in the market stalls every day.) When Muscovites talk angrily about the "blacks," it is these Armenians, Azerbaijanis, Georgians, and so on that they're talking about. And Russians have an expression they use when things go well: *"Now* we're living like white people!"

Language

For the first time since I was a teenager trying to get up enough courage to call a girl for a date, I am terrified of making phone calls. I rehearse, I procrastinate, I have a script in front of me; finally, eyes shut, I take the plunge. Why is it so frightening to telephone a stranger in a language you speak imperfectly? Probably because you can't give the puzzled frown that shows you don't understand, or see the hand gestures or facial expressions that might help you comprehend the other person's flood of unfamiliar words.

Who invented this impossible language, anyway, with its double-rooted verbs bethorned with prefixes, suffixes, and infixes? I spent many months before coming trying to improve my Russian. But immersion in an entire country of people speaking this tongue is like war: nothing you can study beforehand fully prepares you. Oddly, I can, however clumsily and incorrectly, usually say what I want in Russian. The problem is understanding the response. Before an interview, I never know whether I'll be able to grasp 90 percent of what someone is telling me, or 50 percent.

My highest rate of comprehension, 99 percent at least, is with Igor Dolutsky, a high school teacher experimenting with new ways of teaching Russian history. He knows how to speak in a lively and simple way, so that even the dumbest student in the class will pay attention and get the point. That's just my speed: I can understand every word. My lowest rate, less than 50 percent, is with retired secret police officers: endless acronyms, bureaucratic jargon, no experience talking to foreigners who know Russian less than fluently.

Happily, these problems don't impede the interviews for my book, for I just have to ask the right questions. I tape-record everything, and later give the tape to a wonderfully skilled transcriptionalist, Tanya Pogossova, who transcribes the answers directly into English. If in an interview I'm not following what someone is telling me, all I have to do is say, "And then what happened?" or

"Tell me a little more about that!" or "And why do you think this is so?" just to keep the person talking. And a few days or weeks later, I'm able to read it all in English. Sometimes I'm amazed at what's there. What luxury!

Bureaucracy II

Our friend Hermann finally gets through on the phone from Germany, and says he is coming to visit for a few days; can I reserve him a hotel room? I walk over to the hotel two blocks from our apartment. The clerk shakes his head disapprovingly. An American citizen making a reservation for a German citizen? It can't be done. Reservations for foreigners, he says, can be made only by a telex—from the country a visitor is coming from. Or, he concedes grudgingly, my strange request could be discussed if it is made in writing, on embassy stationery.

Hermann sleeps on our couch.

A Dacha

The spur-of-the-moment invitation comes in a phone call from Sergei Kakovkin, actor and playwright, whom I had met in the United States last year at my Russian-language summer school. "Can you come to our *dacha* for dinner? A friend is driving out from the city, and she'll pick you up—in twenty minutes."

The drive is only forty minutes or so. But we have the feeling of going much farther. Leaving Moscow behind us, we soon veer off the highway, then go down a smaller road, past cottages deep in snow, with windows glowing in the darkness. Then comes a short walk along a path trampled down in the snow, and then a feeling that a golden circle has opened to include us.

Sergei's wife, Anna Radionova, also a playwright, rushes out and kisses us all, although she has never seen Arlie and Gabriel before. The house is wooden, high-ceilinged, ramshackle, with uneven floors and a homemade look: exposed wires and unfinished rough boards. After quickly introducing us to his guests, Sergei takes us up a staircase so steep that it is more like a ladder, to a small loft where he and Anna read and work: a lovely, warm, peaceful spot, its walls covered with bookshelves and with posters, in many languages, of the plays and movies in which Sergei has acted or which one or the other of them has written. It is the work space of people who love their work. There he sits us down in their two reading chairs and casts his arm across the room proudly, as if to say: this space is us, through it you can know us. Would an American do that? Or would he show off, instead, a more public space: a den, a pool, a backyard, a view? Russians have a sharper line than we between in and out, and at this moment we are being invited in. Just as Sergei had shifted to the informal second person singular as soon as we crossed his doorstep.

Except for Fazil Iskander, a well-known novelist, and Alexander Orlov, a director, all the guests are actors and actresses. Much of the conversation is too fast for my Russian, but it doesn't matter: they mime out the various parts when telling a story, or occasionally throw in bits of English and French for our benefit. In the middle of it all, Orlov turns to Iskander and begins a long monologue about how the roots of Russia's miseries go back not only to the Revolution but also to Peter the Great.

What is the source of the almost magical warmth we feel? It is a combination of that all-embracing Russian hospitality and the special camaraderie of artists who have worked together. Twice during the evening, our hosts, Sergei and Anna, mount the ladder-staircase to sit on a step together and survey everyone's enjoyment from on high, as if they are triumphant directors watching a performance on opening night.

To combat the food shortages, many of the guests have brought a dish or a bottle with them. Amid the food on the table are huge piles of *blini*—pancakes with jam and sour cream, traditionally eaten today, the day before the beginning of Lent. To drink, there is vodka, Georgian wine, and strong, cloudy, greenish *samogen,* or moonshine, made in the nearby village.

After dinner, Sergei says, "Let's go for a walk in the forest!" We pull two sleds for the children. We tramp twenty minutes or so down a road, under filigrees of black branches against a sky whose ghostly whiteness reflects the light from distant Moscow. At a little pond, there is a slope the children can sled down in the moonlight. On the way back, Orlov explains that on this feast day it is supposed to bring you happiness if you roll or fall in the snow. He pushes Gabriel down in the snow, saying, "Happiness! Happiness!"

Telephones II

One day the phone stops ringing. We can still make outgoing calls, but for an entire week, we receive none. Finally I discover what's happened: they've changed our phone number. Without telling us.

What, I wonder, happens to one's old number in such a situation? Almost certainly, it is immediately given to someone else. One piece of evidence suggesting this is another telephone adventure. We are trying to reach a colleague of Arlie's who has told us he will be coming to Moscow and staying at the Hotel Sputnik. We call the listed number and reach a man whose weary, exasperated voice makes clear he is saying something for the hundredth time: "No this is *not* the Hotel Sputnik."

Further research turns up a new number for the hotel.

"Do you have an American staying there, named Michael Burawoy?"

A pause, a shuffling of papers. "No."

A few minutes later we remember that Michael is a British citizen, and try calling again.

"Do you have an Englishman staying there, named Michael Burawoy?

More shuffling of papers. "Yes."

He's not in, however. And the operator seems unfamiliar with the concept of taking a message.

Right-wingers

One Saturday afternoon right-wingers demonstrate in the Manege square just outside the Kremlin wall. One voice floating out of the loudspeakers is that of Mikhail Nozhkin, an actor: "We are witnessing the breakdown of the country, the breakdown of the state, the breakdown of morality, the breakdown of our historical legacy."

It is Soviet Army and Navy Day, and thousands of the demonstrators are, people say, soldiers out of uniform who have been ordered to come. A good many others are soldiers *in* uniform. Many older members of the crowd are World War II veterans—stolid, dumpy men in their seventies and eighties now, their overcoats paved with battle ribbons. Occasionally one carries a picture of Stalin.

Mingling happily with these Communist Party types are conservatives of a different sort: the monarchists. One sign has a tsarist double eagle and the words FOR THE 21ST CENTURY. Three young men wear uniforms of the Russian troops who fought Napoleon: swords, leather shot pouches, tricornered plumed hats, high leather boots. A man brings up his child to be photographed with them, holding a musket.

Another demonstrator carries a sign bordered with little Stars of David and punning on the word *vzglad* [view], the name of the popular, liberal TV show recently forced off the air, THE DICTION AND ACCENT OF THE RADIO AND TV COMMENTATORS REVEAL THE INFLUENCE ON THEIR "VIEW": AMERICA AND ISRAEL.

Food II

Week by week, we watch the quality of food on sale decreasing. Russians are the most hospitable people on earth, and are forever inviting us to dinner. Perhaps half the time there is no meat. Often they warn us apologetically in advance. The rest of the time, we never know if we are eating up the one decent piece of meat they've been able to get all week. We always take a small canned Danish ham as a gift. When Soviet friends come to our house for dinner, they usually bring hothouse fresh flowers—which, surprisingly, are on sale cheaply everywhere.

Despite its other disasters, and despite a tiny elite living in great luxury at the very top, one thing the Soviet Union achieved was a great measure of economic equality. This is fast vanishing. And as the gulf between rich and poor opens up, the biggest visible gap is between those who have a source of foreign currency— relatives abroad or a job doing business with foreigners—and those who don't. That gulf is fast widening, and visible nowhere more than on peoples' dinner tables.

Privileges

The loudest noise in our four-room apartment is the constant whir of electric meters—four of them. Before we moved in, this was a communal apartment, and at one point held three different families. And so there was one meter for each, plus one for the common spaces—hall, bathroom, kitchen. In the other apartment on our landing, six rooms are shared by four families—ten people altogether.

Several people now have made the same gesture, a sad, envious little shake of the head, when they heard we were renting an apartment. So many people here have to wait half their lives to get out of a communal apartment and into a single-family one. (And even then, single-family often means parents, grown children, and grandparents all living together.) Then we just whisk in here with our dollars and get one. It feels like having white skin in the old South Africa.

Readers

One of the enduring mysteries about Russia is why this nation that has gotten itself into such an awful mess is also one of the world's most literate.

One day a week, to take us grocery shopping at the Finnish store and on other errands, we hire a tiny car and its enormous owner, a retired truck and cab driver, a huge, shy man with a fur hat. Victor speaks a rough, slangy Russian, of which I can understand only 50 percent at best. But, like so many people at all class levels here, he is a fanatical reader. In the car, he reads happily by the hour while waiting for us. One morning I ask him about today's book, by an author I had never heard of. "An excellent example of eighteenth-century style," he says.

One evening, while I am waiting on a snow-covered sidewalk, two middle-aged women slowly walk past me. Each carries a plastic shopping bag. By the light of street lamps, one is reading aloud to the other from a book of poetry.

At a food store near us, an older man with a pleasant face seems to have the job of stocking the shelves—easy work because there's not much food. One evening I find him sitting in a chair by the shelves, reading Varlam Shalamov, the great short-story writer of the *gulag*. "I've read that same book in English," I tell him. We agree Shalamov is a great writer. "And it's important," the man says, "that these things be *documented,* by someone who speaks with the authority of having been there." I agree, and he smiles and says, "Then we are"—and he uses one of those dizzyingly long Russian compound words—"thinkers-of-similar-thoughts!"

Food III

Dinner with Marina, a schoolteacher. She tells us the sources of all the food on the table. The butter came from her father in Byelorussia, sent on the train—"there is no butter in Moscow." The smoked fish came from a relative in Leningrad. The mayonnaise came from the weekly food package given to teachers at her school. The caviar she purchased: one day she and her fellow teachers were given the chance to place orders. She bought twenty-three cans—one for herself and the rest for friends. Eventually, they will give her food in return. She quotes the proverb: "It is better to have a hundred friends than a hundred rubles."

There are two words for friend in Russian: *droog,* which means close friend, and *znakomi,* or acquaintance. The close friendships, with people in that inner circle, are closer here than in the United States, I think. It is a closeness born of privation, of being dependent on your friends for basic necessities that money sometimes can't purchase, like food. There is no question that Russia needs sweeping economic reform: people must eat. But I fear that an economy where anything can be purchased for enough money will destroy some of the close human relationships that were paradoxically forged by scarcity and oppression.

Spring

The weather has turned warmer. The snow is melting, and we see what it has been covering. Sidewalks are badly cracked, except for the broad one in front of the big building next door to us, the headquarters of the Russian Republic. The streets are full of potholes. Most buildings need a paint job. Thousands of them, even the landmark former mansions in the center of town that are prime tourist attractions, have their plaster peeling off, leaving jagged, irregular patches of exposed brick. The whole city has a battered look, as if a giant hailstorm has passed through.

Two months after our arrival, the promised desks have still not arrived. Now the problem is the lack of a truck.

The mysterious piles of pipe, one old, one new, remain in the vacant lot across the street, no longer covered with snow. Every day or two someone comes along and bangs on a piece of pipe, seeing if he can find something useful. One day one of the salvagers even has a welding torch.

The melting snow has disclosed several rough-edged, gaping holes between the sidewalk and the darkened basement of our building. Each evening, as our footsteps approach, a flock of dark shapes scurry into one of these holes a few feet from our entry door: rats.

One week millions of radishes suddenly appear all over Moscow, sold at eighty kopecks a bunch by women in kerchiefs in front of every Metro station. Either this is the first vegetable of spring or a huge trainload of radishes has arrived from somewhere.

Bureaucracy III

For Gabriel's spring vacation from school, the three of us are planning a trip to Novosibirsk and Karaganda. In terms of distance and the size of the cities, it is roughly as if we were going from New York to Denver, to Dallas, and back to New York.

The woman in the Moscow ticket office of Aeroflot, the state airline, is happy to sell us tickets from Moscow to Novosibirsk, and from Karaganda back to Moscow. But she can't sell us tickets from Novosibirsk to Karaganda. Are there no flights? I ask incredulously. Probably there are, she says, but she has no way of finding out about them from here. Eventually we solve this problem the way all travelers in the USSR do. If you're going from A to B to C and back to A again, you call ahead to a friend in B and get him or her to buy your ticket to C.

Crime

A visit to the home of Misha Shevelov, a journalist at *Moscow News*. We drink a bottle of Abkhazian wine, which Misha says was brought to the newspaper by a delegation of Abkhazians wanting more coverage for their homeland's problems. The Abkhazians, in the western Caucasus, are now locked in a bitter dispute over land and power with the more numerous Georgians. Some Abkhazians living in Moscow take part in the city's organized crime—some of it controlled by rival ethnic gangs from the Caucasus. As this delegation was leaving the newspaper, one member said to Misha, "If you ever have anyone you need, you know . . . taken care of . . . let us know." Another added: "And if he's a Georgian, we pay *you.*"

Coming back to the apartment sometime after this, I start to walk through the attractive little park across from our building. It is near midnight, and I feel a moment's hesitation. The papers have been reporting shootings in Moscow's parks, in fighting between those different Caucasian gangs. But I've walked through this park coming home from the Metro station countless times before. And besides, a couple is walking on the path behind me. Entering the park, however, I see the cigarette's-end glow of two men smoking on the path up ahead. Their faces are in darkness. They abruptly shout some threat in my direction, in a language not Russian. I wheel around and walk quickly away, as do the couple behind me. This is not more than fifty yards from the militia post that guards the Russian Republic's headquarters.

Magic

For the third time since we've been here, a handwritten chain letter arrives in our mailbox. It promises health, happiness, and good fortune, if only you won't break the chain.

I'm sure you could chart a correlation between the fall in the economy and the rise in promises of magical rewards of all kinds. Hari Krishnas are on the streets here now; Werner Erhard has a big Moscow operation; TV programs show hypnotists and faith healers.

A similar interest in mysticism and Oriental religion swept old St. Petersburg in the last years of Tsar Nicholas II.

Food IV

Out to dinner at the house of Natasha, an artist who lives in a communal apartment, living in the same room in which she paints. Dinner is: fried potato pancakes, raisin bread, white bread baked around a layer of cabbage, and rolls with a filling of chopped potato. Irina, another guest, says, "Somehow they've seen to it that every generation experiences hunger. To us it is coming later than to our parents' generation; to our children, earlier. A few years ago all the conversation you heard on the bus was politics, politics,

politics. Now all you hear is the prices and locations of milk, meat, and vegetables."

May Day

For the May Day holiday, trios of red flags are mounted in special sockets on the sides of buildings all over town. The Ministry of Geology building near our Metro station is covered with a three-story-high portrait of Lenin. Nearby, a street lamp has fallen off its pole, and someone is poking through the innards, trying to salvage wire. A few blocks away, on the riverbank, a colorful row of flags has been raised for the holiday in front of the building that houses Comecon, the Eastern European economic union. They are the flags of all the former Soviet satellites now pulling out of this near-defunct organization.

Telephones III

Sometimes there is an excitement about all these missed connections and wrong numbers. One day I pick up the phone to make a call and find myself in the midst of a conversation between two strangers about pension payments.

How do such crossed wires affect the country's telephone tappers? Does the KGB now think that there are secret American dealings with the Ministry of Pensions? The KGB's phones may not work any better than anyone else's, for if you try to call their public information office—a surprising new concession to *glasnost*—all you get is a busy signal, for hours.

Emigration

A current joke: Lenin said communism is Soviet power plus electrification of the whole country; today, communism is Soviet power plus emigration of the whole country.

How many people in Moscow have not thought of leaving? Very few, I think, among those who speak a Western European language. It's one reason why some people are so friendly to us: three times Soviet acquaintances have asked me to help them get American visas. Hundreds of people line up on the sidewalk outside the U.S. embassy daily, but you can go right to the head of the line if you're with an American citizen.

T., a journalist, tells me that he and his wife are thinking of leaving, "not for good, but just for five years . . . until things get better." But I know, and he knows, that that means for good.

Z., a theoretical physicist, says his family will leave before their daughter reaches school age. He is trying to lay the ground-work for getting a job by publishing articles in foreign journals. But many U.S. scientific journals make authors pay publication expenses, and he has no hard currency. A promised invitation to a conference in France has gotten lost in the mail; and the telephone lines are so clogged that people overseas have trouble getting through by fax. The computer programs at his institute are all bootleg copies of Western ones, "and so we must work with no manuals—it's all trial and error." If that French conference invita-tion comes through, he must stay with friends and ask them to pay for his meals. His monthly salary of three hundred rubles ex-changes into about eleven dollars.

Hot Water

One Monday morning in May, there's no hot water. Downstairs I find a tiny typed notice on our entry door:

COMRADE TENANTS:

IN CONNECTION WITH HYDRAULIC TESTING OF THE HOT WATER MAINS, FROM 13 MAY THROUGH 3 JUNE IN YOUR BUILDING THE HOT WATER WILL BE TURNED OFF.

—THE MANAGEMENT

At first I think this is some peculiarity of our building, or perhaps of our part of town, for hot water, like household heat, comes in pipelines from giant plants that serve a whole district. But no, everyone says, they turn it off all over the city every year. For three weeks. Corroded pipes and valves have to be cleaned out.

I can see why. Even though we use only cold water in it, run through a filter like all our drinking water, our teakettle has devel-oped a hard, cracked gray crust on the bottom during the months that we've been here. Heaven knows what the inside of hot-water pipes look like. A newspaper article says that one of those central water-heating plants dates from the last century.

We manage baths by heating pots and frying pans of water on

the stove and dumping them into the tub. There, mixed with cold water from the tap, it gives you a three-inch lukewarm bath. One day, however, a minor disaster occurs: we pour the boiling water from the stove into the tub without putting in some cold water first. The boiling water melts our prized one-size-fits-all rubber bath stopper. Wrinkled and deformed, it now lets water slip out.

However, after several days of experimentation, we partly solve this new problem. If you pile weight on top of the stopper, it presses it down enough to slow the leak. So cans of beans from the Finnish store become part of our equipment for taking a bath.

Slowing to a Stop

Moscow is strewn with stalled construction projects, like the mysterious pipe replacement job across the street. Everywhere are buildings half-built, construction cranes standing still against the sky, scaffolds against the sides of buildings but no one on them. It is such a contrast to my first visit here, in 1963, when the country was in the midst of the Khrushchev-era apartment-building boom. Construction sites were floodlit so that builders could work around the clock. Welders' sparks filled the night air, even in November, as they rushed to finish their work before the worst of winter.

One reason for all this stalled construction now is that the entire collapsing Soviet economy runs partly on barter. The ruble buys less and less. At the glass factory where Arlie is doing research, the plant trades mirrors it produces to get furniture, television sets, and other products for its workers—they can no longer find these things for sale in stores. What can a construction-project manager trade to get his building materials?

Summer

Suddenly the city is very green. Grass is everywhere, the trees are all in leaf. The sun seems to come up around four or five in the morning now. With the weather so much warmer, there are more rats out on the sidewalk when we come walking home in the dark. They scurry quickly into the basement at the sound of our steps.

At last! A truck and a crane arrive at the vacant lot across the street. So they must be finally going to work. Or at least they will clear away that tangle of old, rusted pipe so they can do so. But no—the crane loads the pile of *new* pipe onto the truck, which goes off with it. The pile of old pipe remains.

After three weeks, as promised, we get our hot water back. Rumor has it that in some Moscow apartments, people are now getting only hot water, out of both taps.

Summer has also brought something we never expected on the sixth floor in the middle of a huge city: a horde of mosquitoes. They are breeding, I'm sure, in the pools of stagnant rainwater in our building's uncared-for courtyard. The ten-year-old daughter of some scientists we have met publishes a homemade newspaper for her family and friends. She asks me to contribute an article, and for this I interview Buzz Buzzevich, the mosquito warlord who has settled in some invisible recess on our bedroom ceiling. He tells me his trade secrets: wait till your quarry is just dropping off to sleep, and *then* launch your dive-bombing attacks. . . .

Nostalgia

In the pedestrian underpass at Pushkin Square, a vendor is selling framed photographs of Tsar Nicholas II and his family. The young princesses wear long white dresses and are playing on a lawn. There are now many popular ballads praising the noble soldiers of the White army. Some say that they lost the civil war to the Reds because they fought in too gentlemanly a fashion.

I feel nostalgic for something else, a lost illusion of my own. In the heady late 1980s, when Mikhail Gorbachev began making his changes and introduced free speech at last, it seemed possible to hope that the Soviet Union might evolve toward some sort of middle way in politics, toward a society that would have neither the murderous injustices of communism at its worst, nor the rampant commercialism of the United States. A society that would have both economic equality *and* civil liberties, where the wealth would be owned neither by giant corporations nor by huge state ministries, but, in some way—and wasn't that the original idea?—by the people themselves. A society easy to imagine, but, I see now, less likely to come into being here than almost anywhere.

With ever less food on most dinner tables, people care most about feeding their families, not about experimental new forms of organizing an economy. And with the hold of the Communist Party crumbling, the old elite has found a far better, more lucrative way to hold onto power: privatizing state factories and natural resources right into their own hands.

A further barrier to a more just society here is that entrenched bureaucracy, whose strange ways have bedeviled us ever since we arrived. Its roots are in a profoundly conservative, undemocratic culture that stretches back to the crowds of meek petitioners waiting before clerks wielding quill pens that one can see in nineteenth-century Russian paintings. This is a tradition where most people are willing to take orders, to wait long, to expect little.

Departure, June 1991

For our last ten days in Moscow, our telephone is out. The same is true for everyone in our part of the building. The repair people say there is "a break in the underground cable" that may take a week or two to fix. We think we know the culprits: our basement rats.*

1991

*Six months later, in December 1991, the Soviet Union officially came to an end, dissolving into fifteen separate countries.

The Grand Bargain in South Africa

As you approach any South African city from the air, the colors of the landscape become blue, green, and red. The blue is the thousands of swimming pools in the white suburbs. The green is the lawns in which they are set. The red is the red earth of southern Africa, bared to the sky in the tight crisscross of streets in the black townships, where the roads are usually unpaved, and never paved at all in the shantytowns. In such areas there is little green: you can't keep a lawn watered when two dozen families share a single faucet; trees and bushes don't last where you need every branch for firewood.

On this morning's flight from Johannesburg to Port Elizabeth, every seat in my Boeing 737 is full. All but three passengers are white. If any of them are worried by the prospect, in a few weeks' time, of this country's first democratic election, in which whites will be only some 13 percent of the electorate, they're not showing it. Two white businessmen in shirtsleeves and neckties in the row of seats just behind me are cheerfully making plans about how many unit managers they need per terminal control area, whatever that may be.

Like most other inhabitants of this long-suffering country, these travelers heading for Port Elizabeth this March morning in 1994 are well aware of the Grand Bargain that underlies next month's long-awaited election: blacks get the vote, whites keep the swimming pools. And, more importantly, whites keep the mines, the factories, the vast shopping malls with their Woolworth's and Kentucky Fried Chicken outlets, and all the rest of the more than 90 percent of South Africa's commercial and industrial capital that is under white control. That percentage may even rise, if the new

South Africa attracts the investment from the United States and Europe that nearly everyone here is hoping for.

These are the basic terms of the Grand Bargain, hammered out in three tough years of formal negotiating and in secret, informal talks that began long before that. They form a more somber and intractable truth than the rhetoric about liberation and triumph that you hear from the African National Congress, or than the self-congratulations about South Africa's proud membership in the family of nations that you hear from the governing National Party. The Grand Bargain means that rectifying the grossly unequal distribution of South Africa's wealth may take almost as many hundreds of years as it did to create this wildly unbalanced society in the first place.

One small example: More than 7 million black South Africans, and more than half the blacks here in Port Elizabeth, live in what is euphemistically called "informal housing." This means shacks made out of tarpaper, pieces of billboards or canvas or plywood, with corrugated tin or zinc roofs. Three times in the last year, black residents of the desperately poor Walmer Township have broken into Port Elizabeth's almost all-white Walmer Country Club nearby. And what have they taken? Not golf clubs, and not TVs and stereos (which aren't much use if you have no electricity). They've taken sections of the clubhouse roof. The fabric rain cover from the club's cricket field has also vanished once or twice.

This, then, is the kind of gap between rich and poor that will persist in South Africa for decades to come. And yet . . . simultaneously there is another truth about the historic election about to take place. Which is that it is the most extraordinary, the most heart-lifting, the most soul-stirring event to happen here since the first Dutch settlers opened a trading post at the Cape of Good Hope in 1652 and the long struggle over who was to dominate this rich and beautiful corner of Africa began.

.   .   .

I've come to Port Elizabeth to see how the election campaign unfolds in one city, a city that only a few years ago was a notorious symbol of apartheid at its most harsh. When I was last in South Africa, in 1988, during a long period of brutal repression, this city spreading back from the bluffs and beaches of the Indian Ocean was a war zone. Huge armored personnel carriers, with shiplike

V-shaped hulls to deflect land-mine blasts, roared through the city's black townships. Hundreds of local activists were behind bars, incommunicado for months or years. Almost weekly, government-backed vigilantes torched or robbed the offices of local civil-rights groups and black labor unions.

The city's security police long had a reputation as the country's harshest. In 1988, even at a dignified conference on human rights I attended here, filled with bishops and white members of Parliament, hard-eyed men in plain clothes sat in back rows, taking pictures and notes. In 1985, a death squad here murdered several popular young black leaders. A nationwide survey of former political prisoners found that 93 percent of those arrested in this region (the highest score nationally) reported experiencing "beatings," 34.9 percent "electric shocks," 52.4 percent were "threatened with execution of self or family." Only 4.7 percent (the lowest score of all regions) reported "no physical torture." It was in Port Elizabeth that black consciousness leader Steve Biko was given the beating that killed him.

For a hundred years, this part of the country has been the heartland of black militance. Nelson Mandela and several other top African National Congress leaders have their family roots near here. And when the black revolts of the mid-1980s swept South Africa, hundreds of thousands of people boycotted Port Elizabeth's downtown business district to put pressure on the government, igniting similar boycotts elsewhere.

Today, on the main street of that same downtown, every lamp-post is hung with an ANC campaign poster: JOBS PEACE FREEDOM. Suddenly it is no longer South Africa's political violence that fills TV screens here and in the rest of the world, but the far deadlier carnage now raging in the former Yugoslavia, where nearly 200,000 people are dead, millions more have fled their homes, and the brutal siege of Sarajevo continues.

Today Port Elizabeth is, amazingly, a city at peace. The day after I arrive, eighteen public bodies and political groups, from the local Chamber of Commerce to the South African Communist Party, sign a path-breaking accord that officially begins dismantling a half century of apartheid at the level of city government. With this agreement, Port Elizabeth—many months before it will be required by the country's new constitution—proudly becomes the first major urban area in South Africa to officially declare itself, in effect, one city.

Until now, Port Elizabeth's downtown, its white suburbs, and most of its municipal purse strings have been controlled by an all-white city council; the black and brown areas have been run by appointed white administrators and by district councils with little money or power, chosen in elections that most people boycotted. Now this crazy-quilt is on the way out. A new transitional authority representing all races is in place. And when South Africa holds its first local democratic election, some months after the forthcoming national one, a new city council for all of Port Elizabeth will be chosen by one-person-one-vote.

Much lies on the agenda. A key item is revising the local tax structure, for until now, taxes generated by the central business district, where most people of all colors work and shop, have been mainly paying for things like the immaculately manicured parks of the white suburbs. Then comes the massive job of trying to redistribute library books, street-cleaning crews, new sewer lines, garbage collectors, and a host of other city services more equitably, instead of mostly to the white areas.

The evening that the historic One-City Accord is signed, I go to an ANC celebration party at a white supporter's apartment. People consume huge amounts of red wine, white wine, beer, and brandy, in odd combinations, while gathered around three candles in the Congress colors: yellow, black, and green. One of the guests, a much-liked local black activist with a booming voice, jokes exuberantly about how much *lobola* (a bride-price paid in cattle) he is prepared to pay for the white hostess. His voice echoes out the window and through the beachfront neighborhood. Several people explain to me that he speaks so loudly because blows to the head during his last police interrogation have nearly deafened him. But tonight all that seems far away.

· · ·

The next day I'm in the office of another such veteran. Five years ago, Mike Xego was in prison here. "They came to pick me up about two A.M. I was sleeping, relaxed. All I knew was that all the doors were down, bashed. Dogs, guns, rifles. And they were shouting, 'Where's Mike? Where's Mike? Where's Mike?' One security guy put a rifle to my mother's head. My mother wetted herself, she was so upset. My little cousin-sister, who was one and a half, whenever someone was knocking at the door after that, she began to cry."

Then came the interrogations. Xego sits down on the floor to demonstrate. He clasps his hands in front of his knees. "There was a system called the helicopter. Like this. They would handcuff you. Then they would take a big stick like this." He uses a rolled-up newspaper to show how policemen thrust the stick inside his knees and elbows, pinning him into a permanent crouch. "You'd be passed from one hand to another. Kicked. Tipped over. The blood stops moving. You scream and scream and scream until there is no voice. Then there was the bag method. It was brought from Chile. They took this bag, a dirty old black bag. Somebody comes [from behind], you are not seeing him, and then *whap,* you feel you are in a death trap. You go there [to the interrogation room] at about half past seven [in the morning]. You come back at about half past five or six and you are *dead.*"

Today Mike Xego is an ANC candidate for the regional parliament, third on the party list in a proportional representation system. The ANC is expected to win a big majority of the vote, so Xego is guaranteed a seat and a high position in the provincial government. Xego has spent more than seven of his thirty-seven years in prison, but now he is studying for a degree in public administration at the local university. He vows to finish it after he is in office.

Does he ever run into the policemen who tortured him?

Of course: "They've come to the ANC office to talk to us on a range of security matters. When Mandela comes around, for instance, they always come." He doesn't want to name them: "We were never involved in this struggle to bear revenge. But we shall never forget."

What does he see in their faces?

"Shame. It's painful on their side. They now recognize that we are the leaders. I felt very much humbled. We had told them in the torture rooms that we were not really opposed to them personally, but were fighting the system. They didn't understand it then."

Today, he says, most of the black interrogators have apologized. But none of the white ones.

．　　．　　．

One Sunday I follow Tokyo Sexwale, a top ANC leader and four-teen-year prison veteran who is flying in to spend a day campaign-ing for the ANC in the black townships of Port Elizabeth and the neighboring industrial city of Uitenhage. Contradictory, ever-changing information about his schedule comes from the local ANC headquarters. Sexwale's office in Johannesburg confirms by phone that he has left for Port Elizabeth but doesn't know when he is arriving. Finally he appears at the airport. A broad-shoul-dered, bearded, handsome man in a brown windbreaker, he has an electric smile and great charisma. Voted by women in a radio sta-tion's poll the sexiest man in South Africa, he is married to a white lawyer he met while in prison.

Sexwale's three-car motorcade roars off from the airport at top speed. For reasons unclear to me, the ANC believes that "security" requires candidates to be driven at what seems like 120 miles per hour. Our small contingent of press cars is left behind. For the next half hour, we try to catch up, swerving at one point to avoid a donkey who has wandered onto the freeway. Then groups of black and white reporters, their heads and TV cameras poking out of car windows, encounter each other at dusty intersections in black townships: "Did he go that way? This way? Let's try over there!"

At last we manage to find Sexwale at a township ANC office, a single room squeezed between a butcher shop and a dingy café. From there he moves to a school soccer field for a rally. At first the crowd is small—only a few hundred—because of the confusion over the schedule. But as the sound of a loudspeaker booms out over the township, desolate rows of cinder-block houses on treeless brown hills, more people come streaming in.

A medical worker walks around handing out packets from a big cardboard carton: "Free condoms for everyone!" Because some two million black South African men are migrant workers, forced to live apart from their families for months at a time if they want work, prostitution is common and AIDS is spreading rapidly, ac-knowledged very belatedly by both the government and the ANC. A local ANC official, in fact, tries to usher the condom woman out of the rally grounds.

Sexwale's campaign rhetoric for the day shows the tricky bal-ance the ANC has to walk. When talking briefly and quietly to reporters, he is careful to stress reconciliation: "We are prepared to work with those we hated in the past, with the army, with the police." Then the questions turn to the economy, and to who, under the ANC, might get a larger slice of the pie. (In South Africa, however, you talk about "the cake.") Sexwale mentions antitrust laws and breaking up cartels, but doesn't go any further. He knows the terms of the Grand Bargain. "We have dedicated ourselves to creating a very good basis for the development of small business and medium enterprises. Because the cake is already taken."

But when Sexwale talks to the enthusiastic crowd on the soccer field, his words are aimed at a different constituency: ANC militants in their twenties, with whom he is very popular. He talks of his birth in a Johannesburg squatter camp. He drips scorn on State President F. W. de Klerk. He makes fun of de Klerk's baldness: "The next leader of the government will have *hair!*" And he urges the crowd to spurn de Klerk when the president campaigns near here later in the month:

"Adolf Hitler cannot go to Israel to look for votes! When you mention [de Klerk's] name, you need a brush to wash! So if I mention his name, that means I'm making business for those of you who are selling toothbrushes and toothpaste. He is unwelcome! He is unwanted! They go about today kissing black babies. But we know when they get home they wash themselves! We know them. Away with the government of de Klerk!"

"AWAY!" roars the crowd.

(The next day the National Party indignantly registers an objection to the Hitler comparison.)

After more chants and singing, Sexwale is finally on his way, the motorcade roaring off at Indianapolis 500 speed. The press cars get left behind at the first stoplight, and Sexwale's convoy vanishes over the hills, in a direction different from that of the next announced stop. We never catch up with him.

·   ·   ·

While the ANC'S election campaign is more like a tumultuous religious revival, the ruling National Party is running a classic, ward-by-ward, house-by-house machine effort in which any American municipal party boss would feel at home. The National Party has no hope of winning this election. But it is almost certain to place second, which will guarantee the party a deputy presidency, plus at least one cabinet seat for each 5 percent of the vote received.

The National Party's Port Elizabeth headquarters is a two-story suite of downtown offices. Stickers and placards from past campaigns are on view; stacks of cardboard posters of de Klerk are piled in the hallways. The walls are filled with businesslike lists of *Sateliet Kantore* [branch offices]. A computer and fax machine hum.

Franz Smit, forty-six, a member of the old all-white parliament and a candidate for the new one, is running the National Party campaign here. His initial uneasiness with an inquiring American visitor (never a favorite species to most Afrikaners) quickly gives way to a professional's pride in displaying his well-organized canvassing operation.

Smit's strategy is determined by racial statistics. Port Elizabeth is the largest city of the Eastern Cape province. The region has, according to Smit, 273,000 whites, 10,000 Indians, 246,000 Coloureds, as South Africans of mixed racial ancestry are known, and more than 2.3 million blacks. The blacks, he admits, will largely vote for the ANC, although there are some exceptions that the NP has easy ways of influencing, such as servants in white homes: "the domestics and gardeners—and you know how many of *them* there are!" The whites are no problem: the great bulk of them will vote NP. And they're all already in Smit's computers from previous all-white elections. That means his all-out effort now is to woo the Coloureds.

This is not a vain hope. The native language of the great majority of South Africa's 3.3 million Coloureds is the traditional one of the National Party, Afrikaans. Economically the Coloureds are much better off than blacks, and there has been tension between the two groups—much of it encouraged over the years by apartheid's elaborate system of divide and rule.

Smit has opened thirteen branch offices in Port Elizabeth's Coloured districts. And the fifty-three thousand file cards stacked alphabetically on tables in his head office here reflect his systematic attempt to reach everyone in that community. He shows me the questions on each card with blanks for answers: number of people in household over eighteen? Support NP? Support another party? Need transport on election day? Name? Address? Telephone? One reason this type of canvassing and phone-banking operation can work is that most urban Coloureds *have* telephones. Most blacks do not.

Ironically, the National Party did not even open its own membership rolls to nonwhites until 1991, a year after F. W. de Klerk released Nelson Mandela from prison and began the historic moves toward a new constitution. But to win followers in the new South Africa where everyone can vote, the party that created apartheid is now fielding a rainbow array of candidates from all South Africa's racial groups.

The Coloured vote will probably break down along class lines, with better-off shopkeepers and professionals tending to vote for the National Party and the working class for the ANC. But not entirely. One morning I visit the National Party branch office in Port Elizabeth's poorest Coloured neighborhood, Helenvale. Because of layoffs in the local auto industry, unemployment in Helenvale has been measured at 78 percent. Men in blue workmen's jumpsuits cluster all day at intersections, hoping, usually in vain, to be hired as temporary laborers by white employers who occasionally cruise by in pickup trucks. Pavements are cracked and pitted. Factories, warehouses, and even a church are surrounded by high walls topped with coils of razor wire. Windblown garbage is everywhere, and scraps of colored plastic grocery bags have stuck to the razor wire.

The house I stop at is divided into four two-room units, their tiny yards separated by vertical sheets of plywood. Altogether some forty people occupy these eight rooms, sharing one water faucet and two cinder-block pillbox outhouses. Several of the forty are receiving pensions or welfare. Not one has a full-time job.

It seems odd to find a house like this as the local outpost of the party that constructed apartheid. But a National Party sticker is on the window, and, inside, in the cramped living room of John Davids, fifty-eight, hang pictures of Joseph, Mary, Jesus, and F. W. de Klerk.

Davids and two neighbors, Vernon Arendse, twenty-five, and his brother Cyril, thirty, all say they are former ANC supporters who have switched to the National Party. "My problem was that the ANC people were violent," says Davids. "They intimidated people. Me, as a church leader, I didn't fit in with their ways. They burned shops down." (Five years ago, rioters destroyed a number of

Coloured-owned shops nearby. Some are still charred shells, others are rebuilt with bars or thick wire mesh over the windows.)

Why the National Party? Davids answers: "The only [white] people I had contact with were National Party people." He was a tractor driver on a cattle and sheep farm near here for some years, he says; the owner was a good man who treated him well.

The Arendse brothers have a different beef with the ANC. Both used to work at a local boiler-making plant. When they didn't want to join a strike a few years ago, black pro-ANC union members threatened to burn their house down. When the dispute was finally settled, the company rehired the black workers, they say, but not the Coloureds—"there are two hundred still out."

I have no reason to doubt anything Davids or the Arendse brothers say, but there is clearly an additional reason why they are supporting the National Party: money. Davids is given a telephone and rent payments for the use of his living room as a Party office, and the Arendses and eleven others who are canvassing house-to-house in their neighborhood are paid a fee for every filled-out card they turn in. In a community with 78 percent unemployment, that matters. And so, too, does the fear that if South Africa's cake is reapportioned, the blacks, who are even lower in the racial and class hierarchy, may get whatever new slices can be found.

·   ·   ·

Many smaller parties are also competing in the election, and one of them is the Pan Africanist Congress. The PAC split off from the ANC in 1959, fueled by militant black nationalism. For a brief moment it captured center stage in the resistance movement. But during the long years of repression and exile it declined into a morass of competing factions and antiwhite racism. Its small military wing made sporadic attacks on whites, whom it called "settlers," even after the ANC's guerrillas had laid down their arms. The name South African is regarded as white, and PAC members refer to the country as Azania. PAC supporters murdered the white American graduate student Amy Biehl in Cape Town in 1993. But recently the PAC decided to contest the new election, seeking support among black township militants who feel the ANC has made too many compromises.

Few people expect the PAC to get more than 1 or 2 percent of the vote. But the party has two curious advantages. One is that, as a result of a public drawing, it will be the first party listed on the ballot. The other is that its candidate for president, Clarence Makwetu, looks strikingly like Nelson Mandela. The reason these things matter is that more than half of South Africa's new electorate is illiterate. The ballot where voters mark their "X" therefore contains, on each line, a party's name, initials, logo—and a photo of its leader.

I spend the better part of a day following Makwetu on a campaign swing through Port Elizabeth and Uitenhage. A big, solemn man in a pin-striped suit, Makwetu's resemblance to Mandela is indeed uncanny: both are tall and wide-shouldered, with broad faces and high cheekbones; Makwetu is about ten years younger. He spends the day visiting an orphanage, a public hospital, a TB sanatorium, and a barren, windswept cemetery where he lays a wreath on the mass grave of twenty-nine protesters, the youngest fifteen years old, who were killed by police in 1985.

One member of his staff, I notice, wears a T-shirt with a drawing of an AK-47 and the slogan of the PAC's military wing: "One Settler One Bullet."

The PAC shares the ANC's mad conviction that security lies in high-speed driving. When we leave the TB sanatorium, the convoy speeds off so fast that three members of the entourage are left behind. They include Mr. One Settler One Bullet. A Coloured reporter and I offer them a ride in our car. As we bounce over the rutted township roads, skirting children, cows, and goats, I ask them about various PAC policies. Finally, as we arrive at the next stop, I can't help asking the man in the T-shirt about his slogan: "Does that apply to me?"

"No, not you, man. Don't worry," he says, with a ghost of a smile, as he gets out of the car.

Who, then, does it apply to?

"If you are a resident of Azania," says one of the others, "you must be loyal to the country. That's a characteristic you find in every country in the world. If you are loyal to majority rule, then you are an African! If you're against it, then you are a settler."

The climax of Makwetu's campaign day is a rally in a sports stadium in a black township called KwaNobuhle. Perhaps twenty-five hundred people, many of them teenagers, are in the grandstand when we all walk onto the field. Most of the local journalists following Makwetu today are black or Coloured, but there are two whites besides me. A portion of the crowd in the stands begins chanting "One Settler! One Bullet!" as we enter the stadium. Occasionally over the next hour or two the chants erupt again: "Settler! Settler! Bullet! Bullet!" But the mood is festive and relaxed, not angry.

There are warm-up speakers, chants, songs, oral poets reciting in both English and Xhosa, a children's dance troupe, and then a long speech by Makwetu, which he reads ponderously from a text, alternating the two languages. Despite the PAC's checkered and violent history, Makwetu is a numbingly drab speaker: Discrimination must go; women play a crucial role; de Klerk must go. Makwetu is anxious not to antagonize anybody, including local white businessmen, from whom he hopes to raise money for his party's near-empty coffers: even the Audi he is riding in today is on loan from the local Volkswagen factory.

"*Izwelethu iAfrika!*" the crowd chants: Africa is our land! "Genuine liberation begins with repossession of the land," says Makwetu. Indeed it does, for on the eve of the election, the 13 percent of South Africans who are white own 85 percent of the land. But here, too, Makwetu has few specifics. Many white farmers, using black laborers, have owned the same farm for half a dozen generations. How do you begin to redistribute this land more fairly without setting off massive white emigration and capital flight? This is something no one has an easy answer to; it is one of the harsh realities that forced the Grand Bargain.

As the speechmaking at today's rally continues, four people come walking slowly onto the sports field. They shake hands with the rally organizers, then with the journalists, then stroll past the rostrum. They are monitors from the United Nations. They wear blue baseball caps, blue arm bands, and blue vests with the UN emblem. Several hundred UN observers are in South Africa, and there will be many more as election day draws closer. They have fanned out across the country, attending campaign events large and small, and mediating disputes when asked.

Intellectually, I know all the UN's problems and failures. But why, most unexpectedly, do I suddenly find a lump in my throat at the sight of these four people in blue: two men, two women; black, white, and brown? Their presence is a reminder: the whole world is watching.

I ask the four where they are from. One woman is from India. One man is from Switzerland. One woman is from Nigeria. And the fourth?

"I am from Bosnia."

His name is Zeljko Jerkic. "I'm from Sarajevo. My parents are there still. I can do nothing there. I can here."

1994

Fishhooks and Chickens

Few places on earth have seen their indigenous cultures more shattered than the Amazon. The jungle is eroding before road builders, loggers, cattle ranchers, and slash-and-burn farmers. Their numbers drastically shrunken, thousands of remaining Amazon Indians are migrating to towns and cities in search of work, on the poverty-stricken margins of the machine-based civilization that has largely destroyed their own. But the news from the Amazon is not entirely bleak. In one unheralded corner of the rain forest, there is a small but startling migration in reverse. Indians are pulling their children out of mission schools, are leaving the frontier towns, and are rebuilding their traditional dwellings deep in the forest. And all this is happening, amazingly, in the benighted country of Colombia.

When we picture Colombia, we think of guerrilla warfare, paramilitary death squads, cocaine cartels. And that picture is true. Paradoxically, however, of the nine countries that share the Amazon watershed, Colombia has done by far the most to preserve the endangered rain forest and its people. Colombia has set aside in perpetuity more than one quarter of the nation's entire land surface as protected areas for the Indians. And, most remarkable of all, the country's new constitution says that Indians living in these areas may choose, if they wish, to live completely outside the normal framework of government.

Some of the Indians who have made this rare reverse migration live on the Mirití River, a long, winding stream on which, for a stretch of about 280 miles, there are no towns and no white people whatever. The Indians who have returned here in recent years want to live on this river as their ancestors did, earlier in the century and, as far as we can tell, for thousands of years before that. Few groups of people anywhere on earth have chosen so deliberately to turn their backs on the modern world. Recently I got an unexpected chance to spend a week among them.

.   .   .

Martin von Hildebrand is a fifty-year-old Colombian Indian rights activist. Some months ago, he had to spend a week traveling on the Mirití for his work, and he invited me to go along.

We met first in Bogotá. As he approached down a busy street, Martin von Hildebrand seemed the opposite of what I had expected of someone who had devoted his life to rain forest Indians. Exuberantly cosmopolitan, he looked completely at home in Bogotá's elegant downtown, as, it seemed, he would in many other capitals. He is trilingual in Spanish, English (his mother was Irish), and French (he went to a French school in Bogotá, and to the Sorbonne). He also speaks German, Italian, some Greek, and Tanimuca. Tanimuca is an Amazon language spoken by about 140 people; Martin knows all the adult Tanimuca speakers in the world. He first worked among Indians as an anthropologist, then served five years in the government, helping set up the huge areas of protected Indian land, which are called *resguardos*. Today he runs a foundation that supports Indian rights. A stocky, sandy-haired man of medium height, he walks with a pigeon-toed gait at a pace that seldom drops below five or six miles per hour.

"By the way," I asked over lunch, "what are we going to eat on this trip?"

"Oh, the Indians will feed us," Martin replied cheerfully. "And if we're out on the river—they live quite far apart, you know—I usually just mix a little manioc flour with the river water. It makes a sort of paste that's really very good."

That afternoon I hastily went to a Bogotá grocery store and bought what I hoped would be a week's supply of crackers, nuts, raisins, and the like.

In the evening we were joined by another traveling companion and a mutual friend, Hermann Hatzfeldt, a German environmentalist. Early the next morning the three of us boarded a two-engined turboprop, the once-a-week plane to La Pedrera, a small river town near Colombia's border with Brazil. Our luggage included a ten-horsepower outboard motor. In La Pedrera, Martin explained, we would rent a canoe to put it on.

After several hours' flying, the plane descended out of the clouds. The flat jungle spread out below in all directions, rivers snaking through it in endless, rounded zigzags. It was as if brown ropes had been thrown across a bright green carpet, bunching up in loops that almost touched each other. This weekly flight is La Pedrera's main link to the outside world, for, despite a wishful line on a map put out by Colombia's Ministry of Economic Development, no roads reach the town, and it has no cars.

Landing felt like arriving in a Graham Greene novel. Some three hundred people live in La Pedrera, and at least a quarter of them turned out to meet the plane: submachine-gun-carrying soldiers in sweat-stained green fatigues; the police chief, joking with everyone and inspecting all baggage; traders; prostitutes; nuns. The airstrip was at one end of the town's dirt main street. Scrawny dogs nosed through beer cans and scraps of garbage lying in the gutters. At a small trading post and general store, the proprietor weighed tiny bags of gold dust given him by wizened mestizo prospectors, and dispensed beer and supplies in return. A platoon of soldiers in T-shirts and combat boots came down the street on their daily run, jogging in step and chanting.

Martin immediately went to work on the day-long job of getting permission for us to go upriver. This meant having papers stamped and signed by the police chief, the local army commander, and the mayor. At the police station, the chief sat at a rickety desk beneath a picture of Christ and frowned curiously at my passport. Because of the heat, he had taken off his uniform after meeting the plane, and now wore only a T-shirt, bathing trunks, and sandals. On the wall hung a "Wanted" poster of a drug lord. Flies buzzed in and out. On a little hillock outside, small, whitewashed stones were arranged to read DIOS Y PATRIA, but rain had muddied the slope and some of the stones had slid downhill.

We ate dinner in La Pedrera's one restaurant—an open-sided shed, whose water supply was a barrel underneath the roof's drainpipe. Abruptly at 9:00 P.M., the town's diesel generator shut down for the night, and all the lights went out.

The next morning, Martin rented a twenty-foot dugout canoe from a local mestizo fisherman. With it, to run our outboard motor, came one of the fisherman's nine children. A bright, black-haired, teenage boy named Famir, he was so lithe and sure-footed that he could walk along the canoe's inch-wide gunwale. At the last minute, we took along a hitchhiker, who smiled with delight at getting a ride on a boat with an outboard motor. She was an Indian of perhaps eighteen or nineteen. Her name was Leah, and she lived in a Colombian border town south of La Pedrera. There she had just married a man who came from the rain forest far up the Mirití River, just where we were going. It is a custom throughout the Amazon that a new bride must go and work for several months in her mother-in-law's garden. Her new husband had had to stay in town at his job, and so she was making a journey of hundreds of miles alone, to a family and a remote jungle community that she had never seen.

.   .   .

At last we hoisted a big plastic barrel of gasoline into the canoe, and set off. For the first few hours we headed up the Caquetá River, a tributary of the Amazon. Sometimes a freshwater dolphin broke the surface with a splash, and once a small fish leapt into the boat. Pelicanlike birds circled overhead, cawing. At midday we turned up the much smaller Mirití River. Immediately the color of the water changed, from muddy brown to lighter yellow-green. Now for the first time it felt as if we were traveling inside the rain forest: the river was narrow and the dense wall of trees loomed high on each side, hung with vines and unbroken for mile after mile.

Why has Colombia turned all this land into protected *resguardos* for the Indians? Partly the move is due to determined pressure from the Indians themselves. "It is not the government that gives us a *resguardo*," a group of Amazon tribal leaders declared recently. "When the earth was created and delivered by the gods to the indigenous tribes, then and there the *resguardos* were created. . . ."

Several other things also lie behind the government's apparent largess. One is the drug trade: because of it, Colombia has been desperately eager to gain some good press overseas. Another is that the Colombian military, unlike its counterpart in Brazil, never linked its dreams of grandeur with developing the Amazon; for years it has been tied up fighting guerrillas, and sometimes labor organizers, elsewhere. Third, Colombia lacks Brazil's huge, horrendously poor peasantry, hungry for Amazon land. And finally, as far as anyone knows, the Colombian Amazon has no big deposits of oil, gas, or metals. For all these reasons, developers have largely left the area alone.

Today the 125,000 square miles of Amazon forest in Colombia's Indian *resguardos*—more land than New York, New Jersey, and the New England states combined—has remarkably few inhabitants: only about fifty-five thousand Indians and some two hundred whites, many of them missionaries. As our canoe headed steadily upstream, hugging the river's inside bank on dozens of hairpin turns, we saw nobody: no houses, no fields, no signs of human life for hour after hour. When the sun grew hot, I filled my hat with river water, and let its delicious coolness seep into my hair and down my neck. The low drone of the outboard motor, the river swishing past, the sense of going deeper and deeper into the endless forest and of being suspended between water and sky put us all almost into a trance.

. . .

Martin wore brown pants, a nondescript green-gray shirt, and a Swiss Army knife on his belt. For him, this was a business trip. During the long hours on the river this first day, he explained his mission.

Some of the Indians who now live on this stretch of the Mirití have spent a few years in Catholic mission boarding schools. Many of the men have worked in La Pedrera or other towns, or on the notoriously exploitative rubber plantations. More recently, some sold coca leaves to drug dealers, who, not surprisingly, turned out to be no more honest or generous in dealing with the Indians than were the rubber planters.

For the Indians, these brushes with the outside world were unhappy ones. And so in the past twenty years several hundred of them have returned to the Mirití rain forest, rejoining some who never left. There they have resumed practice of their traditional religion, which is intricately connected with hunting, fishing, and harvesting rituals and with the medicinal use of rain forest herbs and plants.

However, living off the river and the jungle is enormously easier to do with certain Western tools. Cutting down trees and building a house is much less work with hatchets and machetes made of steel instead of stone. Catching fish is far simpler with a metal fishhook and nylon line than with a spear. "There are a few other things as well," Martin said, "like hammocks. They've used hammocks forever here, of course, but a hammock made out of rope is a lot sturdier than one made out of palm fronds. All in all, the Indians' wants are modest. They build all their own houses and boats from materials of the forest. But for these other things, they need a small amount of income. Not much, maybe the equivalent of several hundred dollars per family per year."

The problem is: how can Indians earn this money without eroding their way of life? If they produce handicrafts or harvest anything from the forest, that means going downriver to La Pedrera. There they're at the mercy of traders, who know that an Indian who has just arrived with a dugout canoe load of pineapples or bananas has no other place to sell it before it spoils. Another alternative—young men from the forest becoming migrant workers at a small gold mine near La Pedrera or in the shantytowns of Colombia's cities—is even worse. Jobs are scarce, wages are low, disease is rife. Many migrants never return.

The Indians' dilemma poses a larger question. Is it possible to partake only selectively of the Western way of life? Can you dip only one foot into the twentieth century? If this can't be done here on the Mirití, where the Indians live so far from the outside world, it probably can't be done anywhere. Martin heads the Gaia Foundation, based in Bogotá and London, which has offered to help the Indians deal with this dilemma. Some months earlier, he had traveled up the Mirití discussing with Indian leaders how their people could earn those few hundred dollars per family without further eroding their traditional way of life. Now he was coming back to learn what decisions they had made.

.   .   .

Toward sunset, we turned off the Mirití and up a small side stream of strangely dark water, called Black Creek. We had reached the home of Fausto Tanimuca.

Indians here often have Spanish first names; the last name is the name of the tribe. Fausto was the elected *capitán,* or combination chief and shaman, of people living on this part of the river. He was a small, dark-skinned man with an intense, frowning face. He invited us to take seats on low stools in the middle of his *maloca,* or chief's communal house. This was a large, round, one-room building with a palm thatch roof held up by tall poles.

After Fausto and Martin had talked for a few minutes, Martin said, "Come! We must have a bath in the creek. That's the first thing you do after arriving at someone's *maloca,* after you've been properly greeted."

A swim? What about crocodiles? Piranhas? Martin and Hermann took off their clothes and plunged in. I gingerly followed. From the water, Martin called out: "Now, if a boa attacks you, you must poke out his eyes!" He tipped back his head and roared with laughter. But boa constrictors must not be too active here, because just upstream some women were bathing and were dipping babies in the water. It felt wonderful to wash off the day's sweat. Our legs looked amber in the black water.

Returning to the *maloca,* we sat back down in a circle with Fausto and several other men. Someone passed around an old coffee can filled with green powder, with a hollowed-out piece of tapir bone as a spoon. This was pulverized coca leaf, mixed with ashes of the burned leaves of another plant.

Coca in this form is a mild stimulant, which supposedly reduces hunger and increases alertness. To chew the coca, you shovel several bone loads of the fine green powder into your mouth, and form it into little wads that stay between your gums and cheeks for several hours. For the first few minutes, before everyone can generate enough saliva to moisten this unappetizing mix, little clouds of powder puff out of the mouths of the men talking, like gusts of green steam. People sound as if they were talking with mouths full of wet cigarette ashes. Unfortunately the coca tastes that way too. It didn't do much for me.

We were almost on the equator, and the sun set swiftly. The inside of the *maloca* went from light to dark. Fausto pointed to where we should hang our hammocks. Famir, our boatman, and Leah, the young Indian woman making the long trek to her mother-in-law's garden, shared a hammock, chastely head-to-toe, talking and giggling softly far into the night.

Fausto and Martin and the other men resumed talking. About what, I could not tell. But from my hammock, I was struck by the unfamiliar rhythm of the talk. It had no repartee, no interruptions. Fausto would talk for maybe twenty or thirty minutes; then Martin would talk for almost as long; then Fausto would talk again. This rhythm surely has to do with living not only without telephones or TV but also in a place where it can take all day to reach your nearest neighbor's and a week to paddle to your *capitán's maloca.*

In the morning I asked, with Martin translating, if Fausto would let me ask him a few questions. Yes, the answer came back. But then Martin added: "Don't necessarily expect an answer to each question. It doesn't work that way. You share thoughts. You give your thought, then he gives his thought. Maybe you get an answer to a question, maybe not. Or maybe you get the answer the next time you come up the river, after he's had time to meditate about it."

I began by saying how peaceful it had felt to spend the night in Fausto's *maloca.*

"Not everyone can build a *maloca,*" Fausto replied. "It must be a person with the right thought, with the right knowledge of the world, who can properly look after what is sacred. And then he must find the right place for the *maloca.* Just as the animals of the forest find and own the places that are their homes."

I then asked: Can Indian culture survive all the pressures from the white world?

Another unexpected thing about Amazonian conversations is their silences. Fausto now said nothing for a few minutes. Finally he spoke, walking about and punctuating his words with rapid hand gestures.

"The white world is a world that must be respected. It has so many things: machines that pick you up at one place and put you down in another. It's another path, another way of being, an extremely complicated way of being. One has to respect it, even if one can't understand it. But what the white people call development is destroying our culture. We see it when our people go down the river to town and get drunk.

"We can't go back to the days of stone hatchets. But people have started going to town to sell fish and food. I myself have had to do this, instead of being here to cure the sick and attend to people.

"With my shaman-power I have made a barrier on the river, so that our people will not leave and white people will not come up. I have put a net around people so they will stay here. But if a few people leave, it is like a fish finding a hole in the net—then all the other fish go through it."

Fausto is wary of all offers of help, even from a longtime friend like Martin. "Behind this aid, is there another intention? The people from where the sun was born [Europe, the source of the Gaia Foundation's funding]—will they come and invade this territory? Is their aid opening a path? We say that if a person eats too much tapir meat, he becomes like a tapir, even if he looks like a human being. It's the same with this aid: if we become too dependent on it, people will still look like Indians, but will be Europeans inside."

And what would that mean?

"The white people's garden is money. We have a garden; it gives us food. If it does not, we are in despair. But with white people, if they have no money, they are in despair."

Fausto then gave us a tour of his garden, which filled a large forest clearing five minutes' walk from the *maloca*. The rain forest topsoil is surprisingly thin, a layer of only a few inches above clay. This means you can only cultivate the garden for three years. After this you cease planting and weeding, although you can still harvest some fruit. But other fruit that drops off the trees fertilizes a variety of plants with medicinal uses. It also attracts small animals nosing around for something to eat, which makes the former garden a hunting ground. Slowly the forest then takes back the land; it will be restored and ready to use as a garden again about a generation later. In the meantime you plant a series of other gardens elsewhere.

Tilling land so sparingly means that people must live far dispersed, seldom more than three or four families in one spot. Spreading his hands wide, Fausto talked about how important it was for these family clusters to be several miles apart, so that the land will never wear out. How opposite this is, it struck me, to the constant tendency of the industrial world: to bring people together in one spot.

"The priests have always pushed for villages," Martin told us later. "Behind that is the basic idea: you'll be better off living like *us*. If you have everyone in a village, then you can get everybody to come to mass. You'll find a little village of twenty mud houses, clustered around a church. Like a little plaza in Spain. People still hunt in the forest, but after a while they can't find any animals: there's too much demand when you concentrate so many families in one spot. Same with the garden—you can use the same soil only for those three years or so. So pretty soon people are having to walk an hour or more each way to get to fertile land. Then they give up and depend on the market economy. And to do that they have to have money. And to have money they have to have a job. And to find them jobs the government comes in and—if they're lucky—pays them a pittance for doing something that they would do anyway, like building a path through the forest. And there, in a single generation, you've turned the Indians into *poor people*."

. . .

Amazon Indian cosmology contains an extraordinarily subtle understanding of the rich but fragile environment, and, above all, of the carrying capacity of the land. Gerardo Reichel-Dolmatoff, Colombia's most eminent anthropologist, spent much of his life studying an area only fifty miles north of the Mirití. The Indians there know that the thin soil of the rain forest will support only a limited population. "The number of children is kept low and couples with many children are criticized quite openly as socially irresponsible," writes Reichel-Dolmatoff. Women take herbal mixtures that make them temporarily sterile. And for long periods couples must not have sex: for some days before a man goes hunting, for example, or if the man is an apprentice shaman. In effect, many rain forest tribes practice birth control.

Rituals show an awareness that the forest and rivers can support only a limited amount of fish and game. You must not eat birds' eggs, spawning fish, or certain animals during their breeding season. Other rules restrict the amount of hunting still more. Each type of animal, for example, is associated with a certain constellation, and can be hunted only when those stars are in the sky. The shaman makes sure all these practices are followed, acting, Reichel-Dolmatoff says, as a sort of "ecological broker."

After our night at Fausto's, we headed farther up the river, traveling eight or nine hours a day in the outboard canoe. In the next two days of travel, we passed only three other boats. One was occupied by an Indian couple Martin knew. Two dogs and an ancient rifle lay between them in their small dugout. They were hunting tapir. Martin asked how many bullets they had, and the answer came back: "One."

Worried about guerrillas and the drug mafia, the government has made it almost impossible to buy bullets. For smaller animals, many Indians have therefore gone back to using traditional blow-guns, which shoot darts tipped with curare, a poisonous resin taken from certain plants.

Perhaps three or four times a day, we passed a palm-thatched house or two. People ran out at the sound of the motor; Martin knew them all, and exchanged news and gossip and small presents. The Indians gave us plantains and papayas, and, at one house, a jungle delicacy: smoked rat. Martin ate it with relish.

People were usually barefoot. The men often wore just a pair of bathing trunks; the women a T-shirt and short skirt. Clothing was introduced by the missionaries, and I suspect the Indians often don't bother about it when no whites are around: once or twice people seemed to be hastily putting on their clothes as our boat rounded a bend and came into sight.

At least once a day, we all dove into the river. The farther we went, the happier Martin became. Sometimes he would strategize with Hermann about which members of parliament he should lobby about rain forest issues on a forthcoming trip to Germany. Then, abruptly, he would say in Spanish to our boatman, "Famir! Stop the motor!" For a few moments we would drift slowly back down the river. We could now hear all the sounds of the jungle: the splash of water against the banks, parrot calls, the chatter of monkeys. In the air fluttered hundreds of brilliant butterflies: red, yellow, blue, green. We never saw the monkeys, but the dense upper branches of trees shook and rustled from their leaping.

At one point we stopped and talked to an Indian on the river-bank. With Martin interpreting, the man asked the names of the countries Hermann and I were from, which did not seem familiar to him. Then he asked me, "In your land, where does the sun rise?"

I explained that, unlike here, it did not rise directly in the east, nor pass directly overhead. He then understood that we were from far away indeed, and not likely to meet again. When we said good-bye, he added, laughing, "I'll see you in heaven!"

· · ·

Our final destination was a *maloca* some 260 miles upriver from La Pedrera, home of a *capitán* who is leader of about half the people on the Mirití. Toward evening of our third day on the river, the boat slowed and pulled up to the bank. A crowd of young men and children came down to the water to help carry our things up a steep bluff of slippery clay. We walked for a few minutes along a path, Martin setting his usual breakneck pace, and came to the biggest *maloca* we had seen so far. We ducked our heads to enter the door, and shook hands with the *capitán,* Faustino Matapi. Faustino had several hundred people in his domain, Martin explained, and for more than twenty years had been a major leader in the battle for Indian land rights. He and Martin had much to discuss, and we would be here the next three nights. For Leah, the young woman we had given a ride to, it was almost the end of the journey. Her new mother-in-law's garden was five hours' walk through the forest from here, and the next day, Faustino said, he would provide a man to guide her.

Faustino was a short man with wiry black hair, streaks of red dye on his cheeks (it is the men here, not the women, who wear make-up), powerful shoulders, and an aura of great seriousness and dignity. At sunset, one of his men carried burning resin on a stick around the inside of the *maloca,* to purify it by scaring away germs and making the building invisible to evil spirits. It smelled pleasantly, like incense. Faustino then offered us some tobacco to smoke, a special honor. It was a large, whole tobacco leaf, rolled up tightly with a small hole in the middle.

Dinner was boiled chicken, and then manioc bread, which is a staple food here. The bread is baked in round, flat loaves about twenty inches in diameter. It is unleavened and mushy, perhaps three-fourths of an inch thick, and looks and tastes something like white rubber. Also for dinner was some sort of stew, which, for extra zest and protein, had worms added to it. Martin, though not I, devoured it with gusto. I also declined some large, live ants. "Don't eat the heads; they're too sweet," said Martin, "but the body is really delicious."

. . .

Unexpectedly the following morning three other visitors arrived at the *maloca* in a big forty-horsepower outboard. They were Indians, but they wore something we had not seen so far: life jackets. "They probably grew up on one of the rivers, and swim like dolphins," said Martin. But life jackets are white people's wear, and therefore a badge of official status.

Colombian law now gives Indians on the *resguardos* the right to live completely outside the normal structure of government, ruling themselves through the traditional *capitáns*. But if it wants, an Indian community can instead choose to incorporate as a municipality. Colombia's provincial governors are lobbying the Indians hard to do this: the more municipalities, the more people a governor has to govern, and to collect votes and taxes from. These men in life jackets were representing the governor's office in the provincial capital several hundred miles away. The governor, they said, wants to send an airplane to bring Faustino and the other *capitáns* of the Mirití to a special meeting where he can explain the many benefits of municipality status. These will include new housing, electricity, schools, TV, and short canals through the forest here and there to eliminate those long hairpin bends on the river and reduce travel time.

Happily, the visitors' mission was unsuccessful. After several hours of talk and coca chewing, Faustino told them no. But their visit was a sobering reminder that when an Indian community here makes a choice of how it wants to live, the choice is not made once and done with, but must be made again and again, against repeated pressures for "development."

.   .   .

Night sounds in the *maloca*:

The men sit on their low stools, talking with Martin. Their uninterrupted half-hour monologues carry the echo of such a different pace, a different sense of time. From the other side of this immense circular space, lit only by a candle and several dying fires, comes a soft splash as women pour leftover cooking water onto the *maloca* floor; the clay soil quickly absorbs it.

Finally, all are in their hammocks. Two small children sometimes share one. Once or twice a baby cries; a woman or girl reaches over to rock its hammock, and then all is quiet. A child urinates on the floor; this, too, is quickly absorbed and the clay is soon dry. Late in the night, a little girl whimpers one word over and over. An old woman in the hammock next to her gets up and throws a piece of wood onto the embers of a cooking fire. The flame flares up. The girl is immediately still. She had been afraid of the dark.

Toward morning, a rainstorm patters on the roof, then blows away.

We are sharing this *maloca* with nearly two dozen people altogether: Faustino, his wife, and their children; his brother and his family; and three women and four children from downriver, the first contingent of visitors coming to a harvest festival that will take place here next week. The *maloca* is huge, the size and shape of a small circus tent. Its circular wall is about five feet high, made of thin, rough-hewn boards set in the ground. Overhanging this wall, the palm thatch roof slopes steeply up. A dozen feet or so in from the wall a circle of twenty palm trunks, stripped of their bark, support the roof. Then, farther in and high above the center of the *maloca,* this main roof ends in a rectangular opening, of perhaps ten by fifteen feet. Each corner of the rectangle is supported by a taller, thicker palm trunk some thirty feet high. The rectangular opening is covered by a gable roof open at the ends.

The design is ingenious. It completely protects you from rain, but through the open gables it lets out smoke from the cooking fires. The rising smoke blackens the inside of the roof, conveniently killing insects that would otherwise eat holes in the palm thatch. As a result, a *maloca* roof needs to be replaced only every ten to fifteen years—a life span similar to that of the flat tarpaper-and-gravel roof of my house in San Francisco. Besides letting out smoke, the open gables let in daylight—enough to read by for most of the day. Now, at night, lying in a hammock, through one of these openings I can see the stars.

Dawn. The triangle of sky in the gable turns from black to gray to blue. The young men are up first, slipping out of their hammocks to go down to the river to bathe. I hear their shouts and the drumlike sounds of hands slapping the water. When bathing at dawn, men scrape their skin with piranha teeth, rub pepper in the scratches, then get into the water to soothe the burning. This toughens the skin and makes callouses—useful armor for slipping through underbrush when you're hunting.

Then the women and children are up, and I hear babies sucking at their mothers' breasts. A little girl near me begins to sing, high and sweetly. She is rocking a baby in her hammock. As sunlight seeps between the boards of the wall, dogs and chickens, who have been shooed outside during the night, once more roam the *maloca* floor.

Martin seems to need very little sleep. He wakes up, stretches, and, still in his hammock, immediately begins talking. "We have to get this damned municipality thing *stopped.* I've got to work on this in Bogotá." Then he bounds out of his hammock, and, at his usual five-miles-per-hour pace, heads down to the water for an early-morning swim.

For a long time, I lie in my hammock. A bunch of bananas hangs on the *maloca* wall; a woman takes one and smilingly hands it to me, breakfast in bed. Later people give us palm nuts and small, round pineapples, just picked. A beautiful little bird, with a blue head and green wings, hops across the floor and makes off with a piece of my manioc bread.

Through a triangular open gable now comes a majestic shaft of sunlight that hits the earth floor, like the light from a high cathedral window. Even though I can't understand a word anyone is saying, I have rarely felt so relaxed, so connected to the natural world around me, of night and day, of forest and water, of earth and sky.

I find my mind going back a week, to a moment when I felt just the opposite. I had flown from San Francisco to South America via Miami, and had spent the night in an airport hotel there. The hotel was actually part of the airport; you did not go outdoors to reach it. In the room itself, as in an airplane, the small window was sealed shut; a constant whoosh of temperature-controlled air came from a vent. All day in one airplane; the night in this sealed room; all the next day in another airplane. During those thirty hours or so, I never saw the sky or sun except through glass, all the air I breathed had been processed and blown by a machine, and my feet had never touched the earth.

.   .   .

Back in the *maloca,* it occurs to me that I have never before lived, even for a few nights, in a building that is circular. A round building has no corners you can withdraw to. And a *maloca* has no rooms. Think of everything that is allowed by rooms. Differences of privilege: who gets the master bedroom, who gets the corner office. The division of functions: separate spaces for eating, sleeping, working, cooking, and leisure. But here the *maloca* is church, living room, kitchen, bedroom, nursery, playroom—and even graveyard, for the dead are buried, rolled in their hammocks, just beneath where they slept in life.

(One of the few things that does not happen in the *maloca* is the procreation of its next generation of inhabitants. For that, a couple finds a secluded patch of garden or forest. But first they put down banana leaves to keep away the ants.)

In Indian mythology, the circularity of the *maloca* represents the cycle of the year, with each of the central four posts standing for a season. *Malocas* usually have twelve poles in the outer ring of roof supports, symbolizing the twelve lunar months. This circularity also stands for the uterus. The center of the *maloca* floor represents the navel of the world, a sacred spot where no harm can come to you.

Missionaries "realized early on the religious significance of the *maloca* and its role as the center of the Indian's universe," writes Peter Bunyard in *The Colombian Amazon.* "A vital first step in getting the Indians to abandon their traditions . . . was to get them to give up using their *malocas.* Without the *maloca* the rituals would become meaningless." It is strange how worldwide is this conquest of the circular by the rectangular, whether the conqueror is church, corporation, or state. I think of the teepees of the North American Plains Indians, replaced by the cinder block houses of the reservations, or of the round Zulu huts of South Africa, replaced by the brick matchboxes of Soweto.

Studying Faustino's *maloca* from the vantage point of my hammock, I can see only two Western artifacts used in its construction. One is the door hinges. The other is a long inverted V of corrugated tin, just a few inches wide, fitted over the crest of the gable roof—at a sharp angle it is hard to get a tight seal with palm thatch. But every other part of the building is material from the forest, put together in the same way in which people have been building *malocas* for thousands of years. Ropelike lianas, firmly knotted, tie the rafters and vertical beams together.

Besides clothing, one of the few other visible traces of European influence is a small, faded picture of Jesus and Mary fastened to the *maloca* wall. "The idea of worshiping a *virgin* the Indians have always found a bit *odd,* really," Martin explains. "They don't get it. Jesus, on the other hand, they accept as the white people's god—and as the god of merchandise. Why? Because at the mission station upriver, the priest operates a little shop, to supply flashlight batteries and so on. But he won't open the shop for you unless you come to mass first."

The Indians around me in the *maloca* on average seem several inches shorter than Americans or Europeans, but with rare exceptions they look healthy. Those who are unhealthy tend to die young. No medical statistics exist for people like these; Martin says that usually at least one or two children per family do not live to adulthood, and that adult life expectancy may be about fifty. But one thing everyone agrees on is that every measure of public health declines when Indians move to towns and cities, which almost always means living in tin-shack slums. Here in the *maloca* none of the children have the swollen bellies of the malnourished. Most adults seem to have all their teeth. They are not, after all, consuming Cokes and Mars Bars, but only food that comes from the river, the forest, and the garden.

All day long, a laughing flock of children runs in and out the *maloca* door. A young man throws a pebble across the dirt floor for them, and they race after it, squealing. How inadequate are our usual measures of well-being. These Indians have zero physicians, telephones, or automobiles per capita. Those who have been to school have dropped out. They produce almost no goods and services of monetary value. They are depressing their country's per capita GNP. In the eyes of a foreign-aid worker, they are in urgent need of "development." In the eyes of a statistician, they are the poorest of the poor. But they are rich in much that has no price.

·   ·   ·

It is tempting to idealize such a life. But one aspect of it falls far short of paradise. The women do all the work.

The men seem to spend their time mainly sitting in a circle, chewing coca leaves, receiving visitors, and talking at great length. Women take care of the children, do all the cooking, and almost all the gardening. It is a woman who sweeps the dirt floor of the *maloca* at least once a day with a twig broom. During our three days in Faustino's *maloca,* the women, young and old, carry in big baskets of manioc root from the garden and make a huge supply of manioc bread for the visitors coming to next week's harvest ritual. But during the ritual itself women will not even be allowed in the *maloca.* The dance is for men only.

Furthermore, these rubbery manioc loaves must be the most labor-intensive bread on earth. First the women peel a tough brown skin off the manioc. Then they grate the white root into a pulp by rubbing it against a washboardlike plank, embedded with stones or thorns. Then they vigorously pound the resulting mush with a stone, over a woven sieve, to force out all the liquid, which contains a form of cyanide. Only then do they have the raw material to start baking with. For most of each day, groups of women and girls scrape and pound and press and knead for hours at a time.

When teenage boys reach manhood, they can sit in the circle and chew coca with the male elders; women are allowed to do this only after menopause—and even then we see only one or two who do so, and they seldom speak. A woman having her menstrual period can't enter the *maloca:* we see one woman sitting on a stool outside the door. Among the Indians he studied across the border from here in Brazil, the French anthropologist Claude Levi-Strauss noted that "after death, the souls of men are embodied in jaguars; but those of women and children are carried up into the air where they vanish forever."

.   .   .

Because the dense rain forest makes cross-country travel so difficult, ethnic groups tend to be very small. Fifty-five known tribes live in Colombia's Amazon rain forest, each with its own language. Faustino, however, is the elected *capitán* of people from several different tribes. This is not Yugoslavia.

Certainly the spirit of the society around me now seems anything but nationalistic or martial. In our three days living in Faustino's *maloca,* I never see anyone scold or punish a child. One afternoon we find a man from the *maloca* standing by the river with a small boy in his arms. His child has a fever, he explains, and he hopes that being next to the running water will soothe the boy and make him feel better.

Although I am awed by the harmony of the life of the *maloca* I see unfolding each day, at the same time it feels extremely fragile. The menace that lurks outside the *maloca* is not bulldozers that will come crashing through these trees but more subtle things. These women grating manioc, rubbing the hard white roots for hour after hour against the thorn-studded board: What if they knew there was a hand-cranked grinder that could do the job in a tenth the time? Would they then feel the grinder to be a need, like fishhooks and machetes? How would their lives have to change so they could get enough money to buy a grinder? And then, if the people in one *maloca* have a grinder, would the people in another *maloca* who don't have one feel poor? Right now, the very idea of being poor does not yet exist here. But how easily it could be introduced, and how hard to uproot.

.   .   .

As the days go by, I find myself feeling differently about the rain forest itself. Think of all the connotations of the word "jungle." It implies a tangle, a thicket, a place of steaming heat, swamps, danger. I had worriedly asked Martin beforehand: should I bring mosquito netting? Snake bite medicine? Boots? But mosquitoes rarely bother us, and we wear sandals. One afternoon Martin and Hermann and I walk for several hours on a forest path that begins at Faustino's *maloca*. In a few minutes the laughter of people bathing in the river is behind us. The trees are so high that the light down on the forest floor is deep, gentle green; it feels as if you are walking on the bottom of a fish tank.

Lianas wind their way up tree trunks and around branches. The trees are immensely tall, their trunks thin. One tree that looks strikingly different from the others is the *bamba*, which has strange, vertical, buttresslike roots that begin above ground, jutting out huge and flat from the base of the trunk, like fins at the base of a rocket.

The forest has an extraordinary ability to recycle. Probably thirty or forty people live in Faustino's *maloca* and in several other wood-and-thatch buildings within a few hundred feet. The community has no garbage pit and no latrines. Yet this does not seem unsanitary. The Colombian euphemism for defecating, says Martin, is "sending a telegram to the mayor." If you come back to the same spot in the forest the next day, your telegram of yesterday has completely vanished. The heat and humidity here produce some of the most vigorous microorganisms on earth.

Returning hot and sweaty from our forest walk, we swim up a little muddy-green creek that flows into the Miriti here. The creek is so narrow that tree branches meet in a continuous archway above us; hanging vines come down to the water and graze our heads. To come back downstream, we just float.

.   .   .

Finally the day came when we had to leave Faustino's. It had taken us three full days to come up the river from La Pedrera; going back, with the current, would require only two.

As before, Martin talked to people along the way. At each stop, as at Fausto's and Faustino's, Martin had long, coca-chewing conferences about the mission that had brought him on this trip: how did the Indians plan to earn enough money to buy the fishhooks, machetes, and other items they wanted without destroying their way of life? They had deliberated over this question for months, and each time it took them several hours to give Martin all their reasoning.

The answer was the same at every stop: chickens.

"They considered every alternative," Martin explained to Hermann and me over the sound of the outboard motor. "They're expert canoe builders, but they say, 'If we make too many, we'll cut down all the good trees.' Sacred objects of any sort they don't want to sell. They thought about fish, but say, 'Then there'll be too few fish in the river and our children won't have anything to eat.' Plus, they don't have any way to store the fish: that would mean a freezer, and a generator, and diesel fuel. And if you have electricity it could lead to television and all sorts of other things the *capitáns* don't want.

"They like the idea of chickens because they have some anyway, and you can raise chickens without destroying the forest. And there's no investment needed. I think it'll work: if a chicken is worth three or four dollars, say, then with two chickens you can buy a machete. A hammock might be six chickens. There's a modest market for chickens in La Pedrera and the other towns. Another nice thing about chickens is that you can easily transport them long distances."

We had proof of this on board our boat, from whose stern came an occasional despairing squawk. At Faustino's *maloca*, Famir, our teenage boatman, had traded a T-shirt for a chicken, and the bird was now traveling back down the river with us, toward Famir's family dinner table in La Pedrera.

Martin had discussed with the Indians how the Gaia Foundation he works for could help them carry out the chicken plan. "It's important that any help to them not be seen as charity. Ideally, they have to be able to sell the chickens without making the long trip down to town. The plan is for the foundation to get a boat, one big enough to have a cabin. It can be a sort of traveling shop. We'll stock all the things they want: fishhooks, knives, hatchets, needles and thread, matches, and so on. Just the necessities. No food, that's important. And because we're buying the supplies in bulk, we can get cheaper prices. Then we'll buy the chickens from them. All transactions will be barter, no money. Selling the chickens then becomes our problem, not theirs.

"Once we get the boat, it should become a self-sustaining operation. If it works, people can copy the model on other rivers. If it doesn't work, then people will drift out to the towns, they'll go back and forth, and slowly the culture will disappear. We have to make it work. We're not going to have this chance again."

During these two long days going downriver, I asked Martin how he got first interested in the Indians.

"The first time I came here was to do some anthropological fieldwork," he said. "But I just got . . . carried away. I traveled through the forest by canoe, for five months, from one end to the other. I've written academic articles and taught anthropology at a university and all that, but I've never been that kind of scholar at heart. I think most anthropologists believe that *they* have something to contribute to humanity by writing about the Indians, not that the Indians have something to contribute. And how can you work peacefully when the people you're studying are perishing? I don't want to write the definitive book about the last of the Yucuna. I want to help them to not be the last."

. . .

It had rained off and on while we were at Faustino's, and the river was now much higher. In places where the banks were low, a powerfully flowing sheet of water spilled into the forest, making the tops of the trees shake, and sweeping dead branches off the forest floor. I washed some laundry in the river, but in the humid air and intermittent rain, I never managed to get it dry. (When I finally got back home some days later, it was still damp, smelling mysteriously of the Mirití River.)

At the end of our second day coming downstream, we stopped at one last *maloca* Martin had to visit, and when we got on the river and started the outboard motor again, it was long past dark. The night was moonless. From time to time rainsqualls swept over us. Martin sat on the bow of the canoe and played his flashlight on the water, trying to spot floating logs and branches before we hit them. As we approached La Pedrera it showed no lights, for the electricity was shut down for the night.

The next morning much of the town again turned out to watch the weekly plane land its handful of passengers. One, in a white summer dress, was the wife or girlfriend of an army officer. In his boots, cap, and pistol belt, he greeted her hungrily, not letting go of her waist as they walked down the dirt street into town.

Then we got on board. La Pedrera, like most of the Amazon rain forest, is near sea level; Bogotá, several hours away, is nestled high into the side of the Andes. As our plane climbed toward the capital, the crew began breathing oxygen, taking turns with a single mask. There was none for the passengers. I felt light-headed. Even the energetic Martin looked groggy and wilted.

Downtown Bogotá is filled with skyscrapers, shopping malls, freeways. Arriving there felt like reentering that world of the Miami airport. There were beggars on the streets, though; one anguished, haggard woman pressed her face against the window of our taxi, imploringly pointing to her mouth to show that she had nothing to eat. It was haunting to see the dark skin and jet-black hair of her entirely Indian features. How short a time ago did her ancestors live in a riverside *maloca* or other Indian dwelling, and on what sidewalk or park bench did she sleep now?

The TV in my hotel room was filled with endless conflict: Bosnia, Somalia, the British royal family. Even the sports news showed a basketball coach sobbing because his team had lost a game. To my surprise, the rains of the past week, which we had experienced mainly as peaceful thrumming on the *maloca* roof, had flooded low-lying cities and towns all over the Amazon basin. The TV showed emergency crews going down streets in boats to rescue people from the tin roofs of their homes. We had seen absolutely nothing like this. The Indians of the Mirití know better than to build their *malocas* on a floodplain.

.   .   .

That night Martin took Hermann and me to dinner at the Bogotá home of Gerardo Reichel-Dolmatoff, the dean of Colombia's anthropologists. He and his wife live in an apartment filled with photographs and art objects collected over a lifetime of studying the country's Indians. The Austrian-born Reichel-Dolmatoff, in his eighties, was a tall, august, imposing man, very formal and very European. His first question was, "What shall be the language of the evening?"

Reichel-Dolmatoff talked, among other things, about shamans. The Indians believe that illness or misfortune is often sent to you by a malevolent shaman of another tribe; your shaman's job is to send the trouble back where it came from. This seems ridiculous to many Westerners, Reichel-Dolmatoff said, but he saw it differently. "The Indians play out these inevitable human conflicts—but only in the realm of the imagination." He gestured at his TV set. "We do it with guns."

He went on to describe "purification rituals," an important part of Indian life. Before an Amazon Indian makes a major step, like going deep into the forest to hunt, or setting out on a long journey, he fasts or eats only certain foods, and prays or meditates.

In the middle of this dinner-table conversation about purification rituals, a curious thing happened. For the first time in my life, I fainted.

Everyone was very helpful and comforting as I came to, on the floor but undamaged. This happens often to visitors who've just arrived in Bogotá, they said, because of the sudden change of altitude. Our hosts kindly suggested we finish dinner in the living room, so I could remain lying down. Oddly, after this embarrassing interruption, the talk took a deeper turn. Hermann asked Reichel-Dolmatoff, "What can we learn from the Indians?"

As in one of those *maloca* conversations I had overheard, Reichel-Dolmatoff remained silent, for so long I wasn't sure he had heard the question. Finally he answered: "Patience."

Suddenly, flat on my back, I wondered if my fainting was not a symptom, in a way, of supreme *im*patience. From yesterday to today, Hermann, Martin, and I had made the greatest imaginable transitions. From sea level to nearly nine thousand feet. From a hammock in a dirt-floored *maloca* to a high-rise apartment. From swimming naked in a jungle river to wearing coats and ties. From munching papayas sliced off the tree to eating *poulet en croûte*. From breathing some of the most oxygen-rich air on earth to being in a big-city's traffic fumes. Was I not arrogant to think that I could make such a drastic set of transitions without this telling on my body? And was I not impatient to make this sudden leap between altitudes, oxygen levels, foods, and spiritual universes so suddenly, and without first undergoing the equivalent of a purification ritual?

That question has lingered and broadened in my mind. Is there not an impatience, an arrogance to it, when we so blithely use technology to shrink time and distance? And, more important, what is the price of that impatience anytime we use technology to dramatically alter the natural world?

I cannot say that my life has changed since I returned from

Colombia. I still fly in jet planes, use a computer, and depend on the myriad of other machinery and circuitry that we think of as an essential part of our lives. But I've found myself thinking more about the price of all this. In the back of our minds, we've long known that it's high. If every person on earth consumed as much energy and produced as much waste as each American or European, life on our planet could not go on. We would soon run out of breathable air, drinkable water, and much more.

Several times a week I climb to the top of a high hill in the middle of San Francisco. The city spreads out below me in all its glory, for there is a majesty to our extravagance. A distant murmur rises from endless streams of automobiles and trucks. As night falls, hundreds of thousands of lights go on; the smoggy air and the heat escaping from buildings and pavements makes them shimmer. At anchor in the harbor are the oil tankers, whose supplies keep the spendthrift city running. I know that everything I see cannot last, in this form. If there is still someone able to stand on this hilltop five hundred years from now, he or she will see a different scene, a less ecologically profligate way of living.

An Indian in a *maloca* would not feel that way. Whether *that* life lasts is dependent on people living in the San Franciscos of the world, and on what we do to the earth's air, its oceans, its ozone layer, its very temperature. There is nothing inherent in the way of life of the *maloca* to cause its self-destruction. How strange it is that today we should consider that a remarkable achievement.

I now sometimes wonder what people from that world would think if they looked down from my urban hilltop. Their universe is so centered within one building; ours is so infinitely spread out. Members of one family live scattered in different cities, the food we eat is grown in different countries, the contents of a single desktop manufactured on different continents. The innards of my dishwasher, the fruit on my table, the shirt I wear—I do not even know where these things originally came from. Surely there is a link between that diffusion and our abuse of the earth and its riches.

The survival of people like the Indians of the Mirití matters not only as an issue of human rights and self-determination. In addition, their culture's very existence poses a set of questions to all people, especially to that majority of us who have lost all cultural memory of earlier ways of life, and who must devise afresh our own ways of living more lightly on the earth.

1995

PART THREE

War and Other Literary Pleasures

Preceding page: German and Russian soldiers fraternizing after the Eastern Front cease-fire, 1917.
Photo by Novosti/Corbis-Bettmann.

Paragon of Porkers

FREDDY THE PIG

The moral center of my childhood universe, the place where good
and evil, friendship and treachery, honesty and humbug were de-
fined most clearly, was not church, not school, and not the Boy
Scouts. It was the Bean Farm.

The Bean Farm, as all right-thinking children of my generation knew, was the upstate New York home of Freddy the Pig and
his fellow animals. They are the subject of twenty-six books by
Walter R. Brooks, a former New York advertising man and staff
writer for the *New Yorker,* that appeared between 1927 and Brooks's
death in 1958. One of Brooks's many triumphs of tone is that his
human characters are surprised, but only *mildly* surprised, that
Freddy and the other animals talk. The laconic, bewhiskered Mr.
Bean, whose farm they live on, barely says a word, so he appears
the unusual one.

Brooks had many admirers, from my fifth-grade classmates to
the mighty Lionel Trilling, who called the books "delightful."
Other loyalists have claimed Freddy as the ancestor of more famous
literary pigs, such as those in George Orwell's *Animal Farm.* In
fact, in *Freddy the Politician,* the animals foil a crafty gang of wood-
peckers who try to seize control of the Bean Farm by making
extravagant promises—a revolving door for the henhouse, catproof
apartments for the rats, and so on. In his book *Fairy Tales and
After,* the critic Roger Sale points out that *Freddy the Politician* "not
only preceded Orwell's work but is a good deal more careful with
its materials and, for that matter, shrewder about its politics. . . .
The actions emerge much less mechanically than do Orwell's."

Freddy enthusiasts have called him a porcine prince, a pig of

235

many parts, a paragon of porkers, a Renaissance pig. Although lazy, he accomplishes a lot, because "when a lazy person once really gets started doing things, it's easier to keep on than it is to stop." As the problems he faces require, he is by turns cowboy, balloonist, magician, campaign manager, pilot, and detective. But Freddy is the most unheroic of heroes: he oversleeps, he daydreams, he eats too much, and, when not suffering from writer's block, he writes flowery poetry for all occasions. When he gets scared, his tail uncurls.

Walter R. Brooks's gentle genius shines even brighter in his villains. Take, for example, Watson P. Condiment, the comic-book magnate, who has six big houses, fifteen big cars, and a yacht. A blustery blackmailer, he is "a tall thin man who always looked as if he had a stomach ache. That was because he did have a stomach ache." But the animals can thwart Mr. Condiment's evil plans because "people who read comic books will believe almost anything."

.   .   .

Almost all the other villains foiled by Freddy are also from the Establishment. General Grimm is "short, stocky and red-faced and looked as if his uniform was too tight for him but nobody had better mention it." Mr. Gridley, the high school principal, "never came close to anybody he was talking to but always stood off several yards and shouted." The bank president, Mr. Weezer, has glasses that fall off any time anyone mentions a sum over ten dollars.

The pompous, timid Senator Blunder flees the scene when pursued by the animals because "should I be struck down, into what hands would fall the reins of the ship of state?" The fabulously wealthy Margarine family tears up farmers' fields with fox hunts in *Freddy Rides Again*. (The fox, of course, is a friend of Freddy's and the Margarines are undone.) And, until he is exposed by the animals, a conniving real estate man pretends he is a ghost and haunts houses he wants the occupants to sell. Brooks also takes a few digs at the space program and at the FBI—Freddy's bumbling Animal Bureau of Investigation often misses the evidence right under his snout.

Poking fun at generals, realtors, bank presidents, and the like was unusual fare for children's books of the 1940s and 1950s. In a subtle, low-key way the books even prefigured the spirit of the rebellious decade that followed.

In *Freddy and the Bean Home News,* for instance, the animals start their own paper because Mrs. Underdunk, the rich, haughty newspaper owner, and her editor, Mr. Garble, distort the news. When the evil Mr. Condiment hits Freddy, Freddy thinks: "He slapped me because I am a pig. . . . If I were a boy or a man he wouldn't have done it." And when Freddy becomes mayor, he solves the traffic problem by banning all parking within city limits.

Small wonder, then, that some of the children who grew up on these books went on to found alternative newspapers, to march for civil rights, and to become ardent environmentalists. Still, you don't have to be in the 1960s generation to appreciate Freddy. As with all books that last, their attraction is broader and deeper. Essentially they evoke the most subversive and radical politics of all: a child's instinctive sense of fair play. Brooks speaks powerfully to his young readers' moral sense without ever overtly moralizing. The local sheriff tells Freddy's sidekick, Charles the rooster, that he will get much tougher penalties for pecking the face of a rich man than that of a poor one. Truer words were never spoken. But how can a reader feel preached at when it's someone talking to a rooster?

In the early 1980s, says Dave Carley, a Toronto playwright, he "stopped in at a children's library to see if they still had any Freddy books. The librarian told me that she was photocopying pages and binding the books with hockey-stick tape because they were in such demand." Carley found others, he told me in a telephone interview, who remembered the books as fondly as he, and formed the Friends of Freddy, who meet every two years for a weekend of book trading, talk, and pork-free dinners.

"I grew up in Peterborough, Ontario," Carley says. "A Friends of Freddy member from there told me recently that when he was a boy, there were two thugs who came to the library on Saturday mornings. The bigger one blocked the door and the smaller one ran upstairs and checked out all available Freddy books. I had to confess that these two were my brother and me."

The nearly two hundred Friends of Freddy include Michael Cart, former director of the Beverly Hills, California, public library, who is writing Walter R. Brooks's biography; Lee Secrest, an Atlanta actor who says he kept himself sane in the army by reading Freddy books concealed inside a copy of *Time;* and Henry S. F.

Cooper Jr., who for many years covered the space program for the *New Yorker*. "They represent the very best of American fantasy writing for children," says Cooper of the books. "They are the American version of the great English classics such as the Pooh books or *The Wind in the Willows*."

Carley adds: "A lot of people in the organization are writers and journalists. It was such a painful thing when you read the last Freddy book that you felt moved to go out and write your own book."

Above all, it is Brooks's moral world that sticks with his readers. "I distinctly remember learning things from the books that I could apply to my own life," Carley says. "For example, that if somebody says, 'To be frank with you,' it means they're lying." *Village Voice* writer Geoffrey Stokes points out that the Bean animals had a "one-animal, one-vote rule in place long before the human Supreme Court established our version." Wendy Wolf, a New York book editor, learned that the Nuremberg defense is no good. "Like when the children of Simon the Rat say, 'Our father made us do it,' they're told: 'Forget it, you're going to jail.'"

·   ·   ·

Starting in the late 1960s, the twenty-six Freddy books began to go out of print, one by one. Finally only one was left. Then in 1986 and 1987, with prodding from the Friends of Freddy, Brooks's publisher, Alfred A. Knopf, reissued eight titles. The new paperback editions carried introductions by Brooks's biographer, Michael Cart, and won great praise from reviewers. Sadly, however, all copies of the eight republished books are now gone. Says Cart: "It's enough to make your tail come uncurled!"

I asked about a dozen editors, writers, librarians, and children's book experts why these books are apparently less popular today than they were half a century ago. Some people said that maybe the Bean Farm now seems too quaintly rural. Others wondered if the books were too long for today's short attention span. A few suggested that children now want more action and adventure, faster-paced plots, more violence. Everybody mentioned television.

"We were very, very disappointed not to be able to keep the books in print," says Stephanie Spinner of Knopf, who worked on the Freddy reissue. "But it's harder and harder to sell a paperback book that doesn't have mass appeal. We really did give it our best shot."

Then, going over my notes one last time, I suddenly realized something. Like Freddy floundering through one of his detective cases, I had missed a clue right under my snout—evidence that I was asking the wrong question. Between 1927, when Brooks wrote the first book in the series, and 1958, when he died, 340,000 Freddy the Pig books were sold. This was considered a grand success: the books all stayed in print for decades. Between 1986, when Knopf started reissuing the books, and 1993, a mere 86,000 Freddy books were sold. This was considered a failure and the books went out of print.

But wait! Look at the numbers again. From 1986 to 1993, Knopf sold almost exactly the same number of Freddy books *per year,* on average, as during Brooks's lifetime. Furthermore, because they reprinted only eight of the twenty-six titles during this later period, often a particular book sold *more* copies per year than it had forty or fifty years earlier. I tracked down some sales figures to verify this. *Freddy the Detective,* for example, sold 1,098 copies in 1940 and 1,181 copies in 1950. But when it was reissued, sales were higher: 1,810 copies in 1990, for instance. Still, in 1991 it was taken out of print.

What has changed so drastically, then, is not Freddy's appeal for young American readers. It is how many copies of a children's book a publisher now has to sell to keep it alive. One reissued title, *Freddy Goes Camping,* sold 16,000 copies between 1986 and 1993. A respectable number, you would think, but it wasn't enough to keep the book in print. According to Betsy Hearne, editor of the *Bulletin of the Center for Children's Books,* "there's a shift to something like the best-seller syndrome in the adult market, where something flashes across the sky and then goes out of print right away."

Behind this sea change in children's publishing are several forces. One is that almost all major publishers are now owned by big conglomerates, as heartless as Mr. Condiment or Mr. Weezer. They demand the same rate of profit from children's books as they get from coal mines or steel mills or factories making plastic wrap. Another is an obscure but far-reaching change in the way tax laws are applied, making it harder to depreciate the value of goods in inventory. Since 1980 this has made it much more expensive for publishers to keep unsold copies of backlist titles in their warehouses. Finally, during the Reagan years, Congress slashed federal money for public and school libraries—just as these libraries were already being savaged by state taxpayers' revolts.

All this hit publishers hard. Before the 1970s, some 85 percent of American children's books were sold to public and school libraries. Today, with the collapse of library budgets, that figure has plummeted dramatically—no one is sure by exactly how much. It is more difficult for publishers to make money selling children's books to bookstores: the stores take a commission; they return unsold books, and they generally carry paperback editions of older titles, which have a far smaller profit margin than the hardcover editions libraries buy.

Freddy's fans have not given up, however. A "Freddy Forum" has opened on the Internet. The Friends of Freddy still have their biennial convention; their *Bean Home Newsletter* still appears regularly. But despite their efforts, the Freddy books, for the first time since 1927, are no longer sold. For books so widely beloved as classics, this is outrageous. To preserve works of similar stature for adults, we have the Library of America, supported by major foundations and the National Endowment for the Humanities. Isn't it time we had a Library of America for children?

1994

Magic Journalism

In his book on the fall of the Soviet Union, *Imperium,* Ryszard Kapuściński at one point visits the worst of the conflicts that erupted as the empire slowly dissolved. It is 1990. The USSR is still officially one country, but two of its constituent republics, Armenia and Azerbaijan, are unofficially at war. At issue is the mountainous territory of Nagorno-Karabakh. The crumbling Soviet central government is unsuccessfully attempting to suppress this bitter fighting, and is also trying to keep meddlesome foreign journalists like Kapuściński out of Nagorno-Karabakh. This besieged enclave, inhabited largely by Armenians, lies completely within Azerbaijan. The enclave can be reached from Armenia only by air. The Soviets control the airports at both ends. How can Kapuściński get there?

Armenian friends come up with a solution: he will pretend to be a pilot for the Soviet state airline, Aeroflot. They dress him up in an Aeroflot uniform, and enlist the collaboration of the plane's real pilots, who are Armenians.

First, at the airport in Armenia, crowds of exasperated passengers who've been waiting for seats for days take him for a real pilot and mob him. Then airport *mafiosi* muscle their way toward him through the crowd, alarmed that this unfamiliar pilot might be trying to get in on their on their bribes-for-tickets racket. Silently walking onward in his Aeroflot uniform, Kapuściński follows the commands his Armenian friends whisper in his ear as they smuggle him into the cockpit, and then, once the plane has landed in Nagorno-Karabakh, out of the tightly guarded airport and past the many roadblocks staffed by KGB troops: "Sit down at the controls, and put on the headphones." "Get out and immediately walk straight ahead." "Walk in a decisive way!" "Push your way through the crowd." "Get into the backseat of that car." "Lie down and pretend to be dead drunk."

The disguise works. Kapuściński sees Nagorno-Karabakh and gets his story. But what his Armenian hosts never realize is that his role as a journalist is also a disguise. Here, too, the disguise works. The *Chicago Tribune* calls him the "reporter's reporter . . . the best in the business." *Corriere della Sera* calls him "the greatest living war correspondent." But if a reporter means someone who accurately presents facts conventionally thought important ("The president's press secretary announced today that . . ."), Kapuściński is nothing of the sort. He says that he takes few notes. His dispatches from odd corners of the world would be a magazine fact-checker's nightmare. If the work of contemporary Latin American novelists, sprinkled with trees that walk and birds that talk, is magic realism, Kapuściński, a Pole, has created a kind of magic journalism.

Consider, for example, his first book to be translated into English, about the fall of Haile Selassie, *The Emperor: Downfall of an Autocrat.* Soon after the emperor was deposed, Kapuściński went to Ethiopia and interviewed members of the former ruling circle. In the book they speak in long monologues and are identified only by initials. But can it be that there really was a Minister of the Pen? A keeper of the third door? A purse-bearer to the emperor's treasurer? A functionary of the Department of Processions in the Ministry of Ceremonies? A servant whose job was to wipe off the shoes of dignitaries on which the emperor's dog had urinated? And a royal pillow-bearer, who slipped the right-sized pillow under Haile Selassie's feet when he sat on thrones built for taller emperors? And can it be that all these people, speaking in uniformly elegant phrasing, were willing to tell their stories to a Polish reporter?

Entering this rich and strange world, you soon realize that it doesn't matter if these people literally exist, or if Kapuściński made them all up, or if the answer is somewhere in between. The mosaic their stories form is one of the most haunting portraits we have of autocratic power and its delusions. At home, in a Poland still under the thumb of the Soviets, people got the message: the story was adapted for the stage and performed throughout the country.

Imperium, too, has its share of magic. Kapuściński tells us that the skins of seven hundred calves were needed to make the parchment for a certain medieval book. That Turkish soldiers were about to push the greatest of Armenian composers off a cliff when he was saved by his pupil, the sultan of Istanbul's daughter—and that, having seen the abyss, he was struck dumb forever. That for making the best Georgian cognac, the wood for the barrel must come from an oak tree that stands not in a grove but by itself. That the national epic of the Kirgiz people is forty volumes long. That during storms in the great Turkmenistan desert, travelers "are seized by a water madness" and ravenously drink their entire supply. That in Yakutsk the winter is so cold that the air freezes into mist, in which corridors are carved by the bodies of pedestrians; from the shape of the corridor, you can tell who has walked by. That at Siberian funerals, both corpse and mourners are dressed in white.

Readers can search the *Encyclopaedia Britannica* in vain for confirmation of any of these details. I seem to have not noticed the mist corridors when passing through Yakutsk myself a while back. And I saw no funeral-goers in white in other Siberian towns where I stayed longer. But maybe I visited Siberia at a less ghostly time than did Kapuściński. And perhaps a certain amount of ghostliness is appropriate in describing an empire that is, after all, now dead.

.   .   .

Fables are often born when things cannot be said directly, and this is the route through which Kapuściński came to his magic journalism. For some twenty-five years (until he lost his job with the 1981 declaration of martial law in Poland), he roamed the Third World as a correspondent for the Polish government press agency. He wrote books as well, but these, too, had to get past the censor. He learned to write in allegory. Besides the book on Ethiopia, there were more on the final days of other dilapidated, collapsing empires: *Shah of Shahs,* about Iran, and *Another Day of Life,* about the end of Portuguese rule in Angola. Living under an unelected government in a restless satellite of a huge neighbor, Polish readers well knew what imperial system Kapuściński was really thinking about.

But in learning to transcend Communist censorship, Kapuściński ended up transcending something else as well: conventional journalism. He learned that truth consists of much more than collections of facts. He learned that the most memorable quote may be one that was never spoken. And he learned that truth lies in the stories people tell you, even when they are not true.

The results were extraordinary. Salman Rushdie called *The Emperor* "a real work of art." Such works are a reminder of how difficult, and perhaps silly, it is to always draw a line between fiction and nonfiction. *The Emperor* probably has less in it that's true, in the most literal sense of the word, than might a very autobiographical novel written by an official of Haile Selassie's court. By convention, you are a novelist if you shape something imaginative out of the raw materials of your life experience. If you have to flash a press card to have that experience, we normally think, it puts you in a different category. But what Kapuściński does is to bring the skills of a fine novelist to just those sorts of experiences.

Perhaps the most distinctively Kapuścińskian device is his way of slipping seamlessly from a description of someone into a monologue or conversation going on in the other person's head. In his book on Iran, for example, he listens in as the shah thinks about his army: "The army must always have money. It must have everything. The army will make the nation modern, disciplined, obedient. Everyone: *Attention!*"

There are fewer such passages when Kapuściński travels through Russia in *Imperium,* perhaps because he speaks the language fluently and therefore real conversations displace the imaginary ones. The times he does slip into the imaginary ones are often just those moments when someone refuses to talk to him. For example, after encountering a taciturn steward on the Trans-Siberian Railroad who seems fearful of talking to foreigners, he hears the dialogue in the steward's head:

A foreigner is . . . an infiltrator and a spy! Why is he staring so out the window, what does he want to see there? . . . Did he take notes? He took notes. What did he take notes of? Everything? Where does he keep those notes? With him at all times? That's not good! And what did he ask? He asked if it's far to Sima. To Sima? But we're not stopping in Sima. Precisely. But he asked. And what did you say? Me? I said nothing. What do you mean, nothing! . . . You should have said that we already passed Sima, that would have confused him!

.   .   .

Another strength—and occasionally a limitation—of Kapuściński's style is that he is above all a miniaturist. His best passages
have as a springboard some episode he observes, and they are usually only three or four pages long. There are miniessays in his
Russia book, for example, on how the fatal penalties for asking
questions changed the entire style of Soviet conversation, and on a
meeting of striking Arctic coal miners that soon gets taken over by
the mine's managers, because they're the only people around who
know how to run meetings. A brief encounter with two gang
members leads to a compact, brilliant, two pages on the rise of
organized criminals. Kapuściński places them as the sons and
grandsons of the *bezprizorny*—the millions of orphans produced by
the Russian Civil War and the great famine of the early 1930s,
who wandered the country's roads and lived by theft.

One of these meditations can feel forced when it goes on for
longer than the few pages that seem to be Kapuściński's natural
length. This is true, for example, of a rambling epilogue to *Imperium* that has the unmistakable look of something added at the
publisher's request "to bring the story up to date." Remarks about
the prospects for Boris Yeltsin and the Russian economy feel as out
of place here as would an afterword about prospects for the whal-
ing industry at the end of *Moby Dick*. Each writer is after bigger
game.

Kapuściński's style has several other signature traits. One is his
ability to capture the essence of something with one swift, sure
brush stroke. The image, for instance, glimpsed through a train
window in the Ukraine, of an abandoned part of the vast Soviet
arsenal: a row of new artillery pieces sunk deep into the mud, only
the gun barrels and shields protruding.

Another characteristic note is Kapuściński's attraction to mar-
ginal characters, the polar opposite of the "newsmakers" most reporters seek out. In his book about the last days of Portuguese
Angola, he notices a woman who still tends a shop full of lace
wedding dresses, sitting as mutely as her mannequins; there are no
more customers. In *Imperium,* even when Kapuściński meets a politician, what he takes away from the encounter is often something
about the person's marginality. In Baku, he talks to the leader of
the Azerbaijani National Front. "I know what he will tell me
about the situation in Baku, so I do not ask him about that." The
man is a writer in the Azerbaijani language. For political reasons,

the Azerbaijanis want to abandon the Cyrillic letters imposed on them by the Soviets, but can't decide whether to go back to Arabic script or to start using Roman letters as do their linguistic cousins, the Turks. What intrigues Kapuściński is that this writer is stranded without an alphabet.

. . .

Now Kapuściński no longer needs to write in allegory, and his book on the USSR feels less phantasmagoric than some of the earlier ones. The Soviet Union is the biggest collapsing empire story of them all, and he is free to tell it straight. Although there are two long sections about earlier visits, most of *Imperium* is based on travels through the USSR in its final three years: 1989 through 1991. But Kapuściński's Soviet Union is not the Soviet Union of historians like Richard Pipes or Roy Medvedev or the late Isaac Deutscher (although he is clearly familiar with their work). He has little interest in questions that concern them, such as models of capitalism and socialism—words scarcely mentioned in this book. And it is certainly not the Soviet Union of the foreign correspondents who daily chronicle who's in or out in the Kremlin. Kapuściński's angle of vision is completely different. It is, above all, that of a Pole.

After trying for centuries, Poland won independence from Russia only after the First World War. During and after the Second, the Russians brazenly moved the entire country several inches leftward on the map: Poland's borders were shifted from east to west by 150 to 200 miles. In this process, the Soviet Union absorbed a big swath of Polish territory, including Kapuściński's home town, Pinsk.

He gives us a searing, firsthand picture of the Red Army's arrival in Pinsk after the Hitler-Stalin Pact of 1939. At night Soviet soldiers barge into the house looking for his father, a Polish officer. Drunken artillerymen fire their howitzer at the local church tower. One by one, neighbors, friends, classmates, his schoolteacher disappear, deported to Siberia. His mother makes him and his sister sleep with their clothes on, in case it's their turn next. Winter comes. From behind bushes, the fearful seven-year-old Kapuściński watches secret police troops check the boxcars full of deportees, pulling out the bodies of those who have frozen to death during the night. A lesser writer might have gone on longer, told what happened to his family, told how he survived. Ka-

puściński stops after a spare, unforgettable fifteen pages. This is
his prologue.

In the remainder of the book, Kapuściński's interest, above all,
is in the other Pinsks of the Soviet Union: the non-Russian outlying territories that felt Russia's weight. Although he seems to have
spent weeks or months (he is always vague about time) in Kiev, to
have visited St. Petersburg, and even to have lived in Moscow for
periods that included the August 1991 coup attempt, he has little
to say about the three historic capitals. Instead most of his reporting is about the empire's fringes: the Caucasus, the Don region,
the Arctic, Siberia, the former *gulag* center of Magadan, the Central Asian republics. One striking chapter is about the death of the
Aral Sea. Thanks to the diversion of river water to a massive irriga-
tion project (another disaster in itself), lifeless villages of fishing
boats now lie in the middle of the desert. Nature, as well as people, was among the imperial victims.

Of a piece with his perspective as a Pole is the way Kapuściński constantly measures what he sees in the USSR against
his long experience in Asia, Latin America, and especially Africa.
Unlike the many intellectuals in Russia and Eastern Europe who
can be as racist as any Colonel Blimp, he has an acute sense of
what the former Soviet bloc and the Third World have in common.

When Kapuściński sees Tbilisi or Yerevan, he sees Third
World capitals that have impoverished the countryside by draining
population to the metropolis. When he sees the airport in Baku
jammed with frightened Russians trying to get back to Moscow,
he remembers airports packed with fleeing white colonists in Al-
giers and Leopoldville, in Angola and Mozambique. When he sees
how a giant, polluting, chemical combine dominates Russia's
Bashkir region, he compares it to the big mining house, Union
Minière, that long dominated the southern Belgian Congo. A
muddy, desolate slum in Yakutsk reminds him of the *favelas* of
Rio. When he talks with ethnic Russians who claim as much right
to be there as the Yakuts have, he thinks of the Afrikaners in
South Africa. When he hears the xenophobic voice of Russian ethnic nationalism, he compares it to the rise of the Shiite clergy in
Iran, who, just like the old regime, suppressed the Kurds and
other smaller peoples of another multinational state.

The Soviet Central Asian and Caucasian republics, he notes,
were always headed by a first secretary of the Communist Party
from the local ethnic group: "a vizier . . . in accordance with

Eastern tradition, his rule was for life." This is, Kapuściński points out, an adaptation of the long-lasting British colonial system of "indirect rule" through local tribal chiefs, maharajas, and the like.

The analogy between the USSR and the Western colonial powers has certainly been made before, but seldom by someone with such wide personal experience of both systems. I only wish Kapuściński had explored it at more length and more systematically. Being a miniaturist cramps him somewhat here.

For example, an interesting difference between Western Europe's colonies and Russia's is that Russia's colonial territories often exported manufactured goods to Russia, while Russia sent them raw materials, such as timber, oil, and gas. This is the exact opposite of what every British colonial secretary knew a prosperous home country's relations with a proper colony should be. And it is one reason Russia will be far less successful than England, France, and Belgium have been in continuing to draw profits from their former African colonies.

One result of this upside-down imperial economic relationship between Russia and its colonies was that many of the outlying ones—such as the Baltic states and much of Eastern Europe—came to enjoy higher standards of living than Russia itself. The bitter envy this has caused in Russia has helped stir the flames of Great Russian xenophobia.

There are, however, many points of similarity between Soviet and Western colonialism. One is that both systems operated under cover of rhetoric that had little connection to reality. Soviet rule had no more to do with empowering the proletariat than European rule had to do with the white man's burden. As far as Africa was concerned, no one saw more clearly through the fine words to the underlying horror than an earlier Pole whose life had also been touched by both Russia and the colonized world, Joseph Conrad.

.   .   .

Anyone who grew up in Pinsk and saw what Kapuściński did as a boy could be expected to have a keen resentment of Russian imperial power. But someone who suffers under one oppressor all too often turns around and picks on someone else: the Pole turns on the Jew, the poor white on the black, and so on. What gives Kapuściński's voice such integrity is that his early firsthand experience of autocracy and conquest broadened rather than narrowed him. It gave him an unerring moral radar for the abuses and delusions of all autocracies and nationalisms, large and small, whether in Moscow or Yerevan, Tehran or Johannesburg. And that is the ultimate subject of all his major works. The "imperium" of this book's title is not just the former Soviet Union. It is most of the earth.

In Kapuściński's taxonomy of tyranny, a key pattern, as he observed in his book on Iran, is that

> A nation trampled by despotism . . . seeks a shelter, seeks a place where it can dig itself in, wall itself off, be itself. . . . But a whole nation cannot emigrate, so it undertakes a migration in time rather than in space. In the face of the encircling afflictions and threats of reality, it goes back to a past that seems a lost paradise. . . . This is why a gradual rebirth of old customs, beliefs, and symbols occurs under the lid of every dictatorship.

He notes the same thing in his journey around the unraveling Soviet Union, seeing the upwelling everywhere of what he succinctly calls the Great Yesterday. The Great Yesterday emotionally fuels both small peoples, like the Bashkirs, and large ones, like the Russians, where "poor old women in Moscow abandoned the bread lines they had been standing in, gave up buying bread, to march down the street shouting the slogan 'We will not give back the Kurile Islands!'"

The other feature that Kapuściński observes is that all multinational empires produce the compulsion to classify everyone. He arrives in Baku with a high fever, but instead of asking him what caused this, an Azerbaijani woman first asks his ethnicity. "Like peasants the world over who begin each conversation with reflections on the subject of crops . . . so in the Imperium the first step in establishing contact between people is a mutual determination of one's nationality." He later meets another Azerbaijani, who detests above all the late Andrei Sakharov. Why? Not because of what Sakharov stood for, but because Sakharov's wife was part-Armenian.

When Kapuściński carries out his feat of derring-do, donning his Aeroflot pilot's uniform and flying into Nagorno-Karabakh, the story he brings back is not the war reporter's usual portrait of heroic defenders holding out against heavy odds. It is, instead, a heartfelt meditation on the madness of nationalism, racism, and religious fundamentalism.

> Anyone stricken with one of these plagues is beyond reason. In his head burns a sacred pyre, which awaits only its sacrificial victims. Every attempt at calm conversation will fail. He doesn't want a conversation, but a declaration. . . .
>
> [O]ne can envy both the Armenians and the Azerbaijanis. They are not beset by worries about the complexity of the world or about the fact that human destiny is uncertain and fragile. The anxiety that usually accompanies such questions as: What is truth? What is the good? What is justice? is alien to them. They do not know the burden that weighs on those who ask themselves, But am I right? . . . Their world is simple—on one side we, the good people, on the other they, our enemies.

Kapuściński, however, is one of those who do ask such questions. And beneath the seductive dazzle of his style, it is the undercurrent of his humanity that makes his work, otherwise so spread out in geography and time, a whole. The frightened seven-year-old boy in Pinsk, peering out through the bushes at the secret police troops, went on to spend his entire working life looking into their very souls.

1994

The Pleasures of War

What follows is a confession, of something I have successfully kept secret for years. The only excuse I can make for what I am about to disclose is that adults enticed me into this vice while I was still a child.

When I was nine or ten, British cousins began sending me children's books for Christmas. At least in the 1950s, when I was growing up, books published in England smelled different. They had an acrid, faintly briny smell, as if there were a shortage of fresh water, and seawater had to be used in making the paper. I still remember that smell, which accompanied the anticipatory thrill of opening a new package of Christmas books from England. These were all war books: novels for boys about one Major James Bigglesworth, of the Royal Air Force, known as Biggles.

For Biggles, World War II was a long, long war indeed. He fought on every front, from the fall of France and the Battle of Britain to North Africa and Italy, from Burma and India to secret missions behind enemy lines. For a time Biggles headed a special RAF squadron of misfits: pilots kicked out of other units for being rude to commanders, or for taking dogs into combat, or for hunting foxes on the airport grounds. But, aces all, they rallied to their country in her hour of need.

The German squadron they opposed was always headed by Biggles's archenemy, a sadistic Prussian aristocrat named Erich von Stahlheim, who wore a pince-nez. And, on the last page of each book, while the victorious Biggles watched von Stahlheim's smoking Messerschmitt plummet toward earth, out would pop a parachute, so you knew he would live to fight again.

Once addicted to books about combat, I could never shake the habit. This meant living a double life. For while in college in the

1960s, I was an organizer of the first big student peace march on Washington. During the early 1970s I was organizing and demon-strating against the Vietnam War. In the 1980s I attacked U.S. intervention in El Salvador and Nicaragua in print and on the air, and once even went on an eight-campus speaking tour to decry Ronald Reagan's insane military build-up. Yet during all those years, one of my great pleasures in life has remained curling up in the evening with a good book about war.

The author of the Biggles books was Captain W. E. Johns, a curiously anonymous-sounding name about which I've wondered: does it disguise an ever-changing syndicate of authors like those who have produced all the hundreds of Hardy Boys and Nancy Drew books? Whoever he was, or they were, Biggles was a splen-did creation. After Biggles fought in every conceivable battle of World War II, he went on to fight the Communists in various places, although none of this was anywhere near so exciting. Which brings up an important point for us addicts of war books: not any war will do.

Don't, for example, get misled by all those sentimental afi-cionados of the American Civil War. The Blue and the Gray, the tragedy of a house divided, and so on. No, for serious war buffs, the best war, *the* war—with rare exceptions, which I will get to later—is World War II.

This has to do with what one is looking for in reading war books. Squeezed into a seat on a bus or exhausted after a long workday, who wants tragedy and complexity? I'm talking about those times when you haven't got the energy to tackle Jorge Luis Borges or to look at that new translation of Robert Musil. What a reader needs at such moments is action, heroes, and villains. Espe-cially villains. For that, how can you do better than World War II? The pleasure of seeing Hitler get his just desserts never pales.

Disapproving critics will object that this is not sufficient ex-planation for bibliomilitaromania. Aren't you people who are at-tracted to such books being covertly drawn to . . . ahem . . . violence? Guilty as charged. But this addiction of ours is very different from that involving the violence in films and TV, which hundreds of studies show makes viewers more likely to go out and pull triggers in the streets. So far as I know, no study has shown that we lovers of war books are more likely to go out and start wars. If that were so, they'd have to ban everything from much of Shakespeare to the *Iliad*—where, incidentally, Homer observed that "men grow tired of sleep, love, singing and dancing sooner than war."

If we are to enjoy some vicarious violence, then, why not do so on a global scale, from Leningrad to El Alemein, Berlin to Guadalcanal, Normandy to Okinawa? And in contrast to most shoot-'em-up movies and TV shows, war books easily allow you to separate an emotional identification with the participants from any desire to be in their shoes. This is a particular luxury of reading about a distant time and place. I can read with pleasure about the ominous ring of steel closing in on the icy ruins of Stalingrad partly because it makes me happy that I'm *not* there, and can instead, in a few moments, turn out the light and fall asleep under a warm blanket.

· · ·

One word of advice for the war-book reader: avoid the sort of writer who talks of war solely in terms of generals and who talks of generals as if they were slow-motion boxers. "Rommel advanced his Panzer Grenadiers against Bradley's center while testing the American flank with a feint from the motorized S.S. divisions on his right. . . ." No, you want war from the bottom up, from the mud of the trenches, from the deck of a destroyer, from the cockpit in the sky, where it really happened.

The dedicated World War II zealot can find thousands of volumes on the subject (and at least a major part of one bookstore: The Military Bookman, 29 East 93d Street in New York City). But let me mention just a few of my favorites.

The premier American nonfiction writer on World War II was the late Cornelius Ryan. In *The Longest Day* (D-Day), *A Bridge Too Far* (the battle of Arnhem), and *The Last Battle* (the fall of Berlin), he pioneered a distinctively cinematic style, cutting back and forth between people in various corners on both sides of a battle. A consummate craftsman, he knew something that lesser writers working on a large historical stage all too often forget: keep your characters distinct enough so that readers won't get them mixed up. A few of the people he focuses on are generals, but many more of them are ordinary foot soldiers or civilians: a Berlin zookeeper, a spy for the Russians, a French peasant, a Dutch housewife. All three volumes are excellent; the last is the best, although surprisingly the only one not to have been made into a movie.

The best line of photo books on the war is put out by Time-Life, which knows, like the publisher of the old Biggles books, that the way to exploit helpless addicts like me is to publish an endless series. Time-Life's World War II collection runs to several dozen volumes. If you have any imaginable subfetish within the war—the Norwegian underground, say, or the Aleutian Islands campaign—there will most likely be an entire volume on it. Avoid, by the way, the rival photo series, Ballantine's *Illustrated History of World War II,* which clutters bookstore shelves everywhere: bad printing, dull layout, poorly written text.

Alexander Werth's *Russia at War* is a panoramic picture of the struggle between the Soviet Union and Germany, where the outcome of World War II was really decided. Werth was a correspondent in Russia at the time, and often interrupts his narrative to zero in on a section of the front or a newly recaptured city that he personally visited. *The 900 Days,* by Harrison Salisbury, another wartime Moscow correspondent, tells of one of that war's most harrowing battles, the siege of Leningrad. The Russian government now uses the figure of 27 million as the official World War II Soviet death toll, military and civilian. To see what the Nazi-Soviet war felt like to German soldiers, who risked freezing or starvation if they were not killed by Russian bullets, turn to Guy Sajer's vivid, powerful *The Forgotten Soldier,* probably the finest infantryman's memoir of the war.

The neophyte World War II addict might be content with books about D-Day or Pearl Harbor, but we hard-core types demand more. Virginia Cowles's *The Phantom Major* tells how the imaginative British commando leader David Stirling, using camouflaged jeeps hidden in Libyan caves behind German lines, destroyed some 250 Nazi planes on the ground in surprise attacks by night. William Stevenson's *A Man Called Intrepid* is one of several histories of the war's best-kept secret, which has come to light only in recent years: from the beginning, the British had broken the main German code and were reading the radio messages of the Nazi high command.

Finally, two of the best-written, most moving personal accounts of the war are Elmer Bendiner's *The Fall of Fortresses* and

Lothar-Gunther Buchheim's novel *The Boat.* Bendiner served on B-17s bombing Germany; Buchheim, aboard German U-boats. From opposing sides they write with uncommon eloquence about living day after day with the fear of imminent death, with the helpless sense that whether you survive or not has absolutely nothing to do with anything in your control. Buchheim's extraordinary photographs appear in another book of his, *U-Boat War.*

．　．　．

I said earlier that there are a few exceptions to my rule that World War II is the best war for readers. These exceptions mostly are obscure or bizarre corners of other wars. Quite a few candidates crop up for consideration here, but I shall resist the temptation to talk about the use of balloons in the Franco-Prussian War or the guerrillas on horseback in the Boer War or the real story of the Charge of the Light Brigade. Instead, a mere three campaigns.

The first is the saga of the Russian fleet in the Russo-Japanese War. When the two countries began fighting each other in 1904, most of the Russian navy was in the Baltic. With great fanfare, this aging and decrepit armada, some forty-two ships in all, set out on the eighteen thousand-mile voyage to Japan. The story is told with a fine, dry wit in Richard Hough's *The Fleet That Had to Die.*

Everything went wrong from the start. On some Russian battleships, luxurious, armor-protected officers' quarters on the upper decks had been so lavishly built up that the ships turned out to be top-heavy and in danger of capsizing when they reached the open sea. The convoy had to travel at a speed where it would not lose the slower ships. This meant circling the globe at about eight knots, with frequent time out for breakdowns. While officers dined on fowl and champagne, the enlisted men shoveled coal into blazing engine-room boilers in the tropics, ate salt beef, and secretly produced revolutionary propaganda. Sailors grew so mutinous that one vessel was turned into a prison ship, loaded full, and sent home.

At last the convoy neared Japan and the long-awaited confrontation with the Japanese fleet. Just as this climactic moment approached, the Russian admiral in command lapsed into a strange melancholia. Silently he watched Japanese ships come within range without ordering his gunners to fire. Then he seemed to come to life at last, but ordered his long line of warships into two mysterious abrupt turns that left them milling about and nearly colliding with each other. In the confusion, the Japanese navy closed in. The Russian ships had now been sailing for seven months; in the space of a day the Japanese sank or captured virtually the entire fleet, winning the war and igniting the Russian Revolution of 1905.

The second campaign is the story of the Eastern Front in World War I. Almost all the war's vast literature is about the blood-soaked trenches of France and Flanders, but in fact more than a third of the casualties took place on the other side of Europe, where Germany and Austria-Hungary fought Russia. Despite those funny little spikes on their helmets, the Germans were their usual efficient selves. But Russia and Austria-Hungary were huge, creaky, multiethnic empires on the point of collapse, whose portly generals, weighed down by medals and gold braid, were some of the most incompetent men ever to lead soldiers into battle.

In the Austro-Hungarian army, for example, three-quarters of the officers were of German stock, but only one enlisted man in four even understood the language. The resulting muddle is the subject of Jaroslav Hašek's *Good Soldier Schweik,* the marvelous comic novel that fully deserves its status as a classic and will long outlast the overrated *Catch-22.* One disaster after another befalls the bumbling Schweik and his inept comrades, who wander through 750 pages without ever managing to find their way to the front.

On the Russian side of the lines, things were no better. Top army commanders got their jobs through their connections at court. One army corps, writes W. Bruce Lincoln in his *Passage Through Armageddon,* was commanded by a general who "was unable to conduct operations because his nerves could not stand the sound of rifle fire." Soldiers were selected for the Pavlovski Regiment of the Guards for having, like its founder Tsar Paul I, turned-up noses. While Russian soldiers died by the hundreds of thousands in late 1914, special trains still rushed fresh flowers each week from the Crimea to the imperial palace in St. Petersburg.

The Russian commander in chief was Grand Duke Nicholas Nikolaevich, who, according to Lincoln, let it be known that after-dinner conversation at his headquarters should be on "diversionary themes not concerning the conduct of the war." Nicholas Nikolaevich's main military qualifications were royal blood and height: at six feet six inches he towered impressively over all other officers, which was considered a great asset. At army headquarters, the Grand Duke kept hitting his head on door frames. Aides pinned pieces of white paper to them, warning him to duck.

In 1915, the Germans reinforced their inept Austro-Hungarian allies, and pushed back the Russian forces for hundreds of miles. Faced with this disaster, Tsar Nicolas II himself took over as commander in chief. But he knew even less of military matters than his uncle, the Grand Duke. He watched parades, toured the countryside near headquarters in his Rolls-Royce, played dominoes, and issued peculiar orders, such as one promoting all the officers who happened to attend a ceremonial dinner. "I do not read newspapers here," he cheerfully wrote to his wife at a time when the Russian army was losing seventy-five hundred men killed or wounded per day. Later he added, "My brain is resting here . . . no troublesome questions demanding thought." To the French ambassador he remarked, "The life I lead here at the head of my army is so healthy and comforting!"

Added to this befuddlement at the top was ignorance at the bottom. At the start of the war, Russian troops tended to fire on all airplanes, including their own; never having seen any before, they were sure such exotic machinery must be German. "Telegraphs would suddenly stop working," writes Norman Stone in *The Eastern Front 1914–1917,* "and investigation of the lines to the rear would reveal a party of soldiers cooking their tea with pieces of telegraph-pole." More such details can also be found in Alan Clark's *Suicide of the Empires: The Battles on the Eastern Front 1914–1918.* The famous journalist John Reed provides a firsthand account in his *The War in Eastern Europe.*

To also recommend it, the Eastern Front had what all wars need, which is of course the cavalry. Using horses against machine guns was suicidal, but officers whose ancestors had been cavalrymen for generations could not bear to recognize this. Among those who survived the carnage, good sportsmanship prevailed: "The Austrian officers captured were usually invited to breakfast in our mess," writes Paul Rodzianko, a Russian colonel, in his *Tattered Banners.* One day Rodzianko and a captured Austrian officer recognized each other—from an international horse show just before the war. "'The horse I rode is with me now,' I told him, and for half an hour we talked the 'shop' of horsemen, as if no war had come between us."

One final campaign worth reading about is another distant front of World War I, in Africa. At the outbreak of war in 1914, a few hundred German officers leading black African troops were stationed in the colony of German East Africa, today's Tanzania. For the next four years, a far larger British and South African force vainly pursued them for several thousand miles all over east and central Africa. Under the command of the bicycle-riding General Paul von Lettow-Vorbeck, the German forces lived on captured British supplies and on hippo and elephant fat and maize. At the end of the war, they were still fighting, invading British territory. The story is told in various books, including von Lettow-Vorbeck's own *My Reminiscences of East Africa* and Byron Farwell's *The Great War in Africa.*

African soldiers died by the thousands, but for their white officers, there was something gentlemanly about it all. At one point, General Jan Smuts, who commanded the Allied forces, sent a messenger under a white flag to tell his rival, who was cut off from all communications with home, that Kaiser Wilhelm II had awarded him a medal. On another occasion, von Lettow-Vorbeck had Smuts in his machine-gun sights but could not bring himself to fire. After the war the two generals became great friends, which is how all wars ought to end, but seldom do. If there is another world war, there may not be any of us left afterward to be friends. They don't make wars like they used to.

1983

Hemingway

HUNTER AND VICTIM

Certain artists have a relatively narrow range but, within it, achieve near-perfection. One thinks of Chopin, of Degas, or, among writers, of Hemingway. In his best work—two early novels and a half-dozen of the short stories—he summed up the sense of loss, the hedonism, the stoicism of the generation that survived World War I, and he made its mood into something universal and lasting. He struck a chord clear and deep; no one has done it better.

Yet when you go in search of the person who composed the haunting understatement of *The Sun Also Rises, A Farewell to Arms,* and the best stories from that fertile decade that began when Hemingway was about twenty-three, he is hard to find. Almost all the photographs show "Papa" as he became: the braggart sportsman posing beside a dead elephant, a giant marlin, a beautiful woman, a Nazi artillery piece, with the proud, bearded, slightly nervous grin that says "I bagged this game." As the years pass, the photos show him more and more surrounded by socialites and sycophants, movie stars and white hunters. The man capable of writing subtle, achingly beautiful stories like "In Another Country" or "Hills Like White Elephants" is invisible.

I have seen only one portrait of *that* Hemingway. It is an oil painting, done in Paris in 1922 by a friend of his, the American artist Henry Strater. It shows a spare, intense young man with a mustache and a downward-looking frown, a frown of both concentration and sadness. There is no grin, no bluster. The painter captured something dozens of photographers missed.

The swaggering, bragging side took over Hemingway's life and eventually his work. It is as if Chopin had composed all those

259

lovely piano pieces in his twenties and then spent more and more time writing fanfares for brass bands. Hemingway's peculiar competitive venom, which is only a minor blemish in *The Sun Also Rises* (where there is a touch of it in the acid, anti-Semitic portrayal of Robert Cohn), gradually expanded until, in the posthumous memoir, *A Moveable Feast,* he slashed away at nearly all his contemporaries, seriously souring an otherwise lyrical book.

.   .   .

The enduring fascination about Hemingway is the tension between the understatement of his best work and the overstatement of his life—which eventually crept into his work as well. There is surprisingly little about that tension in the current spate of Hemingway books. Most are not of lasting interest. A. E. Hotchner has put out a new version of his voyeuristic *Papa Hemingway,* a memoir of the two men's relationship in Hemingway's last years. But far more interesting than any questions the book answers is the one posed by its existence: what made Hemingway hang out with and confide in this third-rate hack? This "new and revised" edition of Hotchner's book appears different from the original mainly by the addition of an appendix lambasting two rival writers on the same turf: Mary Welsh Hemingway, the author's fourth wife, and Philip Young, a thoughtful Hemingway critic. Hotchner scornfully savages the two of them, as if unconsciously mimicking the vituperative side of Hemingway's character.

Worth more time is *Ernest Hemingway: Selected Letters 1917– 1961,* edited by Carlos Baker. In these 948 pages of frustratingly small type, there is a torrent of raw material for many a future psychobiography. Of that great duality in Hemingway's soul, the letters express almost entirely the bluff, hearty, supermacho, high-achiever side. Open up the volume anywhere and you find passages such as "We've killed 3 big bull elk—2 bucks—2 bear—an eagle and a coyote—Grouse all the time—Killed enough meat for the two guides to get married on—." Even to John Dos Passos or Maxwell Perkins, he talks of warfare, bullfights, and boxing.

Except in an anguished letter to his first wife, Hadley, at the time of their separation, that sensitive, vulnerable side of himself that Hemingway drew on for his early work is mostly kept under wraps. One looks in vain for the Hemingway who could so poignantly see the world through Jake's impotence in *The Sun Also*

Rises or through the café waiter's insomnia in "A Clean Well-Lighted Place." The absence is eerie: it is as if Hemingway could express that side of himself to his public, at least for a time but never to his friends.

·   ·   ·

Bernice Kert's *The Hemingway Women* basically retells the author's life from the angle of the women in it—wives, mother, sisters, lovers, models for various female characters. Although the book seems mildly tinged with feminist sensibility, that makes its job still more difficult: how can one do full justice to the lives of a dozen or so women when the one thing they have in common is their connections to one man? The book makes no attempt to answer the most important question about Hemingway and women: why did he, as Edmund Wilson shrewdly observed a long time ago, hate and fear them?

Nonetheless, Kert has some interesting material, some of it missed by Hemingway's authorized biographer, the plodding and insensitive Carlos Baker. Most striking is Hemingway's extreme ambivalence about what he wanted in women. In his fiction—with the one luminous exception of Lady Brett—they tend to be flat and docile, like Maria of *For Whom the Bell Tolls.* Kert quotes Adriana Ivancich, the model for the heroine of *Across the River and into the Trees,* as complaining to Hemingway that she was disappointed at the portrayal of herself: "The girl is boring. How could your colonel love a girl who is so boring?"

Yet in real life, three of the four women Hemingway loved enough to marry were professional journalists, and one of those, Martha Gellhorn, was a talented novelist as well. Hemingway never resolved this paradox in his feelings. In his letters, when he approves of a woman, he usually praises her for being just like a man: "[Hadley] fishes not with the usual feminine simulation of interest but like one of the men, she's as intelligent about fights as she is about music, she drinks with a male without remorse."

Kert is especially interesting on the contrast between Hemingway's third and fourth wives. Hemingway admired Martha Gellhorn's courage as a war correspondent in Spain, but he sulked when she continued to write under her own last name instead of his. When she went off to report World War II from Europe, leaving him behind, he never forgave her. He himself watched

D-Day from a ship; but when Gellhorn wangled her way onto the Normandy beachhead itself (by locking herself in a toilet of a hospital ship heading to pick up casualties), he was furious. Kert points out that wife No. 4, Mary Welsh Hemingway, gladly abandoned her career, took over as housekeeper and manager of the staff of thirteen at the Hemingway Cuban mansion, typed his manuscripts and took care of his correspondence, and accepted his eruptions of abuse without much complaint. That seems to be why this marriage lasted longer than any of the others, until his death.

.   .   .

In that literary heaven where we all get to see our favorite writers from the past, Hemingway is the one I would least like to meet. For one thing, he wouldn't talk books. "Ernest liked to pretend that he knew nothing and had read nothing, hiding his omnivorous knowledge behind the pose of the unlettered sportsman," writes Bernice Kert. "It seemed to Martha that he disliked conversing with people who could read and write." On the rare occasions when anyone could get him to talk about his literary ancestors, he usually did so only in sports metaphors, as when he said he wouldn't get in the ring with Tolstoy.

Furthermore, the persona of the "unlettered sportsman" that he worked so anxiously to project had a viciousness to it. His letters are filled with invective about wops and jigs and kikes. He talks much of the time in a sort of adolescent schoolboy jargon. And looming in the background is the image of women as a castrating menace. Sometimes all these streams come together, as in a 1924 letter inviting a friend to go and watch bullfights in Spain: "It's so god damn swell to know that we will have some of the genuwind [*sic*] together again. Because Boid the number of genuwind all Caucasian white guys in the world is limited. I should say that maybe there were 5 or 6 at the most. That may be an exaggerated figure. There'd probably be a number more if they didn't marry foecal matter in various forms." Yet a year later the man who wrote this was at work on *The Sun Also Rises*.

No men are John Waynes all the way through; in most there is both a pugilistic side and a vulnerable one. In few of us is the pugilistic side so venomous as Hemingway's, and in almost none is the vulnerable side capable of creating such lasting art. Yet when a person has this dichotomy, we usually expect the pugilistic side to give way to the vulnerable in the end: psychoanalysis tells us to expect, in old age, the "return of the repressed." And since what men often repress is their capacity for gentleness, this is what returns later on. In Hemingway's case, what happened was the reverse.

The tension between those two sides was there to the end, right up to the final chapter of *A Moveable Feast,* the last book he wrote. He evokes the days of his first marriage with heartbreaking beauty: "I remember the snow on the road to the village squeaking at night when we walked home in the cold . . . I remember the smell of the pines and the sleeping on the mattresses of beech leaves in the woodcutters' huts and the skiing through the forest following the tracks of hares and of foxes. . . . During our last year in the mountains new people came into our lives and nothing was ever the same again. The winter of the avalanches was like a happy and innocent winter in childhood compared to the next." Then suddenly he becomes the harsh sadist who blames "the rich" (apparently including the woman who was to become his second wife), who took him in, broke up his idyllic marriage, and brought a period of creativity to an end.

The rich have plenty of sins, but this wasn't one of them. The darker side of Hemingway's character has to take the blame here, of course, although it did have a minor accomplice: Hemingway lived in the age of mass communication and he quickly succumbed to its lures. There were similar temptations in earlier times; Charles Dickens and Mark Twain went on lecture tours and enjoyed being in the public eye—but they knew when to stop. Hemingway did not. He let himself be profiled endlessly by magazines, accepted free rooms from a publicity-hungry hotel at Sun Valley, and, by the end of World War II, became as much a character himself in journalists' copy as a creator of characters in his fiction. In his last two decades, he surrounded himself with hangers-on wherever he went, but because of the great publicity apparatus of modern times, his public became his entourage as well. The hunter who in the early years bragged of his prowess only to friends now was photographed with his kills by *Life* and *Esquire.* He is lucky he did not survive into the age of TV talk shows.

He lived in an age when media could easily separate a writer's life and work, and turn the life into a glittering commodity displayed to the public. For someone whose best work was so good but whose personality was so filled with compulsive braggadocio, the temptation was fatal. Hemingway's tragedy was all the greater because he dimly sensed that it was happening, and he spoke and wrote more eloquently than anyone about the duty of a writer to his craft. But he never managed to write about the fatal dichotomy in himself. As with his hero Tolstoy—who praised marriage above all things and then finally fled his own, dying on the journey— there is a depth of tragedy in Hemingway's own duality that even the best of his works does not capture. His own full story would require a writer greater than Hemingway to write it.

1983

The Private Volcano of Malcolm Lowry

Besides being a visionary, drunkard, champion athlete, carpenter of his own wilderness cabin, and author of one of the great novels of his time, Malcolm Lowry was also a letter writer. Perhaps, in our telephonic age, one of the last great letter writers. His most memorable one was written from Mexico in 1946 to an English publisher who was showing signs of rejecting the masterpiece Lowry had just spent ten years writing, *Under the Volcano.*

The letter runs thirty-one pages. Writing it took Lowry two weeks' time, a drinking bout, and a suicide attempt. In it he defends his novel, chapter by chapter, at times almost page by page. It is a curiously naive document, for Lowry assumes (as he apparently did toward everyone) that the publisher was full of goodwill, and also—a still more naive assumption, as far as publishers are concerned—that the man had carefully read the entire manuscript. But I suspect that like so many people who encounter this dense and bewildering novel for the first time, the publisher had given up. Yes, Lowry wrote, his book is slow-starting, but then so are *The Possessed, Wuthering Heights,* and *Moby Dick.* The extraordinary feature of Lowry's letter is that despite his total obscurity—his only published book was a mediocre and forgotten novel of thirteen years earlier—he *knew* he had written a great book.

Today it is easy to agree. Lowry's letter convinced the wavering publisher, and *Under the Volcano* came out the next year. Critics everywhere praised it, but by his triumph Lowry was undone. Reluctantly he journeyed to New York for the mandatory round of literary cocktail parties. In the receiving line of one large reception, he was so overwhelmed by fright that he never opened his mouth for several hours. From Manhattan he fled back to the almost hermitlike existence he had been living in the forest of British Columbia. Then his compulsive drinking began again; the last ten years of his life saw him in and out of psychiatric hospitals in Canada, France, Italy, England, and Haiti. He was deported from Mexico; he wrote endlessly and finished nothing; he fell off a pier while drunk and broke his back; a few years later, he broke his leg. He began suffering a writing block that was literally a *writing* block: he could not hold a pen and could only write by dictating, standing up for eight hours a day, leaning against a table in a position that gave him calluses on his knuckles and varicose veins so severe they had to be operated on. Finally Lowry fled Canada, made a last attempt to find refuge from himself in a Sussex village, and then brought it all to an end with a fatal combination of alcohol and sleeping pills. When he was buried in the village churchyard in 1957, none of his works were in print in English.

.   .   .

Lowry's eclipse has long ended; now everybody wants him. Literary historians have claimed him as an Englishman, a Canadian, and almost an American. The first is most accurate, though it is hard to place a man who was born in England, lived most of his adult life in Canada, found his largest audience in the United States, and, for the setting of his one great novel, chose Mexico.

Under the Volcano takes place on a single day in 1938, the Day of the Dead, when the dead commune with the living. It was a strange twilight time: the blitzkrieg of Poland was only a year away; Mexico's left-wing government had just nationalized foreign oil companies and the British had broken diplomatic relations; scores of Nazi and Spanish Fascist agents had infiltrated the Mexican army and police; and the country's powerful right wing simmered in near-rebellion.

The book's hero is the now out-of-work British Consul in Cuernavaca, a brilliant man of wide reading and travel, a mystic and Cabalist, and a hopeless alcoholic. He begins the day in a bar, and is found there by his estranged wife, who has returned to Mexico to attempt a reconciliation. Together with the Consul's half brother, the two of them visit a filmmaker friend, go to a bull-fight, eat, argue, and separate. Throughout the day the trio's paths are stalked by vultures, legless beggars, scorpions, spiders, deformed pariah dogs, and laughing dwarves.

Spurred on by marvelous rationalizing (having a drink to reward himself for abstaining a few minutes earlier), the Consul drinks more and more. By evening he is drinking alone—in a bar across the street from a military police barracks, headquarters of the local Fascists. Policemen have been following him all day, thinking he is a Communist spy. Their suspicions are confirmed when they check his pockets, for the half brother had been wearing the Consul's coat. The half brother is a British newspaperman about to leave to fight for the Loyalists in the Spanish Civil War; he had left in the Consul's coat pocket his membership card in the Spanish anarchist party and a press cable in telegraphic shorthand, which of course looks like code. "You are de espider, and we shoota de espiders in Mexico," the policemen say. They take the Consul outside and kill him.

The *Volcano's* readers are divided into two kinds: those who find it (as I do) one of the great twentieth-century novels in English, and those who find it (as I did, on my first reading) exasperating, tortuous, thick with heavy-handed symbolism and with minor characters who never come alive. Both views are true, and when you come to love the book it is as you love *King Lear:* a work great in spite of itself, with faults so monstrous they take on a certain grandeur of their own.

Despite its exotic setting, *Under the Volcano's* greatness is a psychological one. For me the heart of it is the way Lowry gets so totally inside the head of a man who exquisitely, almost victoriously, knows he is destroying himself. He destroys himself both through his drinking and through his lingering at the bar that gradually fills with sinister policemen, directed by a silent Spaniard. The bar's musician, under the cover of fiddling a gay tune next to the Consul's ear, whispers a warning in broken English to leave before it is too late. But the Consul stays.

Everything is seen through the Consul's drunken perceptions: the street that rises to hit him in the face, the sudden apparition of phantom animals, an amusement park filled with whirling, malevolent machines intent on harming him. Most dazzling of all is a conversation near the end where the Consul is arguing politics with his wife and half brother. The talk flows back and forth; the Consul responds to his brother with a long and devastating speech, filled with wit and insight and classical allusions, his full intellectual weaponry on display. Only at the end does he realize he has not spoken at all.

.   .   .

Lowry's sad life story is well told in Douglas Day's biography, *Malcolm Lowry*. Lowry was no easy subject, for he spun many tall tales about himself. Day carefully separates them from the life that Lowry really led.

And what a life. The first word that comes to mind for Lowry is helpless. And not only helpless in his disastrous drinking. Apparently he was one of those people incapable of doing certain everyday things like buying an airplane ticket. Lowry never quite knew where he was in foreign cities, wore shirts inside out, forgot to put on socks, lost his manuscripts. For most of his life he lived on a meager allowance from his wealthy parents; even when he was thirty his father didn't send it to him directly, but hired lawyers in whatever country Lowry was in to dole it out to him month by month and to keep an eye on him.

He was equally helpless in his work. Although he wrote voluminously for nearly thirty years, one youthful first novel and *Under the Volcano* were all he ever finished. The other books he could not control. A short story for a contest with a thousand-word limit grew to eighty pages; an unfinished letter to the editor of a British newspaper to over a hundred. A film script he and his wife did was studded with critical comments on film theory and would have run six hours on the screen. He wrote vast prospectuses of all his work, optimistic letters to publishers, charts, outlines, diagrams, master plans that would unite the great muddle of uncompleted manuscripts. That he finished anything was largely due to his second wife, Marjorie. A writer herself, she was his nurse, protector, best critic, and at times almost coauthor.

However, this most helpless of men lived a physically more self-sufficient life than any major writer since Thoreau. Lowry hated cities, and in 1939 he and his wife moved to British Columbia. Theirs was no one-year fling on a farm: for most of the next fifteen years they lived in a series of squatters' shacks built over tide flats near Vancouver.

I visited the spot sometime ago. The beach is covered with smooth pebbles and looks across a fjordlike inlet at mountains that shoot steeply down to the water. Fir trees cover the middle slopes, and on the day I was there misty clouds ringed them, making the peaks above look disembodied and still higher. They are snow-capped even in summer. Lowry dove off his porch into this freezing water every day.

One of the shacks the Lowrys built themselves, on pilings over the water. They drew drinking water from a spring, gardened, cut their own wood, and heard the seawater swirl directly under their living room at high tide, while worrying that tree trunks torn loose by spring floods would crash against the pilings and bring the house down. Through the Canadian winters they wrote with gloved hands the great epic of a sun-baked day in Mexico. Their best friends were fishermen and boat builders who were their neighbors, and who today treasure their relics. When he was drunk Lowry could be terrible (he twice attacked his wife), but when he was sober he was a good man, as generous as he was possessed, and people loved him.

Lowry described this period of his life in the short lyrical novel *The Forest Path to the Spring,* one of his few works besides *Under the Volcano* worth reading today. It is a gentle story, perhaps the work of a man who knew he did not have long to live, almost rhapsodic in its description of the world he could see from his shack: not just the water and stars and mountains, but the ships, the train on the inlet's opposite bank, the red flares of an oil refinery at night. It is filled with a sense of gratitude: for his marriage, for his wilderness idyll, for the few years of happy and sober writing on his great book.

The *Volcano* saved him while he was working on it; once it was finished, he began to drink again. He spent a few more years in Canada, but the local government began threatening to evict the squatters. There were troubles with publishers when he could not deliver promised books. Finally, he and his wife left for their last disastrous trip to Europe. One letter from there gives a picture of how it felt inside his own private alcoholic volcano.

> Dear old Albert . . . I have to confess . . . that in spite of this comparatively lucid burst of correspondence, that I am going steadily & even beautifully downhill: my memory misses beats at every moment, & my mornings are on all fours. Turning the whole business round in a nutshell I am only sober or merry in a whiskey bottle, & since whiskey is impossible to procure you can imagine how merry I am, & lucid, & by Christ I am

lucid. And merry. But Jesus. The trouble is, apart from Self, that part (which) used to be called: consciousness. I have now reached a position where every night I write 5 novels in imagination, have total recall . . . but am unable to write a word. I cannot explain in human terms the incredible effort it has cost me to write even this silly little note, in a Breughel garden with dogs & barrels & vin kegs & chickens & sunsets & mornings glory with an approaching storm & bottle of half wine.

And now the rain! Let it come, seated as I am on Breughel barrel by a dog's grave crowned with dead irises. . . . And I have been kind to in a way I do not deserve. I have to write pretty fast. . . . Please wire if we can meet each other again, leaving quite out of account whether I can do the same for myself. A night dove has started to hoot & says incessantly the word "dream, dream." A bright idea. I remember always your kindness and generosity . . . Malcolm.

.   .   .

When people love a writer they sometimes want to claim him for their point of view. Tolstoy's love of the peasants was really a kind of precommunism; why, if he had lived past 1917 he would have . . . Or: Orwell's writing really shows how any revolution must invariably betray itself . . . and so on. But the claimers are always wrong, for no great writer's work is that simple, even when the writer involved (Tolstoy, for instance) thinks it is.

There is a growing Lowry cult now, and some of the people trying to claim him are mystics. A whole book has been written proving how *Under the Volcano* is based upon the Cabala. Psychedelic prophets claim Lowry as their precursor. And all this is true: he was fascinated by the Cabala, and he also was under the delusion that mescal, the Mexican liquor with which the Consul drinks himself to death in the *Volcano,* had the hallucinogenic properties of mescaline. Yet his reach was broader.

It would be too crass to try to claim Lowry for the Left, but his one great book has a strong political dimension. You cannot say of Lowry, as does the novelist and critic William Gass in an otherwise perceptive essay, that "he had no politics." Really, now: a novel whose hero is murdered by Fascist policemen is nonpolitical? Anybody who seriously thinks this should compare Lowry's vision of Mexico with the strikingly different one of Graham Greene's *The Power and the Glory,* a novel set in the same time and place. Paradoxically, Greene, the famous anti-American radical, was worried about totalitarians on the Left; Lowry, about those on the Right.

A refrain runs through *Under the Volcano:* "They are losing the battle of the Ebro." It is in the mind of Hugh, the Consul's naively leftist half brother, who apparently represented one side of Lowry himself. Like a distant recurring chord, the struggle in Spain is always there. When the band at a bullfight strikes up the tune "Guadalajara," Hugh softly repeats the word to himself, and you realize that he is thinking of the battle. It is Hugh's ID in the Consul's pockets, remember, which causes the Consul to be killed.

The Consul maintains he is above politics, but he is not. He does not choose sides himself, and so in the end his enemies choose for him. In this sense he is the Consul not only of England but also of all the Western nations that wore blinders then and did nothing to stop Hitler, Franco, and Mussolini until it was too late. Infusing the whole novel is a sense of the rising tide of fascism, slowly, quietly, closing in.

Under the Volcano stands in relation to World War II as *Death in Venice* does to World War I. Intimations of a coming holocaust are heard throughout the book, quickening when the Consul sees at the roadside the body of an Indian messenger of the revolutionary government's land reform bank, murdered by the same policemen who will later kill the Consul himself. Lowry had a clear sense of the class warfare going on in Mexico at the time. The novel's political dimension reaches its peak in the stupendous final chapter. As the Consul stands drinking in the wretched cantina that slowly fills with policemen, you feel like shouting: for Christ's sake, *do* something, these people want to murder you! And when they finally do, the end of the long vision the Consul has as he dies makes him stand for a whole world on the brink of war.

> Opening his eyes, he looked down, expecting to see, below him, the magnificent jungle, the heights, Pico de Orizabe, Malinche, Cofre de Perote, like those peaks of his life conquered one after another before this greatest ascent of all. . . . But there was nothing there: no peaks, no life, no climb. Nor was this summit a summit exactly: it had no substance, no firm base. It was crumbling too, whatever it was, collapsing, while he was falling, falling into the volcano, he must have climbed it after all, though now there was this noise of foisting lava in his ears,

horribly, it was in eruption, yet no, it wasn't the volcano, the world itself was bursting, bursting into black spouts of villages catapulted into space, with himself falling through it all, through the inconceivable pandemonium of a million tanks, through the blazing of ten million burning bodies, falling, into a forest, falling—

Enough. I'm not trying to make Lowry into the whole-hearted radical he was not, but merely to persuade you to read him. And to make clear that one reward of doing so is the multilayered richness of his book, and a sense of the social and political world that frames his central character's personal torments.

.   .   .

Words are cheap; many writers learn to use them well. Putting them to Lowry's ends is much harder. Here is William Gass again, and this time he is right.

Although *Under the Volcano* has many flaws, it is strong where most recent novels are weak: it has no fear of feeling. Our finest contemporary work—that of Beckett and Borges and Barth, for instance—as conscious of metaphoric form as it is, with every part internally and wonderfully related; subtle sometimes as Lowry seldom is; scrupulous to maintain a figurative distance between author, work and reader . . . has achieved many morose, acid, and comic effects. . . . Yet [these writers have] been led too far toward fancy, as Coleridge called it, neglecting . . . the full responsive reach of their readers.

What Gass is talking about—and he is far more charitable than I would be—is a whole stream of contemporary writing in love with extended verbal playfulness. It is a stream where the crossword puzzle lurks never far in the background, where English professors wait eagerly for the chance to publish annotated editions. Lowry is a bulwark against that current.

In his essay on Dickens, Orwell says: "When one reads any strongly individual piece of writing, one has the impression of seeing a face somewhere behind the page. It is not necessarily the actual face of the writer. I feel this very strongly with Swift, with Defoe, with Fielding . . . though in several cases I do not know what these people looked like and do not want to know. What one sees is the face that the writer *ought* to have."

Take someone like Nabokov, for instance. Perhaps in the end a more skilled wielder of words than Lowry, and certainly one who produced a far more substantial corpus of books. But when I imagine him, I don't see the face familiar from photographs: I see his study, his dictionaries, his encyclopedia, his thesaurus, his hands clapping with pleasure as he thinks of a pun in several languages, which I must resort to the dictionaries to understand.

But with Lowry I see the face. And Orwell is right, it is not the way he really looked. None of the existing pictures of him look like the man who could have written *Under the Volcano.* That man is not in his study but in a bar, with a look of helplessness and terror and eagerness for the next drink. For even when you do not know his life, you know, when reading the *Volcano,* that the author has *been* there. There is no shred of playfulness, no sense of the writer at his desk. Lowry's first would-be biographer, Conrad Knickerbocker (who must have shared some of his subject's troubles, for he committed suicide in the middle of his research) once wrote: "Lowry could not perform the vital surgery of separating himself from his characters. He suspected at times that he was not a writer so much as being *written,* and with panic he realized that self-identity was as elusive as ever."

Writing can be like psychoanalysis, or like confession: you grapple with your pain, you remember your trauma, you tell the tale, and then you are shriven. But for Lowry whatever protection gained by writing was precariously temporary. After he completed the *Volcano,* his demons returned and his life began a downward curve that ended with his destroying himself just as his Consul had done. Although it took him ten years beyond the one to live out the other, in the end his book was his life. From a writer you can ask no more.

1974

JFK

EVER-CHANGING HERO

In 1960, John F. Kennedy was elected president of the United States with 49.7 percent of the popular vote. But a poll taken after his death showed that 65 percent of the electorate recalled voting for him. What kind of man could cause some ten million Americans to so drastically edit their memories?

That question, posed by William Manchester, is far more provocative than the predictably clichéd answer Manchester gives in *One Brief Shining Moment: Remembering Kennedy,* the latest addition to his lengthening shelf of fawning JFK books. The epigraph to this one is from Malory's *Morte d'Arthur:* "Thou Sir Launcelot, there thou lyest, thou that were never matched of erthely knyghtes hande. And thou were the courteoust knyght that ever bare shield. And thou were the trewest frende that ever bestrade horse . . ." And so on.

Such Camelotry is by now all too familiar. But the question raised by those statistics is still intriguing. Its real answer is not only the conventional one: that Kennedy's tragic assassination gained him a place in our hearts. This it did, but Kennedy's early death, with so many key decisions yet unmade, resulted in something else. It allowed Kennedy to be the last American president who could successfully be all things to all people.

I was a college student when Kennedy was elected. Even though I was active in a student peace group, Kennedy's wit and intelligence still somehow seemed to outweigh the accumulating evidence of his militarism. When a group of us picketed the White House one chill winter day in 1962, he ordered an urn of hot coffee sent out to the marchers, a gesture in typical Kennedy style. It honored our conviction; it seemed to say: we share the same goals, if not the same strategy. Against my better judgment, I have always half-consciously felt that if only he had lived, he would have led the American people into an era of peace—or at least into a world far better than the one we eventually got, scarred by the cold war and by the brutal hot wars in Vietnam and Central America that cost so many lives.

Yet a few months after Kennedy's assassination, when I found myself in army basic training, I was surprised that my drill sergeant, a gravel-voiced zealot who bragged about the commies he had killed in Korea, thought JFK the greatest president of the century. And of course he, too, had good reasons. Hadn't Kennedy increased the Special Forces fivefold and honored them with the symbol of the Green Beret? Hadn't he told a cheering crowd of Cuban exiles that one day their flag would wave over a free Havana?

Kennedy was a complex man, far more so than most of his worshipers or detractors would have you think. Stop and look at the extraordinary variety of roles he played. The remarkable thing is that there was something to all these parts; none of them was faked. War Hero (PT-109). Friend of the Downtrodden (the executive orders on civil rights). Harvard Intellectual (*Profiles in Courage*). Man of Peace (the atmospheric nuclear test-ban treaty). Builder of America's Military Might (a $6 billion increase over Eisenhower's recommended military budget). And all of these disparate selves were laced together with the finest sense of humor in American politics. Criticized for appointing his brother attorney general, he remarked that he merely thought Bobby should acquire a little legal experience before going out to practice law. Rebuked for campaigning with the aid of Joe Kennedy's vast fortune, he quipped that his father had told him he would pay for every vote necessary, but "he's damned if he's going to pay for a landslide."

. . .

William Manchester is the quintessential Kennedy sycophant. He celebrates all of Kennedy's various roles without ever noticing the contradictions between them. His latest book is a pure, distilled version of the myth, almost an official souvenir program of the Kennedy administration.

In keeping with its basic mawkishness, *One Brief Shining Moment* is written in an unusual grammatical voice, which one might call the second-person sentimental. There is a repeated "you" in the book, but the "you" is not you, the reader; it is apparently the author. "Once when you were visiting Hyannis Port, the president said to you, 'Don't you think . . .'"

Ralph Martin's *A Hero for Our Time: An Intimate Story of the Kennedy Years* is of the same ilk. As does everybody who writes about the Kennedys this way, both men resort to certain standard phrases: "keeper of the flame," "passing the torch," "the glitter of royalty," "the sunlit time," and so forth. Although the loftier Manchester ignores the subject, Martin's book has a good deal about JFK's sex life. Claiming to have interviewed many women who were in a position to know, Martin tells us what kind of lover JFK was (too quick); quotes him telling Clare Boothe Luce "I can't get to sleep unless I've had a lay"; and details trysts in New York penthouses and upstairs at the White House. We've heard all this before, but it says something that it can appear in a biography whose very title declares it celebratory. This, then, is yet another of the roles Kennedy played: Don Juan. Accompanied by winks, it too has become part of the myth—verification that the hero of World War II and the Cuban missile crisis was, in the same macho terms, heroic in bed as well.

Giving more pause for thought, though, is one picture Martin casually gives of his hero in action: walking down Worth Avenue in Palm Beach with an aide, pointing out pretty women who caught his eye. The aide made the arrangements, and the women were brought to Kennedy later in the evening. This is not our usual image of Camelot, although perhaps Sir Lancelot also needed but to point his finger and issue a command.

· · ·

Of all of Kennedy's contradictions, the greatest was between his image as a peacemaker and his massive escalation of the arms race.

That he took some major initiatives for peace there is no doubt. And the important treaty banning nuclear tests in the atmosphere was resisted by many top generals and their congressional allies. Manchester tells us of Kennedy's astonishment when, on a speaking tour of western states in 1963, the president found that mention of the new treaty drew prolonged applause everywhere. If he had realized sooner the potential support for this move, indications are that he would have gone all the way, for a ban on underground testing as well, something the world still had not fully achieved decades after his death. What a missed chance.

At times, Kennedy seemed the first U.S. president to see the insanity of the cold war. "We are both devoting massive sums of money to weapons that could be better devoted to combating ignorance, poverty and disease. We are both caught up in a vicious and dangerous cycle in which suspicion on one side breeds suspicion on the other, and new weapons beget counter-weapons." Yet at the same time, he accepted all the clichés of the cold war and slung them about as carelessly and as sweepingly as any other president before Ronald Reagan. The Camelot of old, after all, was home to bloody exploits on the battlefield and to King Arthur's famous sword, Excalibur. In this sense Kennedy did live up to the legend. He raised a campaign alarm about the "missile gap" between the United States and the Soviet Union and continued his huge arms buildup even when shown that the gap was imaginary. He presided over the deepening U.S. military involvement in Vietnam while keeping much of it secret from the public. He backed civil defense—the lunantic, expensive scheme for building a nationwide network of underground bomb shelters.

By sanctioning the Bay of Pigs invasion, Kennedy gave Fidel Castro reason to want Soviet missiles in Cuba, thus setting the stage for the missile crisis, for the humiliation of the Soviet Union ("I cut his balls off," Kennedy said of Khrushchev), and for the long Soviet military buildup that followed. "I want to tell you something, Mr. McCloy," said a Soviet diplomat as he negotiated the withdrawal of Soviet weapons with Kennedy's adviser. "The Soviet Union is not going to find itself in a position like this ever again." As long as that country existed, both superpowers remained locked in the most expensive arms race of all time.

Kennedy's rhetoric of the 1960s rivaled that of Ronald Reagan two decades later, and often implied the same assumptions about America's right to remake the world as we saw fit. As late as 1963, JFK said, "I think it is unfortunate that [Castro] was permitted to assume control in the 1950s, and perhaps it would have been easier to take an action then than it is now."

Kennedy could get away with this contradiction because it was not yet seen as such. He could successfully tough it out with

Khrushchev over the Cuban missiles because at that time the U.S. nuclear arsenal was vastly superior to the Soviets'—a superiority that soon afterward became impossible for either side to achieve again. He could train the Green Berets and at the same time promulgate the Alliance for Progress: the hawks loved the toughness; the doves the vision of peaceful reform.

A nice vision it was, but time proved it largely impossible. From Vietnam to El Salvador, the carrot of aid has seldom persuaded Third World oligarchies to give away any of their land and power. When that strategy for defeating left-wing rebels fails, military power is all that's left—unless a president is willing, like de Gaulle in Algeria, to withdraw from battle and call it a victory. And that Kennedy showed no willingness to do, either in Cuba or in the looming crisis in Vietnam that faced him in his last weeks, or in anything else.

In this respect, he stayed true to his upbringing: his family was success-oriented and ferociously competitive. Bobby Kennedy refused to stop playing in a Harvard football game even when he had broken his leg. Joe Kennedy, Jr., the oldest son, reportedly wept when he heard that his kid brother Jack had beaten him to the punch in being decorated for bravery in World War II. It is wishful thinking to assume that JFK would have gotten us swiftly out of Vietnam. When asked what Kennedy would have done about Vietnam if he had lived, his military adviser General Maxwell Taylor replied, "Far be it from me to read the mind of a dead man, but let me just say this, Kennedy was not a loser."

.   .   .

And yet, and yet, and yet . . . Why can we still not see the pictures of the Dallas motorcade, of the riderless horse in the funeral procession, without the sense that something greater than one man's life was extinguished on that November day in 1963? Why do all of us alive then remember just where we were when we heard the news? Is there a spark of truth in the idea that if those shots had not rung out, things would have been somehow different—not just in the remainder of Kennedy's presidency but beyond?

If Kennedy had lived, the aura of tragedy might still surround our memories of him, but it would be tragedy of a different kind. The real conflict in Kennedy's life was one that history did not allow to be played out. And it was this: John F. Kennedy was a man whose intelligence ranged far ahead of his convictions.

Kennedy's political beliefs were pretty ordinary, cobbled together out of the conventional wisdom of his time: a dollop of welfare liberalism here, a dollop of cold war hawkishness there, all decorated with a few fresh sprigs of inventive schemes—like the Peace Corps—thought up by bright young advisers. His campaign promise was not, after all, for basic change, but to "get this country moving again." His zest for motion and victory applied everywhere with equal fervor: fighting poverty in Appalachia, fighting Castro in Cuba, fighting discrimination in the South, fighting Communists in Southeast Asia. He died before the moral emptiness of this win-the-game approach to everything became clear.

Yet his mind was capable of far more than this. His wide reading of history suggests a man capable of finding lessons in the past. His American University speech a few months before his death suggests at least one of his many selves could see beyond the hero/villain stick figures of the cold war. That wonderful, self-deprecating wit suggests someone potentially capable of self-doubt and irony—qualities in short supply in the White House since then.

Had he lived, we would have been witnesses to his inner struggle, as his perceptions of the world increasingly contradicted the family ideology that life was touch football writ large, where, if you just tried hard enough, you could win. In Vietnam, in Central America, in the tragedy of our inner cities, no easy touchdowns would have been possible. Would Kennedy, faced with all this, have been able to cope with a world where traditional heroism was no longer enough, and a world that neither he nor his country could remake at will? His being face to face with these problems would have been a drama, and perhaps a tragedy, far greater than that of his death.

1984

Remembrance of Africas Past

Traveling in West Africa in the early 1960s, I once arrived at a Ghanaian fishing village just as its people were hauling in the day's catch. Every villager seemed to be involved. Some fishermen were rowing small boats, in which they had taken a giant net some distance out to sea. Groups of older men were at opposite ends of a beach, pulling on long ropes attached to the ends of this net. Young men and teenage boys were swimming in the surf along with the net as it was hauled back toward shore, making sure that breaking waves did not tangle it or spill its precious load of fish.

After a half hour or so, the long net was finally pulled up onto the beach, maneuvered so that the silvery, wriggling mass of fish was concentrated in the center. The swimmers who had been guiding the net through the water walked out of the surf exhausted and immediately lay on the sunbaked dry sand to warm themselves. The women of the village went to work sorting and dividing up the catch, and finally carried the fish off to their huts in flat woven baskets balanced atop their heads. No money changed hands.

I've often remembered this day, for it was the first time I ever saw a complex, communal subsistence economy at work, with tools largely unchanged for centuries. But as I think back on this scene today, another aspect of it seems remarkable: nobody in it paid any attention to me. My companion and I were the only outsiders, and driving the only car, for many miles in any direction. For an hour or more we sat at one side of the beach and watched everything. But no one came over, smiled, frowned, tried to beg, or tried to sell us anything. Everyone, even the numerous children of the village, had eyes only for the more exciting drama of the fish.

Could you have a similar experience today? I don't think so. Of course there are plenty of Third World villages where feeding oneself is still a matter outside the cash economy. But even where that is so, people are, in their imaginations if not in their wallets, increasingly part of a world commercial culture. They are no longer just members of a local community, but would-be consumers of internationally standardized objects and fantasies. Perhaps they still catch their own fish in that Ghanaian village, but I'd wager that by now most people there want cash to buy things like tape decks, infant formula, Chicago Bulls T-shirts. Stray foreign tourists are probably not a major part of the local economy, but I'll bet they would now be immediately recognized as sources of possible handouts or as prospective buyers of local handicrafts. For much of Africa and Asia that cultural sea change came less with the coming of white colonialists than with the aggressive marketing by multinational corporations in the years since colonialism nominally ended.

·   ·   ·

Both Beryl Markham, a white woman who grew up in Kenya, and Wole Soyinka, a black man who grew up in Nigeria, are aware that the societies they knew as children are now transformed. In their autobiographies they refer to that transformation only fleetingly, but their respective elegies to the worlds of their childhoods are all the more eloquent for the understatement.

Beryl Markham sensed that East Africa was changing in the 1930s and headed for Europe and the United States (although she returned to Kenya for the final decades of her life). "Adventure for Nairobi came in celluloid rolls straight from Hollywood," she writes in *West with the Night,* "and adventure for other parts of the world went out from Nairobi in celluloid rolls straight from the cameras of professional jungle-trotters. It was a good time to leave."

Wole Soyinka lovingly evokes the Nigeria of his childhood, rich in sound and smell and tastes—he spends pages of his *Aké: The Years of Childhood* on the food alone. Only once or twice does he shift to the present tense and look ahead in any detail to today.

The hawkers' lyrics of leaf-wrapped *moin-moin* [a black-eyed bean delicacy] still resound in parts of Aké and the rest of the town but, along Dayisi's Walk is also a shop which sells *moin-moin* from a glass case, lit by seagreen neon lamps. It lies side by side with McDonald's hamburgers, Kentucky Fried Chicken, hot dogs and dehydrated sausage rolls. . . . Today's jaws on Dayisi's Walk . . . champ endlessly—on chewinggum. Among the fantasy stores lit by neon and batteries of coloured bulbs a machine also dispenses popcorn, uniformly fluffed. . . . A girl pauses at the hair-dressers' and soon, the sound of sizzling joins the disco sounds. . . . Along the same midnight walk of Dayisi the guitarist now darts the young hawker, releasing into the faces of passers-by through his finger on the caller's button, the dulcet chimes of Made-in-Hong-Kong doorbells.

Soyinka, a Nobel Prize–winning playwright, did not grow up in a society bereft of Western influences: indeed, his father was a church school headmaster who spoke English at home with his children. But back then the world beyond his town seemed a distant source of curios, not something intrusive and life-changing. The extended family, the complex relations with aunts and uncles and cousins and stray children and hangers-on taken in by the fluid and ever-expanding Soyinka household, was the center of his universe. Electric light and the radio were wondrous toys, but the most marvelous thing imaginable was the marching band of the local police. Seeing them parade by one day, the young Soyinka followed on behind, ending up totally lost, miles away.

One pivotal episode in *Aké* foreshadows the erosion of the complex culture of magic and ritual and legend Soyinka knew as a boy. The radio begins to talk of Hitler and the war, and this becomes part of the local madman's fantasy.

> Paa Adatan patrolled the . . . area, furious that no one would take him into the Army and send him to confront Hitler, personally, and end the war once and for all. 'Ah, Mama Wole, this English people just wan' the glory for den self. Den no wan' blackman to win dis war and finish off dat nonsense-yeye Hitler one time!' . . . He spat his red kola-nut juice on the ground, raging.

One day a British army convoy stops in town. The soldiers buy food (the store has quickly doubled its prices), then head back to their trucks. Paa Adatan, the madman, gets things mixed up and thinks these are Hitler's troops, invading Nigeria, and that they have robbed the shops. He sings and curses at them; he waves his sword at them and threatens to annihilate them with his magic gourd. Worried by the sword, several soldiers jump him from behind and tie him up. They leave. Paa Adatan is crushed that his powers failed to work. He smashes his magic gourd underfoot. "He walked slowly away. He moved with a sad, quiet dignity. He . . . vanished bit by bit as the road dipped downwards before it turned sharply away. . . . I never saw him again."

.   .   .

The Africa that Beryl Markham recalls with equal grace in *West with the Night* is a very different one: Kenya from before the First World War to the 1930s. And the vanishing of the world she evokes is seen through her trade, aviation. Markham was the first woman professional pilot in Africa. She writes in the tradition of Antoine de Saint-Exupéry and a few of his peers: pioneering poet-aviators for whom flying was at once a craft, a perpetual voyage of discovery, and a means of experiencing the natural world afresh. Those dimensions of flight have all but disappeared from skies where scheduled jetliners fly on automatic pilot.

Markham had to contend with giraffes and zebras who strolled onto homemade runways, with a complete lack of modern navigational instruments, and with the British government, which had a rule that the express permission of the Royal Air Force was required for any woman who wanted to fly across the Sudan's vast crocodile-ridden swamp, the Sudd. Exactly why the RAF thought women more vulnerable to the crocodiles than men is not clear. After overcoming these obstacles, Markham flew people and mail to safaris, took medical supplies to distant settlements, and was the first pilot to scout herds from the air for elephant hunters. Later, abroad, she was the first to make a nonstop solo flight across the Atlantic from east to west.

That epochal 1936 trip ended with Markham's plane almost vertical, its nose buried several feet in a Nova Scotia swamp. Unlike Lindbergh, she had to fly against the wind. For some reason, certain of her plane's gas tanks could not be equipped with gauges, and the only way she could tell the fuel in them was exhausted was when the engine stopped. Flying at only two thousand feet above the water (the lower you fly, the less the headwind), she once sank down to three hundred feet before being able to switch tanks and get the engine restarted.

West with the Night was out of print for many years, but was reprinted when someone noticed extravagant praise for it in the letters of Ernest Hemingway, who knew Markham in Kenya. It is not hard to see what appealed to him. "One night," she writes of the first time she saw a plane and knew she had to fly, "I stood there and watched an aeroplane invade the stronghold of the stars. It flew high; it blotted some of them out; it trembled their flames like a hand swept over a company of candles."

In recent years, some critics have charged that *West with the Night* was written not by Markham but by Raoul Schumacher, an American writer to whom she was married for a time in the 1940s and 1950s. Schumacher himself made this claim shortly before he and Markham got divorced. Those who believe him point as evidence to Markham's other published writing, which is sparse and not on a par with *West with the Night.* Much the same, however, can be said of Schumacher. Markham's biographer, Mary S. Lovell, argues fairly convincingly that although Schumacher edited the manuscript, the prose is essentially Markham's own.

Whoever wrote it, the book soars.

> My hands had been taught to seek the controls of a plane. Usage had taught them. They were at ease clinging to a stick as a cobbler's fingers are in repose grasping an awl. No human pursuit achieves dignity until it can be called work, and when you can experience a physical loneliness for the tools of your trade, you see that the other things—the experiments, the irrelevant vocations, the vanities you used to hold—were false to you.

For Markham, flight was never a way to conquer the African landscape, but to be more humble before it.

> To fly in unbroken darkness without even the cold companionship of a pair of ear-phones or the knowledge that somewhere ahead are lights and life and a well-marked airport is something more than just lonely. It is at times unreal to the point where the existence of other people seems not even a reasonable probability. The hills, the forests, the rocks, and the plains are one with the darkness, and the darkness is infinite.

Markham was raised on her father's farm as the only white child within two hundred miles. She writes about being clawed by a lion and about hunting by spear with African children. She grew up speaking several African languages and gives a lovely, respectful account of the Nandi legend explaining why there is death: God sent a chameleon to the first man on earth, with a message saying life will go on forever. Then He changed His mind and sent an egret with the news that for all of us, death would someday come. Whichever message arrived first, said God, would be the true one. The chameleon arrived first, but was so excited by his tidings of eternal life that he could not speak. The egret's message prevailed.

.   .   .

For a book mostly set in a country that has gone from being a colony to an independent nation, and has experienced the Mau Mau rebellion and other upheavals along the way, *West with the Night* is curiously nonpolitical. And, perhaps more to the point, Markham does not quite seem aware that the air routes she pioneered and the white hunters and traders and safari-goers she transported had anything to do with changing the pristine Africa she loved. Soyinka, by contrast, is wiser in understanding exactly how his part of Africa has reflected the impact of the outside world.

Like indigenous cultures almost everywhere, those in Africa proved vulnerable not only to colonial rifles and machine guns but also to a more lasting force: the power of the world market economy. I've never returned to that Ghanaian fishing village, but, like the rural Kenya of Markham's childhood and the Nigeria of Soyinka's, I suspect it has changed. And that its inhabitants measure their well-being ever less by their day's catch from the sea and ever more by their possession of goods in brightly colored packages from far across the ocean, both those they have and those advertised and yearned for but beyond reach. Such a change can be far more devastating than that wrought by any conquering army that has come and gone.

1983

Sex Books, Then and Now

The first time I read a great many books about sex was under the covers, with a flashlight, when I was about twelve. In the pre-*Penthouse* generation, *anything* about sex, such as a marriage manual, was almost a form of pornography. Although I had heard rumors of its existence, I had no idea what real pornography was. But in its absence, much tamer material served just as well. Which is interesting, for it shows that prurience, like much else in life, is entirely relative. I still remember phrases from a *Reader's Digest* article, which I read and reread many times, about the horrifying rise of sexual promiscuity under communism. Little did the *Digest's* editors know, as they linked these twin evils and talked about wild parties in Czechoslovakia or orgies at Polish summer camps, that they were furnishing at least one adolescent with his erotic fantasies for years to come. Who knows, perhaps this connection set me on the path to left-wing politics as well.

Back when I was a teenager in the 1950s, the *Digest* was the embodiment of official morality. The same was true of marriage manuals. The people these books described in the various positions for intercourse (and they were only described, never illustrated) were always "the husband" and "the wife." A decade or two later, of course, things began to change. Books appeared with titles like *Open Marriage* and *Creative Divorce,* and one radical activist I know had "Smash Monogamy" written on his wedding cake. But to judge from a sampling of books on the subject appearing a quarter century or so after my under-the-covers-with-a-flashlight days, the pendulum has swung back. Not all the way, but to a state of indecision: an uneasiness about making any moral pronouncements about sex at all.

Consider, for example, *More Than Just a Friend: The Joys and*

Disappointments of Extramarital Affairs, by Dr. Tom McGinnis. The author goes into such detail on the subject that he even gives a long list of "desirable qualities for an extramarital partner" (these are wonderfully contradictory: you want someone who is "open and honest" but can still keep a secret, someone who is "in touch with inner feelings" but can still break things off promptly when necessary). Yet when it comes down to making a final judgment— extramarital affairs, yes or no?—here is his resounding dictum: "If we can draw a single conclusion from all the material presented, it is, simply, that options are available to all of us. No matter what the alternatives, the choices are ours to make."

My old source of secret stimulation takes a more conservative line on extramarital sex in its current anthology, *Love and Marriage,* selected and edited by the editors of the *Reader's Digest.* But, in a significant sign of the times, it argues against adultery not in terms of right and wrong but on the basis that the sex is no better. "Marcia [a wife who strayed] found out the hard way what most well-adjusted married women already know—that sexually speaking, nearly all men are created equal. There are no magic techniques. True sexual satisfaction for husband and wife is the result of cooperation, mutual dedication and a certain amount of hard work."

If we males are all alike in bed, we're in big trouble. How, then, are we supposed to feel superior to each other? I much prefer the more judgmental kind of thinking of the courtesan Ninon de Lenclos, quoted in *Fascinating Facts about Love, Sex & Marriage* by Ruth Birnkrant. What she thought of her favorite lovers is not noted, but one she didn't like she described as having "a soul of boiled beef, a body of damp cardboard, and a heart like a pumpkin fricasseed in snow."

Cosmopolitan's Love Book: A Guide to Ecstasy in Bed also has a zestier view of the world. There is none of the *Digest's* scorn for "magic techniques" here, or, thank goodness, of its depressing warning of "hard work" in bed. "All right, you're tingling with sensuality. Now . . . how do you get *him* to tingle back? You don't have to be ravishingly beautiful! *Every* woman is a sexual being, and all you have to do is send out your own personal sexual messages, the signals that say, *I am responsive . . . I am warm, loving, giving, I like you.* If you've followed the suggestions in Chapters One through Five . . . you do understand and *enjoy* your body.

Now you're ready to project this inner eroticism into the cold, gray world . . ."

First, says *Cosmo,* make your apartment ready: hide your wigs, your three-year-old collection of *TV Guides,* your dog's rubber bone, your sister's wedding picture, your blackhead remover, and your athlete's foot powder. Put out satin sheets and shag rugs, and adjust your bathroom scale to read five pounds lighter. To get warmed up, *Cosmo* offers a veritable Yellow Pages of fantasies to choose from. Here is one from the more traditional end of the spectrum: "You are a young, supple virgin living in Saudi Arabia. You wear see-through pink veils and have soft, glowing, golden skin. One day, while walking in your walled garden, you see a handsome young sheik . . . and give him provocative glances through your veils. He carries you in his arms, lifts you onto a white steed and rides off toward the palace . . ." Some sort of frontier has been reached here: books are now telling us not only what to do in bed, but also what to imagine. In the realm of instructions, it seems hard to go any further.

.   .   .

Sex and marriage manuals have changed in another way as well. In these less-certain days, the guidebooks are selling not just advice but also something else: the hope that lasting marriage still exists. The former generation of sex manuals seemed to be written almost entirely by male doctors; now many are written by husband-wife teams. The source of a writer's authority is no longer the doctor's white coat, but proof that he or she, or he *and* she, have been long married. This is one of the few instances in our commercial culture when a couple is considered more marketable if they are middle-aged, and can be pictured thus on the book jacket. Gray hair and all, their very agedness and coupleness suggest that they have defied the odds and made marriage last.

One example of this genre is *The Romantic Love Question & Answer Book,* by Nathaniel Branden and E. Devers Branden. The entire book is Q-and-A. One typical Q is: "Nathaniel and Devers Branden, you are husband and wife, in addition to which you conduct workshops together, practice therapy together, and you're now writing a book together. How do you manage to survive so much togetherness . . . ?"

Note that the question, besides advertising the Brandens' success at staying married, also touts their therapy and workshop business (a P.O. box address is given, to write to for more information). In this volume, Nathaniel Branden also repeatedly plugs his previous books. To one of them alone, *The Psychology of Romantic Love,* he refers more than twenty times, often quoting himself at half-page length. The Brandens' Intensive Workshops also figure prominently in their advice, with the first word becoming a noun: "A woman asked this question at an Intensive . . ."

The Romantic Love Question & Answer Book is written in an odd voice. An admiring question is asked, and then an "I" answers the question, talking about the Brandens' personal bedroom techniques or how they fell in love or whatever; from the context you have to tell whether it is husband or wife speaking. Some of the Brandens' paths to enlightenment will be familiar to people who have tasted the newer therapies: twelve-hour intimacy marathons, sentence completion ("The scary thing about staying in touch with my partner after sex is————"), and exercises involving talking to oneself in mirrors. One variety of psychotherapy they offer, however, was new to me: consultations—sentence completion and all—by long distance telephone. The Brandens practice in southern California.

. . .

If telephonic therapy in Los Angeles is one pole of marriage counseling, Avodah K. Offit, a New York feminist and Freudian psychiatrist, practices at the other. Her *Night Thoughts: Reflections of a Sex Therapist* is the only one of all these books that I would recommend you actually read. She seems wise, warm, and at peace with herself. What I like best about her book of short, pithy essays is that, in contrast to all the question-and-answer people and against the grain of our age of instant solutions, Offit celebrates the *mystery* in sexuality and stands in awe of its complex connections to human emotion. She notes, for instance, that anorgasmic women often turn out to have had cruel or absent fathers. She finds that the ones who had cruel fathers are easier to treat: hatred is easier to transform into love than is absence.

Offit talks about the role of laughter in sex, about who gets out of bed first (why is it always the man?), and about grief, tenderness, and elation: "Orgasms are most satisfying when they occur at the peak of such feelings—those that mock our mortality as well as those that affirm it." Unlike many of the manual writers, she is wary of telling anyone what he or she *ought* to feel or fantasize; on this point she quotes Coleridge's reply to a woman who wanted him to give her a technique for responding to poetry: "Madam, think you nothing of itself will come, but we must do the seeking?"

She talks about the sounds people make during sex and of how in ancient India lovers were supposed to make a wide variety of bird and animal noises to show their feelings. She is humble: "To describe the kaleidoscope of feelings that foster orgasmic diversity is a task best left to the poets." Not quite true, for she is one herself. Here she is, for instance, wondering why people sometimes cry while making love: "Are we mourning our childhood, our lost parents, our lover soon to be gone, our life soon to be ended? Are we mourning the lives . . . of others who never experienced this love? Is it all mankind we cry for? Why should we now think such thoughts? Maybe we do not weep enough at other times."

I have only one quibble with this otherwise intelligent and graceful book. In an uncharacteristic departure from her usual wisdom, Offit remarks in passing that the great aphrodisiac is novelty in sexual partners. Is it only we repressed children of the 1950s who find something comforting—and even erotic—in someone familiar? Have we been reading too many *Reader's Digests* and not enough *Cosmopolitans*? I would guess that aphrodisia, like standards of beauty, is a product of one's culture. To say that it is mainly a matter of novelty reflects only that we live in a time of short-term relationships, and of an unending barrage of advertising that tells us a hundred times a day to discard the old and buy the new.

To accept this current taste as an eternal axiom leads to the myth that what marriage counselors call "sexual boredom" is both inevitable, and sexual in origin. Is it not likely to be, instead, a mere symptom of dissonance in territories of the heart much more difficult for guidebook writers to chart? Such new myths about sex can ultimately be just as imprisoning as all the old repressive ones we are still struggling to untangle.

1982